By the same author

DAUGHTERS OF ISIS

HATCHEPSUT

THE FEMALE PHARAOH

JOYCE TYLDESLEY

VIKING

VIKING

Published by the Penguin Group
Penguin Books Ltd, 27 Wrights Lane, London W8 5TZ, England
Penguin Books USA Inc., 375 Hudson Street, New York, New York 10014, USA
Penguin Books Australia Ltd, Ringwood, Victoria, Australia
Penguin Books Canada Ltd, 10 Alcorn Avenue, Toronto, Ontario, Canada M4V 3B2
Penguin Books (NZ) Ltd, 182–190 Wairau Road, Auckland 10, New Zealand

Penguin Books Ltd, Registered Offices: Harmondsworth, Middlesex, England

First published 1996
1 3 5 7 9 10 8 6 4 2
First edition

Set in 10.5/12.5 pt Bembo Monotype
Typeset by Datix International Limited, Bungay, Suffolk
Printed in England by Clays Ltd, St Ives plc

A CIP catalogue record for this book is available from the British Library

ISBN 0–670–85976–1

For William Jack Snape

Contents

Plates

Figures

Chapter 1

1.1 The cartouche of King Sekenenre Tao II
1.2 The cartouche of King Kamose
1.3 The cartouche of King Ahmose
1.4 Old and New Kingdom soldiers (after Wilkinson, J. G., 1853, *The Ancient Egyptians: their life and customs*, London, Figs 297, 300)
1.5 The god Amen (after Sharpe, S., 1859, *The History of Egypt*, London, Fig. 94)
1.6 The goddess Mut (after Seton-Williams, V. and Stocks, P., 1983, *Blue Guide, Egypt*, London and New York, p. 48)

Chapter 2

2.1 King Ahmose and his grandmother, Queen Tetisheri (after Ayrton, E. R., Currelly, C. T. and Weigall, A. E. P., 1903, *Abydos III*, London, Plate LII)
2.2 The god Osiris (after Sharpe, S., 1859, *The History of Egypt*, London, Fig. 106)
2.3 The god Horus (after Sharpe, S., 1859, *The History of Egypt*, London, Fig. 108)
2.4 The cartouche of King Amenhotep I
2.5 The cartouche of King Tuthmosis I

Chapter 3

3.1 The infant Hatchepsut being suckled by the goddess Hathor (after Naville, E., 1896, *The Temple of Deir el-Bahari, 2*, London, Plate LIII)

Chapter 4

Chapter 5

Chapter 6

Chapter 7

Chapter 8

Maps and Chronologies

Acknowledgements

Many people have helped with the preparation of this book, and I would like to express my gratitude to all concerned. First and foremost I must thank my husband, Steven Snape, for his unflagging support, encouragement and cooking. Thanks are also due to Eleo Gordon and Sheila Watson who gave practical advice whenever needed, to Bill Tyldesley who provided translations from German sources, and to the members of the Liverpool University S.E.S. photography department, Ian Qualtrough and Suzanne Yee, who produced photographic prints at lightning speed. Plates 5 and 10 are published by kind permission of the Metropolitan Museum of Art, New York.

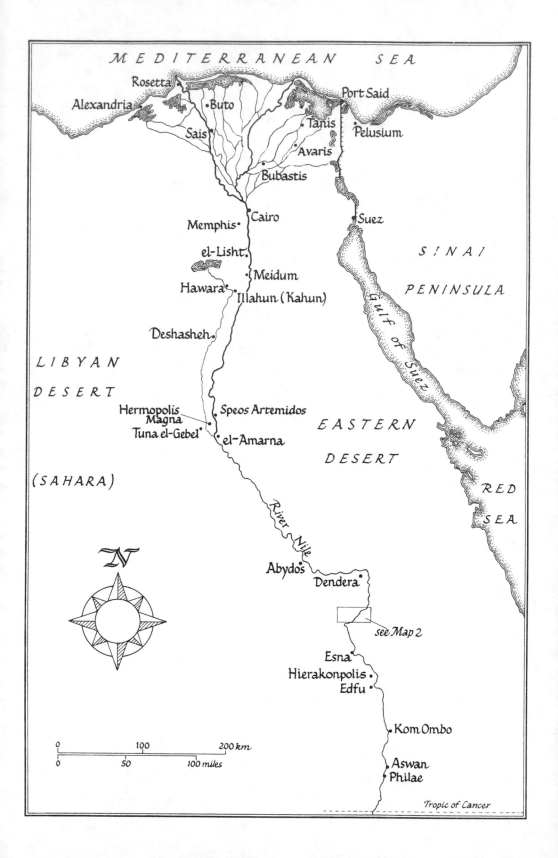

MEDITERRANEAN SEA

Rosetta

Alexandria

Buto

Port Said

Sais

Tanis

Pelusium

Avaris

Bubastis

Memphis

Cairo

Suez

SINAI

el-Lisht

PENINSULA

Meidum

Hawara

Illahun (Kahun)

Deshasheh

LIBYAN

DESERT

Hermopolis

Speos Artemidos

Magna

Tuna el-Gebel

el-Amarna

EASTERN

DESERT

(SAHARA)

RED

SEA

River Nile

Abydos

Dendera

see Map 2

Esna

Hierakonpolis

Edfu

Kom Ombo

Aswan

Philae

Tropic of Cancer

_N_

0   100   200 km
0   50   100 miles

Gulf of Suez

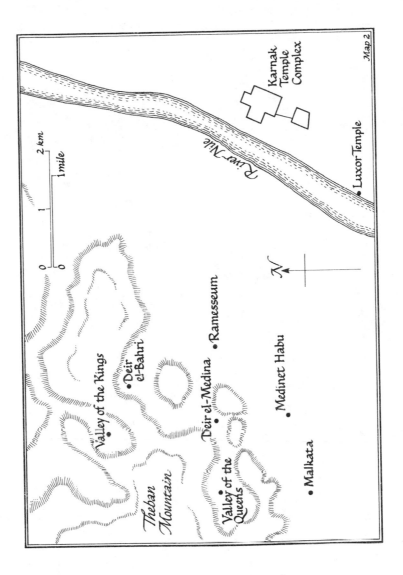

Map 2

Karnak
Temple
Complex

Luxor Temple

River Nile

2 km

1

0

1 mile

0

N

Valley of the Kings

Deir
el-Bahri

Theban
Mountain

Deir el-Medina

Ramesseum

Valley of the
Queens

Medinet Habu

Malkata

Introduction

*My command stands firm like the mountains, and the sun's disk shines
and spreads rays over the titulary of my august person, and my falcon
rises high above the kingly banner unto all eternity.*[1]

Queen or, as she would prefer to be remembered, King Hatchepsut
ruled 18th Dynasty Egypt for over twenty years. Her story is that of a
remarkable woman. Born the eldest daughter of King Tuthmosis I,
married to her half-brother Tuthmosis II, and guardian of her young
stepson–nephew Tuthmosis III, Hatchepsut somehow managed to defy
tradition and establish herself on the divine throne of the pharaohs.
From this time onwards Hatchepsut became the female embodiment of
a male role, uniquely depicted both as a conventional woman and as a
man, dressed in male clothing, carrying male accessories and even
sporting the traditional pharaoh's false beard. Her reign, a carefully bal-
anced period of internal peace, foreign exploration and monumental
building, was in all respects – except one obvious one – a conventional
New Kingdom regime; Egypt prospered under her rule. However, after
Hatchepsut's death, a serious attempt was made to delete her name and
image from the history of Egypt. Hatchepsut's monuments were either
destroyed or usurped, her portraits were vandalized and her rule was
omitted from the official king lists until only the historian Manetho
preserved the memory of a female monarch named Amense or Amensis
as the fifth sovereign of the 18th Dynasty.

Had Hatchepsut been born a man, her lengthy rule would almost certainly be remembered for its achievements: its stable government, successful trade missions and the impressive architectural advances which
include the construction of the Deir el-Bahri temple on the west bank
of the Nile at Luxor, a building which is still widely regarded as one of
the most beautiful in the world. Instead, Hatchepsut's gender has

become her most important characteristic and almost all references to her reign have concentrated not on her policies but on the personal relationships and power struggles which many historians have felt able to detect within the claustrophobic early 18th Dynasty Theban royal family. Two interlinked questions arise again and again, dominating all accounts of Hatchepsut's life: What made a hitherto conventional queen decide to become a king? And how, in a highly conservative and male-dominated society, was she able to achieve her goal with such apparent ease?

It has generally been allowed that the answer to these riddles must be sought in the character of the woman herself. However, this is where all agreement ends as the identical and rather limited set of facts has suggested radically diverse images of the same woman to different observers, to the extent that a casual reader browsing along a shelf of egyptology books might be forgiven for assuming that Hatchepsut suffered from a seriously split personality. Egyptologists, normally the most dry and cautious of observers, have been only too happy to allow their own feelings to intervene in their telling of Hatchepsut's tale and, more particularly, in their interpretation of the motives underlying her deeds. These feelings have tended to coincide with the beliefs common to a generation, so we find egyptologists at the turn of the century, unaware of the complexities of the Tuthmo-side succession and accustomed to the idea of successful female rule personified by Queen Victoria, happy to accept Hatchepsut's own propaganda. To these champions Hatchepsut was a valid monarch, an experienced and well-meaning woman who ruled amicably alongside her young stepson, steering her country through twenty peaceful, prosperous years.

Though unmentioned in the Egyptian king lists, [she] as much deserves to be commemorated among the great monarchs of Egypt as any king or queen who ever sat on its throne during the 18th Dynasty.[2]

As a woman who 'did not fall below the standard of the rest of the 18th Dynasty . . . [having given] early evidence of her capacity to reign',[3] Hatchepsut 'naturally undertook the rule of Egypt, and we are quite justified in saying that the interests of the country suffered in no way through being in her hands'.[4] In summary:

. . . though she has never been considered as a legitimate sovereign, and though she has left us no account of great conquests, her government must have been at once strong and enlightened, for when her nephew Tuthmosis III succeeded her, the country was sufficiently powerful and rich to allow him to venture not only on the building of great edifices, but on a succession of wars of conquests which gave him, among all the kings of Egypt, a pre-eminent claim to the title of 'the Great'.[5]

By the 1960s, knowledge of early 18th Dynasty history had increased, the climate of opinion had changed, and Hatchepsut had been trans-formed into the archetypal wicked stepmother familiar from the pop-ular films *Snow White* and *Cinderella*. She was now an unnatural and scheming woman 'of the most virile character',[6] and one who would deliberately abuse a position of trust to steal the throne from a defence-less child, thereby cutting short the reign one of Egypt's most successful pharaohs, Tuthmosis III. Hatchepsut was a bad-tempered, 'shrewd, ambitious and unscrupulous woman [who soon] showed herself in her true colours'.[7] Her foreign policy – the direct result of her weaker sex – was quite simply a disaster and:

her reign is marked by a halt in the policy of conquests started by Ahmose and so splendidly followed by his three successors . . . [Hatchepsut] was too busy with the internal difficulties which she herself had created by her ambition to interest herself in the affairs of Asia.[8]

With the growing realization that Hatchepsut, a flesh-and-blood woman rather than a one-dimensional storybook character, cannot be simply classified as either 'good' or 'bad', most of these more extreme reactions have been abandoned. However, they have left their mark on the pages of the more popular histories and a significant number of chronicles of 18th Dynasty court life continue to uphold the tradition of the great Tuthmoside family feud. While it is very difficult for any biographer to remain entirely impartial about his or her subject, I am attempting to provide the non-specialist reader with an objective and unbiased account of the life and times of King Hatchepsut, gathered from the researches of those egyptologists who have spent years study-ing, sometimes in minute detail, the individual threads of evidence which, when woven together, form the tapestry of her reign. It is left for the reader to decide on the rights or wrongs of her actions. However, it will almost immediately become apparent that Hatchepsut's story unravels to become three interlinked stories: the history of the king and her immediate family, the history of Hatchepsut's memory after her death, and the equally fascinating tale of those who have since studied and interpreted her. It is impossible to study one without making reference to the others, and I have made no attempt to separate the three.

Writing about the public King Hatchepsut has proved to be something of an exercise in detection, as all too often the archaeological record throws up enough clues to intrigue Hercule Poirot while modestly withholding the final piece of evidence needed to prove or disprove a particular theory. Nevertheless, despite the fact that there are huge gaps in our knowledge, the monuments which testify to her achievements and the propaganda texts written to explain her actions do provide us with the evidence needed to reconstruct at least a partial history of Hatchepsut's reign. The private woman – Hatchepsut as daughter, wife and mother – has been far more difficult to reach as we are lacking almost all the intimate details which can help a historical character come alive to the modern reader. Hatchepsut lived in a literate age, but belonged to a society which did not believe in keeping personal written records. The contemporary records which have been preserved are almost invariably official documents which, by their very nature, rarely express private opinions. We have no intimate letters written to, by or about Hatchepsut and no diaries or memoirs to provide us with a glimpse of early 18th Dynasty court life; we cannot even be sure of Hatchepsut's actual appearance, as all her portraits are formal works of art designed to depict the ideal of the divine Egyptian pharaoh. The real Hatchepsut, therefore, remains something of an enigma, although if we look hard enough at her relationships with the daughter whom she clearly loved and the father whom she adored, or if we consider her obvious need to explain her actions and justify her unusual rule whenever possible, we may feel ourselves able to detect a more complex and less secure personality hidden behind the façade of the mighty king.

This lack of more intimate information perhaps explains in part why Cleopatra VII, a transient and far less successful but infinitely better documented queen of Egypt, has attracted the attention of biographers from the time of her death onwards while Hatchepsut has been virtually ignored by all but the most devoted of specialists. Similarly Queen Nefertiti, short-lived consort to an unconventional king, has, on the basis of one remarkable portrait-head, become immortal, her name synonymous with Egyptian beauty throughout the western world. Hatchepsut herself would almost certainly approve of our inability to pry into her private affairs. All Egyptian kings aspired to conform to the accepted stereotype, and she was no exception. She had no wish to be remembered merely for her sex, which she regarded as an irrelevance; she had demanded – and for a brief time won – the right to be ranked as an equal amongst the pharaohs.

Hatchepsut was a member of the close-knit Theban royal family, a family which had struggled to unite Egypt at the end of the Second Intermediate Period and whose reigns straddled the artificial division between the 17th and 18th Dynasties. To understand the motivation of this family – its fierce militarism, its promotion of the new state god Amen and its liberal treatment of royal women – it is necessary to delve further back, to the period when, for a century, Egypt had been a fragmented country partially ruled by foreigners. Hatchepsut needs to be studied within her own context, and I make no apology for the fact that Egyptian history takes up most of Chapters 1 and 2. Hatchepsut herself was deeply aware of – some might even say obsessed by – her country's recent past, and her reign is characterized by a burning desire to re-create the splendours of the 12th Dynasty, a golden age when Egypt had prospered under a succession of strong kings.

Hatchepsut was by no means the only king of Egypt to attempt to replicate the glories of the past. To the Egyptians, always a highly conservative people, stability and continuity were vitally important signs that all was well within their world. History, correctly interpreted to show Egypt and her rulers in the best possible light, provided an idealized blueprint for the present, so that any pharaoh who could be seen to be emulating the successes of his illustrious predecessors became by definition a good monarch. Although the early 18th Dynasty was a time of architectural, artistic, theological and technological advances, New Kingdom Egypt remained tied to Middle and Old Kingdom Egypt by an unparalleled continuity of language, religion and artistic/architectural convention, and by the idiosyncratic Egyptian view of the world, and the position of Egypt, her people and her gods within that world, which had remained basically unchanged for over a thousand years. The 18th Dynasty monarchs therefore felt the need not only to emulate the physical deeds of their predecessors but also to replicate – on as grand a scale as possible – their rituals, paintings, sculpture and architecture, all of which had become generally accepted as the true and, indeed, the only way of doing things. Throughout her reign Hatchepsut, more than any other New Kingdom pharaoh, stressed the validity of her rule by linking it with both selective aspects of the past – albeit a past re-invented to fit neatly with contemporary concerns – and with the state religion. Thus she was able to justify her unique position to the people, increasing their confidence in her unusual reign.

The Dynastic Period lasted from the beginning of the 1st Dynasty in approximately 3000 BC to the end of the 31st Dynasty in 332 BC. Throughout this period of well over two thousand years, it remained a fundamental principle of religious belief that there should always be a pharaoh, or king, on the throne of Egypt. The modern word pharaoh is a metonymy which has evolved from the Egyptian words *per-a'a*, literally 'great house', a term which was used by the Egyptians when referring to their monarch in much the same way that the modern British refer to 'the Crown' or 'a statement from the Palace', and contemporary Americans speak about 'the White House'. (The words king and pharaoh are used interchangeably throughout this book to avoid stylistic monotony.) Usually there was only one male, native-born king of Egypt at any given time, although occasionally some chose to share their power with a co-regent, and on at least four separate occasions a woman rather than a man officially held the reins of power. During the three decentralized Intermediate Periods there were often two or more contemporary kings ruling over the various regions of the temporarily fragmented country; some of these kings were foreigners who were prepared to abandon their own cultural identity and adopt the traditional pharaoh's regalia in order to conform to the accepted stereotype of an Egyptian king. The king was a necessity. He may not always have been popular with his contemporaries, and indeed a few kings were even assassinated, but these unfortunate individuals were immediately replaced by a new king and there was never any move to establish any other form of government in Egypt.

In the west we have grown used to the idea of the figurehead monarch as nominal head of state; the present Queen of England, for example, remains the theoretical head of both secular and religious life in Britain, although her actual powers are fairly minimal and her existence is in no way vital to the functioning of her country. The abolition of the monarchy and the establishment of a republic would have very little real effect on the day-to-day lives of the majority of the British people. In ancient Egypt, however, things were very different. The pharaoh was accepted without question as an absolute ruler who owned both the land and its people. He was entitled to demand that his subjects worked for him as and when he liked, and the people were bound to serve their master in whatever way he required. At any time the pharaoh could call upon his subjects to abandon their daily tasks and participate in labour-intensive royal projects such as the building of a public monument, for which ignominious and physically demanding work they were paid only subsistence rations. Only the educated upper classes, and those wealthy enough to pay substantial bribes, could hope to avoid this hated conscripted labour.

The pharaoh in turn held some responsibilities towards his subjects. As head of the civil service and the judiciary, it was his duty to ensure that the country functioned efficiently: that taxes were collected from the primary producers, surplus food was stored against possible famine, irrigation canals were excavated, building projects were completed and law and order were maintained throughout the land. The king ran the country with the help of a relatively small band of bureaucrats and advisers selected from the élite educated classes, many of whom were his close relations, and his word was law. As head of the armed forces the pharaoh was also responsible for ensuring that Egypt remained at all times safe from foreign invaders. It was the king who planned military campaigns and who protected Egypt's borders, and it was the king who personally led the Egyptian troops into battle.

However, the pharaoh was no mere administrator or politician – any competent bureaucrat could have performed that function. Indeed, the king of Egypt was no simple human; he had a dual personality. Although he was obviously a mortal, born to a mortal mother, who could suffer joys, misfortunes and sickness like any other Egyptian, when in his official persona the pharaoh was recognized to be the holder of a divine office, an *ex-officio* god on earth. This divinity was inherited along with his title on the death of his predecessor, when the old king became associated with the dead god of the Afterlife, Osiris, and the new king became linked with the living deities Re, the sun god, and Horus, the falcon-headed son of Osiris. His newly acquired divine status separated the king from his subjects and allowed him to speak directly to the Egyptian pantheon, forming a vital link between the humble people and the divine gods and goddesses who controlled their destiny. As the only Egyptian able to communicate effectively with the gods, the king became chief priest of all religious cults; it was the king who took responsibility for ensuring that the gods were served in the appropriate manner. In return the gods agreed to guarantee the prosperity of the land and its people. It was this divine aspect of his role which ensured that the pharaoh became indispensable to his people. Egypt simply could not flourish without a king on the throne.

The lack of a legitimate pharaoh was a clear sign that the gods were displeased, and that *maat* was absent from the land. *Maat*, a word which may be translated literally as 'justice' or 'truth', was the term used by the Egyptians to describe an abstract concept representing the ideal state of the universe and everyone in it; the *status quo*, or correct order, which had been established by the gods at the time of creation and which had to be maintained to placate the gods, but which was always under threat from malevolent outside influences seeking to bring chaos and disruption (or *isfet*) to Egypt. Modern historians have struggled to find the words which provide an adequate explanation of this concept of 'rightness' or 'the proper way of doing things'; perhaps David O'Connor has come closest to reaching the original meaning of the term when he defines *maat* as:

The appropriate arrangement of the universe and human affairs – an effort to summarize the Egyptian world-view in coherent, mythic form. Centuries old by the time of the New Kingdom, the concept of *maat* was a crystallization of a myriad of religious and secular ideas, and its continuity depended upon *their* continuity; nevertheless, its very existence as a formalized statement of Egyptian beliefs helped to perpetuate the ideas and attitudes on which it was based.[9]

Uncontrolled chaos was dreaded more than anything else and a kingless period, which was by definition a *maat*-less period, was therefore something to be avoided at all costs. Times when *maat* was understood to be absent from Egypt, such as the kingless Intermediate Periods, were cited as awful comparatives designed to stress the virtues of more orthodox times; in the pessimistic and much exaggerated late Middle Kingdom text known as the *Admonitions of Ipuwer*, for example, we are told how 'merriment has ceased and is made no more, and groaning is throughout the land . . . the land is left to its weakness like a cutting of flax';[10] a clear and deliberate contrast to the peaceful and orderly late 12th Dynasty when the text was composed. More awful offences against *maat*, such as attempted regicide, were simply omitted from the historical record. Such was the power of the written word that by excluding all mention of a specific deed from a text the deed itself could be understood not to have occurred.

The office of the divine king was itself an integral part of the concept of *maat*, with the king taking personal responsibility for the maintenance of *maat* throughout the land; it was the duty of the pharaoh to preserve *maat* for the somewhat temperamental gods of Egypt. Throughout the dynastic age, the concept of *maat* and the divine nature of the kingship naturally served to reinforce the position of the royal family. By ensuring that the powers and rights of the pharaoh could not be openly questioned without posing a threat to the security of the country (that is, without threatening the presence of *maat*) the ruling élite remained securely at the top of the social pyramid, while the lower classes continued to labour unquestioningly for the good of the state, and the educated middle classes remained both too dependent on the crown and too bound by the customs that they revered to challenge this traditional allocation of resources.

It is, therefore, not too surprising to find individual pharaohs exploiting the concept of *maat* to their own particular advantage, using it to reinforce their own right to rule and to justify any action which might otherwise have proved unacceptable or questionable to the highly conservative Egyptians. Hatchepsut, whose unusual succession may itself have been interpreted by some as an offence against *maat*, instigated a vigorous domestic policy designed to prove beyond any reasonable doubt that *maat* was firmly established throughout Egypt: her large-scale building programme, obvious devotion to the cult of Amen, successful trading missions and restoration of the monuments which had been destroyed by the Hyksos invaders during the *maat*-less Intermediate Period, were all actions calculated to demonstrate the presence of prosperity, law and order. Her people could see that the gods, happy with the new regime, were allowing Egypt to flourish, and the tradition of non-interference with the *status quo* helped to maintain Hatchepsut on her throne.

Archaeological evidence of necessity plays a large part in our reconstruction of ancient Egypt. The shortfalls of the Egyptian archaeological record are by now well known, but they are worth repeating at this point as they have a direct effect on our reconstruction of Egyptian society. Throughout their history, the dynastic Egyptians took the view that, while their temples and tombs should be built to last for ever, their homes, palaces and workplaces were merely temporary structures and should be designed as such. The temples and tombs were either constructed of stone or cut into rock, while less important buildings were built of mud-brick, which was cheap, readily available, easy to work and well suited to the dry Egyptian climate. Unfortunately, while the stone structures have survived relatively intact, the mud-brick villages, towns and cities have crumbled away, collapsing to form mounds of fertile soil that, until the Egyptian government introduced protective legislation, were exploited by local peasant farmers ignorant of their archaeological value. The whole situation has been made even worse by the damp conditions in the Nile floodplain and the Nile Delta, which have hastened the destruction of the mud-brick structures so that the few ancient domestic sites which have survived intact are the atypical purpose-built towns situated away from the damp of the cultivation. The surviving archaeological evidence is therefore strongly biased towards religion and death; we have, for example, two tombs, three sarcophagi and several temples built by Hatchepsut, but little trace of the palaces where she lived her life. Overall, we are left with the misleading impression that the Egyptians were a depressingly gloomy and morbid race.

The history of archaeological excavation in Egypt has also had a direct effect upon our understanding of that country's past. The tendency of early egyptologists to seek out and excavate the more prestigious burial sites, often acting as little more than glorified treasure hunters and grave robbers, has certainly added to the funerary and religious bias in our evidence. Over the past fifty years, with the introduction of more scientific methods of excavation and recording, modern egyptologists have grown to realize just how much valuable evidence was overlooked and even destroyed by their colleagues in the undignified rush to be first to reach the precious 'treasure'. Even the new generation of scholarly excavators, working to the standards of their day, was capable of inadvertently distorting the archaeological record: when, in 1894, Edouard Naville criticized Auguste Mariette's habit of dumping spoil close to the Deir el-Bahri temple where 'it sometimes resulted in his covering important sites with earth or sand, and thus led to his overlooking discoveries to which he himself would have attached high value',[11] he was not to know that some thirty years later an American team led by Herbert E. Winlock would discover a vast number of broken statues of King Hatchepsut directly underneath Naville's own carefully planned spoil heap.

Many of the most productive archaeological expeditions at the turn of the century were funded by wealthy westerners, both individuals and institutions, who were rewarded for their generosity by a share in the finds. This has caused its own problems as valuable collections were routinely split up and dispersed throughout the museums of Egypt, Europe and America. The statuary of Hatchepsut, whose sites have generally been funded by Americans, can now be far better studied in the Metropolitan Museum of New York than in the museums of Luxor or Cairo. While this has almost certainly led to the preservation and display of objects which might otherwise have been condemned to languish in the storerooms of Egypt's over-full museums, it does pose logistical problems for the impoverished student of Hatchepsut-abilia. Hatchepsut herself suffered badly from the fact that the tomb of Tutankhamen, a relatively insignificant king whose burial chamber was stuffed with golden objects, was discovered in 1922, diverting attention away from equally valuable but less obviously exciting work which was just starting at the Deir el-Bahri mortuary temple. From 1922 onwards Tutankhamen entered the public imagination as the instantly recognized symbol of ancient Egypt, and any less spectacular discoveries were generally classified as worthy but dull.

The written evidence used in the reconstruction of Egyptian history comes from two main sources: the formal monumental inscriptions carved or painted on the temple and tomb walls, and the more informal prayers, administrative records, stories and love poems preserved on papyrus and on broken pieces of pottery or limestone chips now

known as ostraca (singular ostracon). Again, this evidence needs to be
approached with an appropriate degree of caution; we should never lose
sight of the fact that the written record is incomplete, randomly selected, and carries its own biases. The monumental inscriptions, for
example, are basically a mixture of religious and propaganda texts which
tell the story that the king him- or herself wished to convey, and which
cannot be taken as the literal truth. The translators of these inscriptions
are faced with problems not just of accuracy but of interpretation; even
the most scrupulous of scholars is aware that he or she is likely to read a
text through the lens of personal feelings. Nevertheless, and in spite of
its obvious drawbacks, this type of evidence, taken in conjunction with
the archaeological data and enlivened by the writings of contemporary
and later visitors to Egypt, can provide modern historians with an in-
valuable glimpse into the life of ancient Egypt.

Those unfamiliar with Egyptian history are often puzzled by the use
of dynasties and individual regnal years to date events. Rather than
providing a specific calendar date, such as 1458 BC, egyptologists will
refer to Hatchepsut's regnal Year 21, while her reign is itself counted as
part of the early 18th Dynasty of the New Kingdom of the dynastic
age. This is done not to confuse but to ensure the greatest possible
accuracy. We know, for example, that Hatchepsut ruled for twenty-two
years, but her precise calendar dates are less certain, and various experts
have suggested differing time-spans for her reign (for example, 1504–
1482 BC; 1490/88–1468 BC; 1479–1457 BC; 1473–1458 BC). The practice of referring to regnal years, followed throughout this book, avoids
the complications engendered by this multiplicity of suggested but unproven calendar dates.

The Egyptians divided their year into twelve months of 30 days plus
5 additional days each year, giving an annual total of 365 days. The
months in turn were grouped into three seasons based on the agricultural cycle: inundation, spring and summer. However, there was no
ancient equivalent of our modern calendar, and year numbers started
afresh with every new reign. In order to be sure of their own history,
the Egyptian scribes were forced to maintain long chronological lists
detailing successive monarchs and their reigns. Fortunately, enough of
these so-called king lists have survived to allow us to reconstruct Egypt's
past with a fair degree of accuracy. The work of the Egyptian priest

and historian Manetho has provided useful corroborative evidence. Manetho, working in approximately 300 BC, compiled a detailed history of the kings of Egypt. This original work is now lost, but fragments have been preserved in the writings of Josephus (AD 70), Africanus (early third century AD), Eusebius (early fourth century AD) and Syncellus (c. AD 800). These preserved extracts do not always agree, and the names given are often wildly incorrect, but students of Egyptian history still acknowledge a huge debt to Manetho, the 'Father of Egyptian History'. It was Manetho who first divided the various reigns into dynasties, and it was Manetho who preserved the memory, if not the actual name, of King Hatchepsut.

Another potential source of confusion is the profusion of slightly different personal names attributed by various authors to the same place or person, particularly when older sources are being quoted. Hatchepsut, for example, is also variously referred to as Hatasu, Hashepsowe, Hatshopsitu, Hatshepsut and Hatshepsuit; her father Dhutmose or Thutmose is now more commonly known by the Greek version of his name, Tuthmosis, and the state gods Amen and Re are often rendered as Amun and Ra. Some authorities have devised their own exclusive variants. Sir Alan Gardiner, for example, consistently uses Pwene in place of the more widely accepted Punt, while Naville, Buttles and other turn-of-the-century egyptologists reverse Hatchepsut's throne name Maatkare to read as Kamara. Unfortunately for modern readers, the ancient Egyptians wrote their hieroglyphic texts with no weak vowels and with an assortment of consonants not found in our modern alphabet, so the correct pronunciation of any Egyptian name must be a matter of educated guesswork. Throughout this book, the most simple and widely accepted version of each proper name has been used, all diacritical marks have been omitted, and the names included in citations within the text have been, as far as possible, standardized in an effort to avoid an unnecessary and confusing muddle for the non-specialist reader.

1

Backdrop: Egypt in the Early Eighteenth Dynasty

I have raised up what was dismembered, even from the first time when the Asiatics were in Avaris of the North Land, with roving hordes in the midst of them overthrowing what had been made; they ruled without Re . . .[1]

Princess Hatchepsut was born into the early 18th Dynasty, at a time when the newly united Egypt was still reeling from the ignominy of seeing foreign kings seated on the divine throne of the pharaohs. Although the 18th Dynasty was to develop into a period of unprecedented Egyptian prosperity, the deep humiliation of a hundred years of Hyksos rule and the widespread civil unrest of the Second Intermediate Period were never fully forgotten, and a concern with replicating the halcyon days of the Old and Middle Kingdoms – and in particular the glorious 12th Dynasty – became a constant underlying theme of early 18th Dynasty political life.

The 12th Dynasty had represented a truly golden age. Recovering from a somewhat shaky start which included the assassination of its founder, Amenemhat I, there had followed almost two hundred years of internal peace and stability which are now widely regarded as forming one of the classical periods of Egyptian civilization. Throughout the dynasty a succession of strong pharaohs ruled over a united land from the new capital of Itj-Tawy (a northern city lying somewhere between the Old Kingdom capital of Memphis and the mouth of the Faiyum), their position as absolute rulers greatly strengthened by a well-planned series of civil service reforms aimed at restricting the power of the wealthy nobles who, after the local autonomy of the First Intermediate Period, might otherwise have been tempted to establish their own independent local dynasties. Twelfth Dynasty foreign policy was as successful as it

was adventurous, and trade and diplomatic links were established
with both the Aegean and the Near East as Egypt abandoned her
traditional insularity and started to play a more prominent role in the
Mediterranean world. There were intrepid expeditions, including a
mission to the fabulous land of Punt, and significant military conquests as a new aggressive attitude towards the south pushed Egypt's
boundary further into Nubia. Within Egypt's newly strengthened borders the eastern desert was exploited for its natural resources which
included gold, the Sinai was mined for turquoise and copper and the
Faiyum was developed for agriculture through a series of innovative
irrigation techniques.

A combination of increasing Egyptian wealth, foreign stimulation
and political stability throughout the Middle Kingdom allowed the arts
to flourish. This was to become the period of classical Egyptian language and literature when many of the best-known texts, inscriptions
and narrative stories were composed. The writings of the Old Kingdom
had been brief, formal and very self-conscious in style. Middle
Kingdom compositions are both longer and far more fluent; the autobiographies[2] recorded on the walls of the private tombs are simultaneously more informative and more imaginative than their Old Kingdom
counterparts while the instructive texts, or *Instructions in Wisdom*, show a
new realism in their desire to stress the chaos poised to overwhelm
Egypt in the absence of a strong king. However, it is for the development of narrative fiction that the Middle Kingdom literature is most
justly celebrated. *The Satire of the Trades, The Story of the Eloquent Peasant,
The Tale of the Shipwrecked Sailor* and *The Story of Sinuhe* all date to this
period, allowing us to trace the evolution of the genre from simple
action-packed adventures taken straight from the oral tradition (for example, *The Tale of the Shipwrecked Sailor* – a *Boys' Own*-style tale of ship-
wreck and adventure including a fabulous snake-like creature) to more
thought-provoking tales told in an increasingly more sophisticated
blend of styles (for example, *The Story of Sinuhe* – the fictional autobiography of a nobleman exiled from Egypt and longing for home).[3]

Artists and sculptors were quick to reflect the new mood of combined nostalgia and realism and their work, while still based on the
traditional and highly formalized style of the Old Kingdom, demonstrates a willingness to portray subjects as individuals rather than stereo-
types. The royal sculptors now felt themselves free to depict a more

human pharaoh; when we look at the portrait heads of the 12th Dynasty kings Senwosret III and Amenemhat III we see strong, serious and somewhat weary men striving to conduct their divine role with regal severity, a marked contrast to the more serene and remote all-powerful god-kings of the Old Kingdom. At the same time the range of private sculpture expanded as ordinary individuals started to be represented in a variety of innovative forms rather than the limited range of statues found in Old Kingdom tombs. Few royal paintings have survived from the Middle Kingdom but the private tombs of Beni Hassan vibrate with colourful life as representations of wrestling, warfare and dancing now join the more restrained scenes found in Old Kingdom tombs.

Large-scale building projects recommenced during the 12th Dynasty, with the form of the pyramid being re-adopted as a means of emulating the Old Kingdom precedent and emphasizing the status of the king and his connection with the sun god, Re. However, there was now to be no single public building on the grand scale of the Giza pyramids. Instead of following their royal predecessors and concentrating their efforts on one solitary mortuary monument, the monarchs of the Middle Kingdom decided to spread their resources rather more widely. The extent to which these kings were willing to construct stone additions to existing mud-brick temples in the provinces is unclear because of the extensive re-modelling which occurred during the 18th Dynasty, but the evidence, where it survives, suggests a construction programme which extended the royal monopoly of stone buildings to the furthest corners of the most distant Egyptian provinces. Unfortunately, many important temples from this period were deliberately destroyed so that their precious stone blocks could be re-used in later buildings, and our knowledge of 12th Dynasty architecture is consequently sadly restricted. Our best-known example is the White Chapel of Senwosret I. This beautiful building, which demonstrates a thorough mastery of stone-working techniques including some impressive relief carving, had been dismantled and used as part of the filling of a pylon built by the New Kingdom Pharaoh Amenhotep III at Karnak. After painstaking reconstruction it is now restored to its former glories and is on permanent display in the Open-Air Museum at Karnak.

All good things must come to an end. Eventually the royal family, which had until now provided one of the longest continuous lines ever

to rule Egypt, found itself without a male heir to the throne. Amenemhat IV, the final king of the 12th Dynasty, was therefore of necessity
succeeded by his sister or half-sister Sobeknofru, who ruled as Queen of
Upper and Lower Egypt for three years, ten months and twenty-four
days before dying a natural death in office. With her death came the
end of her dynasty. Although there was, in theory, nothing to prevent a
woman from becoming pharaoh and, indeed, there appears to have
been no opposition to Sobeknofru assuming this role – although any
unsuccessful opposition would, of course, be difficult for us to detect –
such an obvious departure from royal tradition was a sure sign that
something was very wrong within the royal family, and Sobeknofru's
reign is now generally interpreted as a brave but doomed attempt to
prolong a dying royal line. An alternative view, that she must have seized
the crown as the result of a vicious family quarrel, is now largely discred-
ited on the grounds of lack of evidence. The fact that Sobeknofru's
name was included on the Sakkara king list may be taken as a good
indication that her reign was acceptable both to her people and to the
historians who preserved her memory.

Sobeknofru was succeeded by an unrelated king, and the 13th Dynasty started to follow very much in the tradition of the 12th. However,
no strong royal family was established and there was little apparent
continuity between the monarchs traditionally assigned to this period.
Instead, a succession of short-lived kings and their increasingly powerful
viziers reigned over a slowly fragmenting Egypt, and the country gradually disintegrated into a loose association of semi-independent city
states. A series of freak Nile floods at this time, and the resulting strain
on the Egyptian economy, must have seemed a very bad omen; the
regular rise and fall of the Nile was taken as a general sign that all was
well within Egypt and the 13th Dynasty rulers must have been unpleas-
antly reminded of the very low floods which had heralded the collapse
of the Old Kingdom. They would have done well to heed the omen.
The end of the 13th Dynasty saw the 'official' end of the Middle
Kingdom and the beginning of the Second Intermediate Period (Dynasties 14 to 17), a badly recorded phase of national disunity and foreign
rule sandwiched between the well-documented stability of the Middle
and New Kingdoms.

Tutimaios. In his reign, for what cause I know not, a blast of god smote us; and unexpectedly from the regions of the east invaders of obscure race marched in confidence of victory against our land . . . Their race as a whole was called Hyksos, that is 'king-shepherds', for *Hyk* in the sacred language means 'king' and *sos* in common speech is 'shepherd'.[4]

Throughout the Middle Kingdom there had been a persistent influx of 'Asiatic' migrants from the east, Semitic peoples who were attracted by Egypt's growing prosperity and who were themselves being pressured westwards by immigrants from further east; this was a time of population shifts throughout the entire Eastern Mediterranean region. The new arrivals were accepted by the locals and merged peacefully into the existing towns and villages of northern Egypt.[5] During the 13th Dynasty, however, these groups started to form significant and partially independent communities in the Nile Delta. At the same time the previously emasculated local rulers were gradually gaining in power as national unity began to crumble. Slowly the country resolved itself into three mutually distrustful regions, each ruled concurrently by different dynasties. The Nubian kingdom of Kerma developed in the extreme south, a small group of independent Egyptians controlled southern Egypt from Thebes (17th Dynasty), and the north was ruled by a group of Palestinian invaders known as the Hyksos (15th Dynasty) and their Palestinian vassals (16th Dynasty).[6]

It was the Hyksos invaders who made the deepest impression on the historical record, ruling over northern Egypt for over a hundred years and taking the eastern Delta town of Avaris (a corruption of the Egyptian name *Hwt W'rt*, literally 'The Great Mansion' or 'Mansion of the Administration', modern Tell ed-Daba) as their capital. To the south the native-born Theban rulers remained independent and relationships between north and south were initially peaceful, if distrustful; the southern kings were able to lease grazing land from their Hyksos neighbours and there is even some evidence to suggest that Herit, a daughter of the final Hyksos king, Apophis, may have married into the Theban royal family. The Hyksos were certainly on good terms with the Nubian rulers of Kerma, to the extent that the same Apophis, towards the end of his 33-year reign and no longer on such friendly terms with his immediate neighbours, felt free to urge the Nubians to invade the Theban kingdom in order to distract the Theban army and so protect his own position in the north. A letter written by Apophis to the King of Kush and fortuitously intercepted by troops loyal to the Theban King Kamose, details his plotting:

. . . Have you [not] beheld what Egypt has done against me . . . He [Kamose] choosing the two lands to devastate them, my land and yours, and he has destroyed them. Come, fare north at once, do not be timid. See, he is here with me . . . I will not let him go until you have arrived.[7]

Egyptian legend as typified by Manetho regards the Hyksos as an uncivilized, brutal band of invaders and their reign as a dark, never-to-be-repeated period of chaos and mayhem:

. . . By main force they [the Hyksos] easily seized [Egypt] without striking a blow, and having overpowered the rulers of the land, they then burned our cities ruthlessly, razed to the ground the temples of the gods, and treated all the natives with a cruel hostility, massacring some and leading into slavery the wives and children of others . . .[8]

This lament is, to a large extent, merely the conventional expression of horror at the realization that despised and culturally inferior foreigners could actually conquer the mighty Egypt. Exaggeration was an accepted and even expected component of historical narrative and the Egyptians saw no harm in re-interpreting their own past as and when necessary. The deeply held belief that their land could only flourish under a divinely appointed Egyptian pharaoh was certainly strong enough to distort the historical record in this instance. Archaeological evidence, less obviously biased, makes it clear that the hated Hyksos, far from inflicting barbaric foreign practices on their new subjects, made a determined effort to adapt themselves to the customs of their adopted country. The new rulers retained a few of their own traditions: architectural styles and pottery forms now show a distinct Near Eastern influence, the war goddess Anath or Astarte was quickly absorbed into the Egyptian pantheon as 'Lady of Heaven' and her consort, the Egyptian god Seth, became the chief deity. However, in most other respects the Hyksos surrendered their own identity as, with the zeal of new converts, they immersed themselves in Egyptian culture, adopting hieroglyphic writing, embellishing local temples, copying Middle Kingdom art-forms, manufacturing scarabs and even transforming themselves into Egyptian-style pharaohs by taking names compounded with 'Re', the name of the Egyptian sun god. Far from bringing economic disaster to Egypt, their lands were governed efficiently, making good use of the Middle Kingdom administrative framework which was already in place, and native-born Egyptian bureaucrats worked willingly alongside their new masters to ensure that the Delta region prospered under their rule.

The long-term material advantages of the brief interlude of foreign rule now seem very obvious. Under Hyksos rule, Egypt rapidly lost much of her traditional isolation as trading and diplomatic links were established with a wide range of Near Eastern kingdoms, and the resulting flood of exotic and practical imports both stimulated the economy and inspired the Egyptian artists and artisans. Egypt benefited from the introduction of new bronze working and pottery and weaving techniques; there were exciting new food crops to be tested, and even a previously unknown breed of humped-back cattle. Most important of all was the Hyksos contribution to Egypt's traditional military equipment; it was their improvements, combined with the early 18th Dynasty reorganization of the army structure, which led directly to the evolution of the efficient and almost invincible fighting troops of the 18th and 19th Dynasty Empire. The Hyksos introduced new forms of defensive forts, new weapon-types (more efficient dagger and sword forms and the strong compound bow which had a far greater range than the old-fashioned simple bow) and the concept of body armour to protect the troops. The soldiers – who during the Old and Middle Kingdoms had marched into battle dressed only in the briefest of kilts or loincloths and protected by a long and cumbersome cow-hide shield – were now issued with protective jackets and a lighter, easier-to-handle tapered shield. Their most important introduction was, however, the harnessed horse and the two-wheeled horse-drawn chariot, a light and highly mobile vehicle which, manned by a driver and a soldier equipped with spear, shield and bow, quickly became one of the most valuable assets of the Egyptian army.

In the south the Theban 17th Dynasty ruled over Egypt from Elephantine to Cusae (el-Qusiya, Middle Egypt), successfully continuing many of the Middle Kingdom royal traditions but on a reduced scale and adapted to fit local conditions; the 17th Dynasty royal pyramids were

Fig. 1.1   The cartouche of King Sekenenre Tao II

relatively tiny mud-brick structures perched on top of rock-cut tombs. As the southern dynasty slowly established itself relationships between south and north gradually deteriorated, and open warfare erupted when King Sekenenre Tao II, 'The Brave', came to the Theban throne. A fantastic New Kingdom story which purports to explain the outbreak of hostilities starts by setting the scene:

It once happened that the land of Egypt was in misery, for there was no lord as [sole] king. A day came to pass when King Sekenenre was [still only] ruler of the Southern City. Misery was in the town of the Asiatics, for Prince Apophis was in Avaris, and the entire land paid tribute to him, delivering their taxes [and] even the north bringing every [sort of] good produce of the Delta.[9]

We are told how the Hyksos King Apophis, now a fervent worshipper of the peculiar and so far unidentified animal-headed god Seth, decides to provoke a quarrel by making an intentionally ridiculous demand. A messenger is sent southwards, and he delivers the complaint to the bemused Sekenenre Tao:

Let there be a withdrawal from the canal of hippopotami which lie at the east of the City, because they don't let sleep come to me either in the daytime or at night.

Sekenenre is understandably rendered speechless by this unreasonable request: it is inconceivable that the Theban hippopotami could have been making so much noise that they were preventing Apophis from sleeping in Avaris, some 500 miles downstream. Unfortunately, the end of the story is lost, and we do not know how the king eventually replied, or indeed whether Apophis went on to make even more outrageous demands.

The more down-to-earth archaeological evidence confirms that Sekenenre Tao II fought against the Hyksos in Middle Egypt before dying of wounds sustained in battle: his mummified body was unwrapped by the French egyptologist Gaston Maspero in 1886, and examined by the distinguished anatomist G. Elliot Smith in 1906. The mummy was clearly a disturbing sight, with horrific head and neck injuries caused by repeated blows from a bronze Hyksos battle-axe:

All that now remains of Saqnounri Tiouaqen [Sekenenre Tao II] is a badly damaged, disarticulated skeleton enclosed in an imperfect sheet of soft, moist, flexible dark brown skin, which has a strongly aromatic, spicy odour . . . No attempt was made to put the body into the customary mummy-position; the head had not been straightened on the trunk, the legs were not fully extended, and the arms and hands were left in the agonized attitude into which they had been thrown in the death spasms following the murderous attack, the evidence of which is so clearly impressed on the battered face and skull.[10]

The badly preserved body suggests that the king had been hastily mummified, not necessarily by the official royal undertakers. Sekenenre Tao II was succeeded by his son, Kamose, who ruled for little more than three years yet managed to strengthen the Theban hold on Middle Egypt. After brooding aloud on the unfortunate situation which had divided his land – 'I should like to know what serves this strength of mine when a chieftain is in Avaris and another in Kush, and I sit united with an Asiatic and a Nubian'[11] – Kamose took decisive action. He advanced northwards towards Avaris and southwards as far as Buhen, obtaining control of the vital river trade routes and exacting vengeance on those believed to have collaborated with the enemy, before returning to Thebes where he recorded his daring deeds on a limestone stela at the Karnak temple:

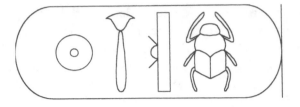

Fig 1.2   The cartouche of King Kamose

O wicked of heart, vile Asiatic, I shall drink the wine of your vineyard which
the Asiatic whom I captured press for me. I lay waste your dwelling place and
cut down your trees . . . I did not leave a scrap of Avaris without being empty . . . I
laid waste their towns and burned their places, they being made into red ruins
for eternity on account of the damage which they did within this Egypt, for
they had made themselves serve the Asiatic and had forsaken Egypt their
mistress.[12]

Kamose died young, possibly killed in action like his father, and was
in turn succeeded on the Theban throne by his younger brother
Ahmose. Ahmose, initially too young to fight, waited for over ten years
before resuming the struggle to unite his country. His victorious campaign against the Hyksos has been recorded in full and somewhat bloodthirsty detail by a soldier also named Ahmose, the son of a woman
named Ibana and a soldier named Baba, who hailed from the southern
Egyptian town of el-Kab. In his autobiography, Ahmose the soldier
aims to impress us with his lengthy military record and his extreme
personal bravery, quoting directly from a New Kingdom proverb: 'The
name of the brave man is in that which he has done; it will not perish in
the land forever.' We learn how, when he had 'founded a household'
(that is, married and perhaps fathered a child), he started his military
service on a ship called *The Northern*. Ahmose sailed north to fight
alongside his pharaoh in the Delta, taking part in several bloody battles
and playing an active part in the sacking of Avaris. The Hyksos and
their kinsmen had been active throughout northern Sinai and in the
Levantine area and, as they retreated from Egypt, King Ahmose followed them eastwards into south-west Palestine, eventually laying siege
to the fortified town of Sharuhen, the last outpost of the Hyksos kingdom. After each successful battle Ahmose, son of Ibana, was rewarded

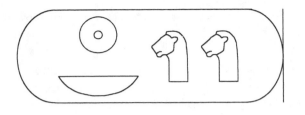

Fig. 1.3   The cartouche of King Ahmose

with booty, including the prisoners he had captured, and he proudly informs us that he was eventually awarded the 'Gold of Valour', one of the highest military honours, for his bravery in battle. His words allow us a rare insight into the turbulent life of an early 18th Dynasty professional soldier:

. . . I was taken to the boat 'The Northern' because of my bravery. I accompanied the Sovereign, life, prosperity and health be upon him, on my feet when he travelled around in his chariot. The town of Avaris was besieged. I was brave in the presence of his Majesty. Then I was promoted to [the boat] 'Rising in Memphis'. There was fighting on the water of Padjedku of Avaris and I made a seizure and brought away a hand. This was reported to the Royal Herald, thereupon I was given the gold of valour . . . Then there was fighting in Southern Egypt, south of this town. I brought away one man as a living captive . . . When it was reported to the Royal Herald I was rewarded with gold a second time.

Then Avaris was sacked. I brought away from there as plunder one man and three women, a total of four people. His Majesty gave them to me as slaves. Then Sharuhen was besieged for three years. His Majesty plundered it. I brought away from there as plunder two women and a hand. The gold of valour was presented to me and, lo, I was given slaves as plunder.[13]

Following the successful expulsion of the Hyksos, Ahmose turned his attention southwards to Nubia, where once again he was followed by his loyal soldier:

[His Majesty] sailed south to Khenthennefer to destroy the Bowmen of Nubia. His majesty made a great heap of corpses among them. I brought away plunder from there, two living men and three hands. I was rewarded with gold again and I was given two female slaves. His majesty travelled north, his heart swelling with bravery and victory. He had conquered southerners and northerners.

When Ahmose writes of capturing a hand he is referring to the practice of amputating the hand, or on some occasions the penis, of a dead enemy so that the true scale of the victory could be assessed. This effective, but to modern eyes rather gruesome, means of counting is attested by several large-scale scenes of victorious New Kingdom pharaohs standing by piles of discarded human body parts.

Following the death of Ahmose the king, Ahmose the soldier continued his military career serving in Nubia under both Amenhotep I and Tuthmosis I, and receiving both promotion and gifts of land as a reward for his loyalty. In his final campaign he accompanied Tuthmosis I to Syria before returning to enjoy a well-earned retirement and a natural death at el-Kab where he was eventually interred 'in the tomb that I myself made'.

A second soldier, also a native of el-Kab and possibly a young relation of Ahmose, son of Ibana, somewhat confusingly named Ahmose-Pennekheb, tells us that King Ahmose undertook a second Asian campaign in his regnal Year 22, fighting in 'Djahy', the general name used for Syria and Palestine, and perhaps reaching as far east as the River Euphrates. Presumably this second campaign was intended to provide conclusive proof that Egypt was once again united under a strong king and well able to participate in international affairs. This region, now under the influence, if not the direct control of Egypt, formed the basis of the Egyptian Empire which was later to be developed by the Tuthmoside kings. By the end of his regnal Year 16 Egypt was the chief power in the Near East and Ahmose was free to consolidate his southern border. Here, as Ahmose son of Ibana has already related, a series of efficient campaigns ensured that control was re-imposed on Nubia and Egypt's boundary was re-established below the Second Cataract.

King Ahmose died after a 25-year rule leaving his son, Amenhotep I, to inherit a country united and secure within her boundaries for the first time in over two hundred years. The Hyksos had been expelled from the north, the Nubians had been crushed to the south and Egypt had expanded into the Levant in order to protect herself from further attack. Although Ahmose was clearly continuing the foreign policies started by his immediate predecessors, to him has gone the credit of militarizing the country and ridding Egypt of the hated foreigners. In honour of this magnificent achievement, history traditionally places Ahmose at the head of the 18th Dynasty, even though his grandfather, father and brother are still regarded as 17th Dynasty kings. Ahmose later became the object of a funerary cult based around his cenotaph at Abydos.

Ahmose had been revered throughout the land for his prowess as a mighty warrior-king. Personal bravery and a good military record now became desirable attributes indicative of a successful monarch, and succeeding 18th Dynasty rulers found it prudent to place great emphasis on their military strength and personal bravery. It was now almost expected that a new king would mark his accession by leading his troops to crush the traditional enemies to the south (Nubians) and to the north (Asiatics). This had not always been the case, although the first king of Egypt, Narmer, is best known in his role of a military leader. Generally, as the Old and Middle Kingdoms progressed and as Egypt continued her policy of self-imposed isolation from the rest of the Mediterranean world, the armed forces had become more and more insignificant, although a royal bodyguard was always maintained. Fighting was not viewed as a particularly noble occupation, being generally associated with periods of civil war when Egyptian fought against Egyptian, and most kings did not choose to exploit the military aspect of their rule. There was no Old or Middle Kingdom standing army; the king relied on an informal militia-type arrangement to gather groups of fighting men together whenever needed, and the small group of professional soldiers who administered these irregular troops were not significant members of the ruling élite.

However, the time of the Hyksos expulsion from Egypt was a time of increasing military activity throughout the entire Near East. Egypt now understood only too well that she was vulnerable to attack and that, with her lucrative interests in Nubia and Palestine, she could no longer afford to remain aloof from world affairs. By maintaining an efficient fighting force, Egypt could remain allies with powerful and well-armed near-neighbours such as the Hittites, who might otherwise be tempted to invade a temptingly wealthy and weak country. The fact that the

Fig. 1.4   Old and New Kingdom soldiers

army could also become a focus for national pride and unity was an
additional and quickly exploited bonus. It was now perceived as excellent propaganda for the king to be seen defending his territory, sub-
duing foreigners and, by implication, maintaining his control over the
population within Egypt, and large-scale scenes of the king, riding in
his chariot, meeting foes in battle or even grasping a handful of enemies
by the hair, became a standard decoration for monumental gateways and
exterior temple walls. This change in attitude may perhaps be understood by considering the approach of present-day monarchies to the
armed services. In early eighteenth-century England, following the civil
wars of the late seventeenth century, the army was deeply distrusted by
the population at large, who saw it as a means of suppressing the rights
of free-born Englishmen. It was therefore rare for a member of the
royal family to be seen wearing a military uniform away from the
battlefield. Today, however, following victory in the two World Wars
and the first-hand experience of those required to do National Service,
the army is viewed as an obvious and acceptable leadership role for
young male members of the royal family and military uniforms are
considered appropriate wear for public occasions such as royal
weddings.

The New Kingdom army was suddenly both popular and socially acceptable, rapidly joining the priesthood and the civil service as one of the acceptable professions for the educated and literate classes. Recruitment soared, and there was a constant demand for able quartermasters and administrators who could ensure the smooth running of a large and complex organization. Alongside the hard-bitten old campaigners who had fought their way up through the ranks there could now be found the ancient equivalent of 'graduate entry' officers: professionals valued more for their administrative skills than their combative abilities. The army was an attractive career option for those who, ambitious but illiterate, were denied entry into the bureaucracy and priesthood, and soon there were whole families who undertook to serve in the army for several generations in return for the right to tenant their own farms. The revitalized and greatly expanded army was organized into highly trained units of infantry, chariotry and more specialized troops: three or four divisions of up to 5,000 men were progressively subdivided into hosts (500 men), companies (250 men), platoons (50 men) and squads (10 men) and a 'Great Army General', often the crown prince, was appointed to take overall command.[14] The pharaoh, of course, remained absolute head of the armed forces.

The monarchs of the 18th Dynasty openly acknowledged that their military successes were entirely due to the superiority of the Egyptian deities and, in particular, to the patronage of their local god, Amen of Thebes. It was no coincidence that the great scenes of the pharaoh as warrior triumphant were carved on temple walls, emphasizing the link between devotion and victory; as Hatchepsut herself was to affirm: 'I have done this with a loving heart for my father Amen . . . My majesty knows his divinity. I acted under his command. It was he who led me, and I did not plan a single work without his doing.'[15]

Throughout the Old Kingdom the most important state god had been Re, the sun god whose cult centre of Heliopolis lay close to the capital city of Memphis, and whose most striking monuments were the pyramids in the Memphite royal cemeteries. The form of the pyramid was designed to associate the dead king with the living god, allowing him to ascend the stairway to heaven so that he might sail across the sky with Re every day. The rise of the Middle Kingdom at Thebes did little directly to reduce the power of Re, although his association with

kingship now became far less obvious than it had been during the
Old Kingdom. The kings of the
12th Dynasty moved their capital
north and recommenced the
building of Re-related pyramids,
presumably as a means of stressing
their newly acquired royal status.
However, they still retained a
loyalty to their local Theban gods
and, as their choice of names –
Amenemhat, 'Amen to the Fore';
Senwosret, 'The Man of Wosret'[16]
– suggests, the provincial southern
deities were starting to gain in national importance. This period
saw the beginning of large-scale
development at the Temple of
Amen at Karnak. The Karnak
temple complex, set in a northern
suburb of Thebes, became, during
the New Kingdom, the largest collection of related religious buildings in the world.

Amen had started life as an insignificant and rather colourless local
deity worshipped in the immediate area around Thebes. However, he was quickly to become
the most powerful god in the

Fig. 1.5   The god Amen

Egyptian Empire, associated with the most important Old Kingdom
deity in the compound god Amen-Re, linked with the fertility god
Min of Coptos in his ithyphallic form and accorded the magnificent
title 'King of the Gods and Lord of the Thrones of the Two Lands'.
Iconographically, Amen most commonly appears as a man dressed in a
short kilt and sporting a distinctive feathered headdress of two tall
plumes. His sacred animals are the goose and, far more importantly, the
ram, and his main cult centre is the Karnak temple at Thebes. Egyptian

gods do not usually come singly but as members of divine families of three; Amen's consort is the anthropoid goddess Mut ('Mother'), a lady who has links with both the mother-goddesses Hathor and Bast and with the fierce lion-headed goddess of war and sickness, Sekhmet, and their son is the local moon-god, Khonsu. Mut's cult centre is an impressive temple enclosure directly to the south of Amen's at Karnak, while Khonsu was worshipped in a temple immediately to the north.

Egypt's new prosperity allowed the 18th Dynasty pharaohs to endow shrines and temples to various gods throughout the land. These new buildings were now built of stone rather than mud-brick and were literally designed to last for all eternity. Major cities

Fig. 1.6   The goddess Mut

such as Thebes and Memphis, previously home to relatively modest mud-brick chapels, now found themselves dominated by massive, painted stone temples. These were typically surrounded by clusters of relatively unimpressive mud-brick buildings housing lesser shrines and administrative offices, the whole temple complex being enclosed by a high, thick mud-brick wall of military appearance, designed to keep the common people out. The Egyptian temple was not the equivalent of a medieval cathedral; it was the private home of the god who, in the form of a statue, dwelt within. The temple gates were rarely thrown open to the general public and, while many townsmen must have worked on the temple buildings, few would have been aware of the mysteries surrounding the daily practice of their state religion. Indeed, although the ordinary people owed an official allegiance to the state gods, they were far more likely to worship their less exalted and more familiar local gods, while folk-religion, including magic, superstition and witchcraft, played an important role in the life of the peasant communities.

By the middle of the 18th Dynasty, Thebes had become a major religious centre with a full range of temples and shrines dedicated not only to Amen and his family but to a whole host of lesser deities. On the western bank of the Nile, opposite Thebes, were the mortuary temples of the kings, the tombs of the élite citizens and, hidden away in the Valley of the Kings, the tombs of the pharaohs themselves. All New Kingdom monarchs showed their extreme devotion to Amen by trying to outdo their predecessors in embellishing the Karnak complex itself, and a considerable amount of Egypt's new-found foreign wealth was diverted towards the Great Temple of Amen so that it grew physically, becoming an economic force in its own right and employing an increasingly large staff to carry out the cult ceremonies and administer the god's extensive portfolio. Theban state religion was now organized on a far more professional basis and the hitherto private deity started to make a series of well-organized public parades through the streets, a tradition which allowed the people to enjoy a day's holiday while subtly underlining the magnificence and omnipresence of the god and his priesthood.

By the middle of the New Kingdom, the religious foundations controlled an estimated one-third of the cultivated land and employed approximately twenty per cent of the population. Amen himself owned not only temples but major secular investments such as fields, ships, mines, quarries, villages and even prisoners of war who had been donated by the grateful monarchy. The income from these assets, together with the routine daily offerings of thousands of loaves of bread and hundreds of jugs of beer plus costlier foodstuffs including wine and meat, was collected by Amen's earthly representatives and was used to pay the temple employees. Surpluses were stored in vast mud-brick warehouses kept safe within the temple walls. Within a very short time the Amen temple at Karnak was second only to the throne itself as a centre of economic and political influence in Egypt.

Perhaps it is modern cynicism which prompts present-day historians to question why the 18th Dynasty monarchs should have deliberately chosen to raise the cult of Amen to state god status, thereby creating an immensely wealthy and semi-independent priesthood capable of posing a threat to the throne. The simple answer, that the kings felt a strong devotion to their patron deity, may well be the true one. However, it is tempting to see the rise of Amen as a more calculated gesture, perhaps aimed at reducing the influence of the northern-based cult of Re. Promoting a new Egyptian state god, one who had demonstrated his powers by granting victory in battle, may have been a shrewd move aimed at unifying a demoralized country recovering from the ignominy of foreign rule. It would certainly have helped the position of the new pharaoh who, as chief priest of all the gods, and indeed as the very son of Amen, had the power to interpret the god's wishes as he saw fit. Hatchepsut herself was to make great use of her filial relationship with Amen, continually stressing the doctrine of the divine birth of kings to support her claim to the throne. However, this mutual dependency could prove to be a two-edged sword. Any public failure by the new god, such as a refusal to grant further victories to the Egyptian army, could be taken as a direct sign that the king himself was failing to perform his duties correctly, and a powerful and wealthy priesthood could ultimately bring about the fall of a weak or inefficient king.

By the late 18th Dynasty, the monarchy was starting to feel itself challenged by the power and ever-increasing wealth of the cult of Amen. Amenhotep II, Tuthmosis IV and Amenhotep III all appointed their own loyal followers to the position of High Priest in an attempt to maintain a degree of royal control over the priesthood, while Amen-hotep III also started to pay more attention to the other gods of the Egyptian pantheon, partially reverting back to Old Kingdom theology by re-allying the monarchy with the sun god, Re of Heliopolis. His son, Amenhotep IV (now known as the heretic King Akhenaten, 'Service-able to the Aten'), took this policy to extremes by completely rejecting the traditional polytheistic religion and imposing a new monotheistic cult based on the worship of the sun disc, or Aten, on his people. This radical change, which included the establishment of a new capital in the desert of Middle Egypt, was too extreme for the conservative Egyptians, and far too much of a threat to the power of Amen. It was doomed to failure. By Year 3 of his successor's reign, the old gods, including Amen, had been reinstated and the new king had changed his name from Tutankhaten, 'Living Image of the Aten', to Tutankhamen, 'Living Image of Amen'.

. . . all the wealth that goes into Thebes of Egypt, where treasures in greatest store are laid up in men's houses. Thebes, which is the city of an hundred gates and from each issue forth to do battle two hundred doughty warriors with horses and chariots.[17]

The early 18th Dynasty rulers broke with tradition when they established their capital at their home-city of Thebes. Thebes, or Thebai, is the Greek name for the southern city which the Egyptians officially knew as Waset but which they referred to simply as 'The City' (literally *Niwt*), and which modern Egyptians now call Luxor. The new capital lay on the east bank of the Nile in the 4th Upper Egyptian province, close enough to both Nubia and the Eastern Desert to be able to benefit from the lucrative trade routes, and far enough away from the northern capital Memphis to have always maintained semi-independent status. Thebes had been an unimportant provincial town throughout the Old Kingdom, and it was not until the civil unrest of the First Intermediate Period that the local Theban rulers started to gain in power and influence. By the time of Ahmose, Thebes had expanded to become an extensive city, and the Theban necropolis on the west bank of the Nile had become the main burial ground for the pharaohs, their families and the higher-ranking court officials. During the 18th Dynasty, however, the old city mound was completely flattened to allow the redevelopment of the Karnak temple, and the residential area was rebuilt on relatively low-lying ground which now lies below the water-table and which is consequently lost from the archaeological record.

Living conditions within Thebes must have been, for all but the most wealthy, somewhat unpleasant during the hot summer months. There was a permanent shortage of building land, made much worse by the extension of the Karnak and Luxor temples, and there was no formal planning policy so that, as the city expanded, the houses were packed more and more closely together, blocking the light from the crowded and twisting streets. The lack of any form of official sanitation combined with the habit of keeping animals within the home to create an undesirable, vermin-ridden environment that must have been highly unhealthy for the unfortunate citizens. However, although many were forced by the nature of their employment to live in the overcrowded towns and cities, Egypt was still a predominantly rural country and the majority of Egyptians lived relatively healthy lives working as peasant farmers in small and politically insignificant agricultural communities. Throughout the New Kingdom it was fashionable to despise city life as a necessary evil while rural life – strongly romanticized – was considered to be ideal. Just as modern city dwellers dream of owning a cottage in the country, so Egyptian officials yearned for a spacious single-storey villa set in its own grounds away from the bustle, noise and smells of the city. For the higher echelons of society, this dream could become a reality which would continue into the Afterlife; their heaven took the form of the 'Field of Reeds', an idyllic rural retreat where noblemen, their wives and daughters would spend eternity supervising the labours of others less fortunate than themselves.

Thebes did, however, boast one example of a well-planned community. The workmen's village of Deir el-Medina, simply 'the Village' to its inhabitants, was founded by Amenhotep I and largely built by Tuthmosis I in order to provide a convenient base for those employed in the cutting and decoration of the royal tombs in the nearby Valley of the Kings and Valley of the Queens. Situated on the West Bank, opposite Thebes and over a mile away from the River Nile, the Village was of necessity built of a combination of stone and mud-brick. For this reason the Village has survived where others, built entirely of mud-brick, have crumbled to dust, and is now able to provide us with a vivid insight into the daily lives of a specialized section of Egypt's middle and working classes. Deir el-Medina experienced over four hundred years of continuous occupation by not only the workmen and their supervisors but their families, dependants, pets and those providing ancillary services such as potters, priests and laundry workers. By the 19th Dynasty up to seventy families – about three hundred people – lived in the modest rectangular houses which had been laid out with all the precision of a modern American city, within a defining wall. Beyond the wall there was a cemetery, a collection of chapels for private worship, and possibly a subsidiary village intended to house the lowest-ranking servants and serfs. Every month a gang of male workers would leave the Village and head for the Valley of the Kings, where they lodged in temporary accommodation for up to twenty-seven working days. Back at the Village, daily life continued as in any normal Egyptian town or city for as long as the king was able to provide the rations which served as wages. During the 18th Dynasty, a period of economic strength and efficient administration, the workmen's Village functioned well.

Although Thebes may be regarded as the new state capital, and certainly as the new religious capital, the idea of the single predominant city was now of far less importance than it had been during the Old Kingdom when Egypt had been ruled from the northern city of Memphis. Memphis was at that time not only the largest Egyptian city, it was the site of the main royal residence and the administrative centre, and nearby were both the royal burial grounds and the major cult centre of Re. In many ways her geographical position made Memphis a far more suitable capital city than Thebes. Situated at the crossroads between the two traditional regions of Upper (Southern) and Lower (Northern, or Delta) Egypt, Memphis enjoyed excellent communications with both north and south. Although an inland city, Memphis, on the River Nile, was the site of the royal dockyards, and the city flourished as a marine trading centre. Furthermore, Memphis made an ideal base for the army. Following the southern campaigns of Tuthmosis I, Nubia, although given to frequent rebellions, could offer no real threat to the might of Egypt. The real danger was perceived as coming from the Levant, where semi-independent city-states were starting to unite under the banners of the powerful rulers of Kadesh, Mitanni and the Hittites. We know that Tuthmosis I built a large palace/barrack at Memphis, and it seems likely that throughout the 18th Dynasty the state bureaucracy was still controlled to a large extent from that city. Unfortunately, little of ancient Memphis has survived to be excavated.

Just as the 18th Dynasty rulers refused to commit themselves to a single capital city, they did not restrict themselves to one principal palace. Instead they adopted a mobile court, perhaps inspired by their experiences of military campaigns, and toured the country with a small entourage, travelling by river to inspect and impose control on the various regions and staying in short-term palaces known as the 'Mooring Places of Pharaoh', which were often little more than elaborate rest-houses situated at strategic points along the Nile. The journey from Memphis to Thebes would have been a slow one of perhaps two to three weeks and it made sense that the less mobile members of the royal household, including the majority of the women, their children and their retinues, were maintained in permanent harem-palaces away from the main royal residences. By the 19th Dynasty the country had become even more de-centralized. The official capital was by then Pa-Ramesses in the Delta but the largest centre of population was still Memphis, while Thebes remained both the main cult centre and the burial place of kings.

The Mooring Places should be considered as palaces in the sense that they provided a home for the king and his retinue, but they should not be imagined as the ancient equivalent of Buckingham Palace or Versailles. The idea of the settled palace, or indeed the settled upper-class household, is a relatively modern one. In fourteenth-century England, for example, even a gentleman of relatively modest means might be the lord of several manors, all of which he needed to oversee in person, while a great lord would own many estates throughout the land. When such a landowner moved from one estate to another he was accompanied by his household (family, dependants and servants), his furniture, plate and clothing, all travelling through the countryside in a style intended to impress his wealth and dignity on the less fortunate locals. A move every two to three weeks would not have been seen as excessive, and it was not until the end of the fourteenth century that the great households became relatively static, moving perhaps two or three times a year.[18]

The palaces scattered along the Nile were never intended to act as impressive stone testimonies to the glories of a particular king's reign; instead they were constructed quickly and relatively cheaply from mud-brick wherever and whenever required. The use of mud-brick meant that the palaces could be designed on the spot to fit the exact requirements of their occupants, unlike the more or less standard plans used for the stone-built temples and tombs. However, the use of mud-brick also meant that the palaces were vulnerable to decay, and we now have few surviving palace buildings. The royal progression from palace to palace ensured that the authority of the king became a reality to those in even the most distant provinces and, at a more practical level, may well have been an efficient cost-cutting exercise. Although each Mooring Place was provided with its own farm and granary this did not necessarily provide enough food for a visit, and it was often necessary to make the local mayor responsible for provisioning the royal household. Local officials presumably came to dread the news of an impending royal visit.[19] A 19th Dynasty scribal exercise gives some

indication of the preparations considered necessary to welcome a
pharaoh:

Get on with having everything ready for pharaoh's [arrival] . . . have made
ready 100 ring stands for bouquets of flowers . . . 1,000 loaves of fine flour . . .
Cakes, 100 baskets . . . Dried meat, 100 baskets . . . Milk, 60 measures . . .
Grapes, 50 sacks . . .[20]

By the end of Ahmose's reign the Egyptian economy was booming.
Egypt was naturally a very wealthy country and once unity and central
control had been re-established it was possible to co-ordinate the man-
agement of her ample natural resources, taxing the primary producers –
the peasants and their landlords – to support the bureaucratic and
priestly superstructure and storing up surpluses to provide against
harsher times. The Greek historian Herodotus commented admiringly:

In no other country do they gather their seed with so little labour. They have
no need to break up the ground with the plough, nor to use the hoe, nor
indeed to do any of the hard work which the rest of mankind finds necessary if
they are to get a crop. Instead the farmer simply waits until the river has, of its
own volition, spread itself over the fields and withdrawn again to its bed, and
then he sows his plot of land . . .[21]

While the farmer's life was almost certainly somewhat harder than the
idyllic existence outlined by Herodotus, it is clear that the peasant
labour force, without undue exertion, was well able to support Egypt's
population of approximately 3,000,000 during the early New Kingdom.
During the period of inundation when the land was flooded and all
routine agricultural work ceased, they provided an unemployed workforce available to work on major state projects such as the building of
royal monuments. The knowledge that the state and temple warehouses
were brimming with grain must have been intensely reassuring to the
18th Dynasty monarchs who knew that repeated famine, just like freak
floods, could bring about a quick change of dynasty.
    Away from the immediate Nile Valley, Egypt was rich in building
stone, both the softer limestone and sandstone and harder, more exotic,
stones such as granite, which was quarried at the First Cataract,
quartzite, which came from the Gebel Ahmar near modern Cairo,

basalt from the Wadi Hammamat in the Eastern Desert and alabaster from Hatnub, Middle Egypt. Although there were no precious gems, the semi-precious amethyst, carnelian and jasper could all be found within Egypt's borders, there was gold in the Eastern Desert and Sinai was mined for both copper and turquoise. The only valuable commodities which were missing were silver and wood; these could be imported from the Aegean and from the Near East as and when needed.

Egypt's newly re-imposed control over Nubia led to increased supplies of gold and highly desirable exotica such as ivory, baboons, pygmies, ostrich eggs and feathers. This in turn provided surplus items for barter with Egypt's Mediterranean neighbours; diplomatic and trading links had been established with Mitanni, Babylon, Assyria, the Hittite Empire and the Greek islands, and Egypt was able to supply gold, grain and linen, receiving silver, wood, copper, oil and wine in return. As the Egyptian sphere of influence slowly expanded throughout the Near East, the treasury coffers opened wide to receive a steadily increasing stream of tribute from client states which, together with the trade surplus, internal taxation and the plunder seized from those unwise enough to resist Egypt's advances, made Egypt the most wealthy and influential country in the Mediterranean world. By the time of Amenhotep III, almost one century after Hatchepsut's reign, an envious King Tushrata of Mitanni was appealing to his fellow monarch: 'So let my brother send me gold in very great quantity without measure. For in my brother's land gold is as plentiful as dust.'[22]

The flourishing economy led directly to a rapid expansion of the civil service as more and more bureaucrats were required to collect, supervise and re-distribute the nation's newfound surpluses. Less than five per cent of the New Kingdom population was literate, and the sudden demand for efficient administrators or scribes combined with the availability of land for private rental from the temples to allow the middle classes a greater political influence, and far greater personal wealth and freedom, than had ever been known in Egypt. The increased demand for scribes led in turn to an expansion in the education system, and we now find many texts written specifically for use in schools. One of these texts, *Papyrus Lansing*, was very specific about the joys – and potential economic rewards – which could be attained through devotion to study: 'Befriend the scroll, the palette. It pleases more than wine.

Writing for him who knows it is better than all other professions.'[23] With
the exception of these school texts, the literature of the early 18th Dynasty remained firmly rooted in the traditions of the Middle Kingdom,
and there was no startling advance in either style or genre at this time.

Most of Egypt's new wealth went directly to the palace, making it
possible for the pharaoh to finance ambitious building works, thereby
enhancing his own status in the eyes of his people and ensuring that his
name, permanently linked to his monuments, would live for ever. Artists
and sculptors, benefiting from the improved financial climate, again
sought their inspiration in Egypt's past, and the artistic conventions of
the 12th Dynasty provided a solid basis for the new-style art. Painting in
particular flourished as, with the new custom of burial in rock-cut
tombs whose crumbling walls were often unsuitable for carving, it was
now necessary to paint funerary scenes. To the modern observer
looking backwards, it seems that there was at this time a new confidence throughout the country and a new awareness of the exciting
foreign influences which were beginning to filter southwards towards
Thebes, so that the art of the early 18th Dynasty may be regarded as
falling halfway between the restrained and formal styles of the 12th
Dynasty and the intricate informality of the Empire. The artists now
appear far more assured in their work and their subjects are depicted
with a restrained professionalism. Gone are the intimate, soul-revealing
pharaohs of the 12th Dynasty; instead we are presented with the
rounded cheeks and faint smile of a king secure in his personal power.
Contemporary private painting, again heavily influenced by the Middle
Kingdom tradition, slowly started to relax and abandon the slightly stiff
poses popular during the Middle Kingdom until 'a new breadth is given
to already established forms, but with a restraint and simplicity which
seems happily suited to the Egyptian spirit'.[24] This growing trend towards less formal artforms was reflected in the more stylish garments
being worn at this time. The standard Old and Middle Kingdom upper-
class clothing (simple kilt or 'bag tunic' for men, long sheath dress and
shawl for women) gradually became less formal and more ornate, until
by the late 18th Dynasty the rather understated Old and Middle
Kingdom elegance had been lost and wealthy Egyptians were dressing
in a far more frivolous style involving yards of closely pleated linen and
rows of elaborate fringes.

★

By the time of Hatchepsut's succession, some fifty years after the re-unification of the country, a well-defined social pyramid had evolved. As in the Old and Middle Kingdoms, the divine pharaoh owned the land and everyone in it; in theory, at least, he remained king, chief priest of every cult, head of the civil service, lord chief justice and supreme commander of the army. He was supported in his onerous tasks by an élite band of nobles, all of whom were male and many of whom were his immediate relations and, one step further down the social scale, by the prominent local families who gave their allegiance to the king and who administered local government. This upper tier of society and their families numbered no more than two or three thousand people, while the total population of Egypt during the New Kingdom has been estimated at between three and four million. The literate middle classes were now enjoying unprecedented prosperity, working as administrators, soldiers, minor priests and artisans while the semi-educated lower-middle classes were apprenticed into trades. The lowest and largest layer of society included foot soldiers, labourers, servants and the peasants who worked the land owned either by the king, the temples or private estates. Herodotus, omitting to mention the farmers who were the main-stay of the Egyptian economy, informs us that there were seven prin-cipal trades: 'These are, the priests, the warriors, the cowherds, the swine-herds, the tradesmen, the interpreters and the boatmen';[25] it would appear that these were the Egyptians whom he himself most frequently encountered on his travels.

At first sight this was a social structure identical to that found in earlier periods of Egyptian history, and indeed the Egyptians themselves rejoiced that their land had returned to the correct social pattern estab-lished at the time of creation. However, subtle changes in emphasis may be detected. The pharaoh remained the ultimate ruler, but he was now all too aware that his authority was not absolute and could, under certain circumstances, be challenged and even lost. Eighteenth Dynasty kings therefore found it prudent to stress the importance of their role by public displays of heroism, wealth and piety, and by the incessant use of self-justifying propaganda texts, myths and ritual. The pharaoh now ruled over a more economically developed country where the army, the civil service and the priesthood had become important state institu-tions; the priesthood in particular was now both semi-independent and economically very powerful. Egypt's increasing wealth had had a beneficial effect on the internal economy, and the literate and skilled middle classes found themselves in great demand. Only the lower classes, in particular the peasants, would have found little change from life in the Old and Middle Kingdoms. These workers continued with the daily routines established by their fathers and grandfathers before them. To the Egyptians, who prized continuity above almost everything, this was a very reassuring state of affairs.

2

A Strong Family: The Tuthmosides

The King [Ahmose] himself said 'I remember my mother's mother, my father's mother, the Great King's Wife and King's Mother, Tetisheri the justified. She now has a tomb and cenotaph on the soil of the Theban province and the Thinite province. I have said this to you because my majesty wants to have made for her a pyramid estate in the necropolis in the neighbourhood of the monument of my majesty, its pool dug, its trees planted, its offering loaves established . . .' Now his majesty spoke of the matter and it was put into action. His majesty did this because he loved her more than anything. Kings of the past never did the like for their mothers.[1]

When King Ahmose decided to honour the memory of Queen Tetisheri, the commoner wife of King Sekenenre Tao I, mother of Sekenenre Tao II and grandmother of both Ahmose and his consort Ahmose Nefertari, he was making an important public statement about the revised status of women, and in particular queens, within the new ruling family. In defiance of previous royal tradition, the Theban rulers of the late 17th and early 18th Dynasties accepted that their womenfolk were capable of assuming a prominent role in state affairs and, most importantly, were happy to acknowledge the unique significance attached to the positions of King's Wife and King's Mother. For the first time since the Archaic Period, 1,500 years before, the queen consorts of Egypt were to be openly celebrated in their own right. Consequently the early New Kingdom is now widely recognized as being remarkable not only for its succession of strong and effective warrior-kings but for its sequence of high-profile, influential and long-lived queens. It was the queens, and not the kings, who were to provide Egypt with an unbroken succession lasting for over a century from Queen Tetisheri, who should perhaps be regarded as the true founder of the 17th/18th Dynasty, to Queen Hatchepsut and beyond.[2]

★

Fig. 2.1   King Ahmose and his grandmother, Queen Tetisheri

The tradition of the semi-invisible queen consort is one which evolved during the Old Kingdom. The queens of the preceding Archaic Period – the 1st and 2nd Dynasties, an unsettled time of gradual consolidation which saw Egypt slowly evolving from a group of semi-independent city states into a single unit – seem to have been strong and politically active women whose role in the unification of their country has for a long time been greatly underestimated. Unfortunately, our information about the personalities of the Archaic Period is severely limited, but four queens (Neith-Hotep, Her-Neith, Meryt-Neith and Nemaathep) have left enough archaeological evidence to prove that women of high birth could wield real power, and indeed one of these ladies, Meryt-Neith, may actually have been a queen regnant rather than a consort.[3] However, following unification and the acceptance of a single divine king ruling over a peaceful country, there was little need for a strong consort and the shadowy and now mostly unknown queens of the Old and (even more so) Middle Kingdoms made little impact on state affairs. Barring exceptional circumstances, such as the untimely death of the king or the lack of a male heir to the throne, royal women confined themselves to family and domestic concerns.

This queenly modesty was entirely in keeping with contemporary views on the conduct proper to married women, particularly during the Middle Kingdom when the sudden disappearance of the queen from royal monuments coincided with a marked decrease in non-royal titles accorded to women. Although Egyptian women could always be included amongst the most legally independent females in the ancient world, with accepted rights which would have been envied by their more protected sisters in Asia, Greece and Rome, there was a clear and well-understood gulf between the work considered appropriate to women and that done by men. As a general rule, men were expected to work outside the home while women remained inside.[4] Similarly, the husband had overall control over external affairs while the wife became Mistress of the House. 'Keep your wife from power, restrain her', argued the Old Kingdom sages. Marriage and motherhood formed the axis of the woman's world and, like any good Egyptian wife, the pre-New Kingdom queen had her clearly defined female tasks which, while not exactly *Kinder, Küche und Kirche* (presumably the queen would not have been expected to do too much cooking), must have been something fairly close. Her duties involved providing her husband with as many children as possible, ensuring the smooth running of the palace, adding silent support to her husband's actions and even, if necessary, acting as regent for a fatherless son. Her primary role was, however, to provide an almost entirely passive complement to her active husband. She was not expected to become a prominent public figure, had no state duties, held few official titles and was powerful only to the extent that she could influence her husband.

From the late 17th Dynasty onwards, we can see a profound change in the nature of the role of queen consort. Casting off her cloak of invisibility, she now emerged to claim a highly public position since, even though her status was still ultimately derived from her relationship with the king, increasing emphasis was placed both on the individuality of each queen and on the divinity of her role. By the early 18th Dynasty, queens were routinely awarded a range of secular and religious titles, owned their own estates which came complete with land, servants and administrators, and were portrayed wearing a range of distinctive crowns. This newly expanded repertoire of queen's regalia was clearly designed not only to stress 'royalness' and the connection with the king, but also to emphasize links with various deities. It had always been

recognized that the role of queen had semi-divine origins, but this
aspect of queenship now became far more blatant. For example, the
new double uraeus headdress, two flat snakes worn side by side on the
brow, was directly associated with the Lower Egyptian cobra goddess
Wadjyt and the Upper Egyptian vulture goddess Nekhbet, but also had
connections with the cults of Hathor and Re. The vulture crown,
which resembles a rather limp bird draped over the queen's head with
the wings hanging down against the sides of her face and the head of
the vulture rising above the wearer's forehead, was a long-established
queen's crown again linked with Nekhbet, while the double plumes –
tall falcon feathers attached to a circular base – had been worn since the
13th Dynasty to stress links with the male gods Min and Amen and
with the sun cult of Re. Depictions of the goddesses Isis and Hathor
now show them wearing similar crowns so that the distinction between
the mortal queen and the immortal goddesses becomes deliberately
blurred.

Why should such a change have come about at this time? For over a century egyptologists, heavily influenced by now largely outdated theories of
kinship and social evolution,[5] have speculated that the new royal family
must have been organized along matriarchal rather than patriarchal lines.
The more prominent role allowed to the queens, an otherwise inexplicable deviation away from normal Egyptian behaviour patterns, could
then be understood as something unfortunate but unavoidable. However, the theorists, in their desire to provide a simple explanation for the
otherwise inexplicable, were somewhat haphazard in their classification.
In its strictest sense a matriarchy involves the complete domination of
the female line with all property and inheritance rights being held by
women and transmitted from mother to daughter, and with the women
holding all the power within the family unit.[6] In such a system the
women may be said to control the men. It is clearly distinct from both
matrilocal kinship systems (where the women remain in their own
homes following marriage) and from matrilineal systems (where descent is traced through the female line rather than the male); in both
these cases the male, either the spouse or the brother, still retains overall
family control. It is also, unhappily for the theorists, clearly distinct from
the situation in the Theban royal family, where there is no suggestion
that the kings ever relinquished their control to their queens.

Although the idea of an archaic female-dominated state has been a popular one amongst both old-fashioned anthropologists and extreme feminist historians, it is now widely recognized that such a state has never existed anywhere in the world. The Theban royal family may have allowed its queens to play a more prominent role in matters of state, but that role never allowed the queen to take precedence over the all-powerful pharaoh while Hatchepsut, the seeming exception to this rule, only sought the powers of a king when she had actually transformed herself into a female king. She would have probably been as horrified as anyone to think that a mere consort could rule in the place of a divinely appointed monarch. The 'power' of the Theban women should instead be seen in its true perspective as an increase in status and perhaps influence rather than a complete reversal of domestic custom.

Perhaps a more accurate explanation for the change in attitude towards the higher-ranking royal women can best be found by considering conditions in Egypt at the start of the Theban royal family's rule. This was a period when, as during the Archaic Period, Egypt was suffering from profound civil unrest. The kings who emerged during the late 17th Dynasty were warrior-kings, their reigns characterized by successive successful military campaigns. Under normal circumstances, and apart from a somewhat vague reference to Queen Ahhotep commanding troops which is discussed in further detail later in this chapter, it is the active Egyptian men who provide military leadership while their passive womenfolk attend to their separate domestic concerns; when the Middle Kingdom pharaoh Amenemhat I asked, 'Has any woman previously marshalled troops? And has rebellion previously been plotted in the palace?' he was posing intentionally ridiculous questions.[7] However, at times of national crisis we often find that traditional roles no longer apply, and that women may be actively encouraged to leave the shelter of their hearths and seek employment without incurring public disapproval. This is precisely what occurred during the First and Second World Wars in Britain when women were expected to play an active part in the war effort, taking over jobs previously reserved exclusively for men.

When a monarchy feels itself to be under threat, we might expect to find the royal family relying on its most loyal and devoted supporters – other family members – to provide much-needed strength and support, regardless of sex. This is particularly true of the close-knit Theban royal family where the queen was often the full or half-sister of the king, was equally descended from the founders of the dynasty and would presumably have the same interests vested in her family. At such a time, when family might be set against family, it would be an act of great folly to overlook the potential contribution of an intelligent and politically astute woman, and a queen or queen mother who could effectively deputize for the king would be a valuable asset. It is, therefore, perhaps not surprising to find that the late 17th and early 18th Dynasty kings followed their Archaic Period predecessors in utilizing their womenfolk far beyond their ability to produce male children.

It is certainly not hard to find parallels for a ruling family where the influence of the royal women is both acknowledged and respected. African kingships have traditionally allowed their royal women to play a conspicuous part in state affairs and it should be remembered that the city of Thebes was geographically close to Nubia whose royal family also included powerful women. However, if we really need a parallel for the Theban royal family we should perhaps look closer to our own time; Kennedy-like clans where the women, although themselves not the holders of supreme office, play an important role in the functioning of the family as a single effective unit of government are not particularly rare, while the British monarchy itself has recently found that a suitable spouse, correctly presented, can help to boost the status of the entire royal family.

Respect for mothers was already a long-established Egyptian custom and not necessarily one which needed to be imported from further south. The Egyptian mother was both loved and revered by her children, particularly her sons, and New Kingdom scribes were constantly stressing the obligation which a young man owed to his long-suffering mother:

Double the food that your mother gave you, and support her as she supported you, for you were a heavy burden to her yet she did not abandon you. When you were born after your months she was still tied to you as her breast was in your mouth for three years. As you grew and your excrement was disgusting she was not disgusted.[8]

Nor were the royal family the only family to emphasize the importance of the female line at this time. We have already met Ahmose, son of Ibana, the mighty warrior from el-Kab. His grandson, Paheri, also a native of el-Kab, was a bureaucrat who rose to become a respected Scribe of the Treasury and Mayor of both el-Kab (ancient Nekheb) and Esna (ancient Iunyt). His magnificent tomb lacks an autobiography like that provided by his grandfather, but includes conventional images of agriculture and feasting which are considerably enhanced by the inclusion of the comments of the participants in each scene. The banqueting scene is particularly illuminating; here we have the opportunity to eavesdrop on the female members of the Paheri family as they relax after a hard day's work. Their comments are perhaps not all we would expect from a collection of well-bred young ladies:

In the third row are the daughters of Kem, viz. [Thu]pu, Nub-em-heb and Amen-sat; also Paheri's second cousin Nub-Mehy, and his three nurses . . . Amen-sat refuses the bowl, and the servant says jestingly, 'For thy Ka, drink to drunkenness, make holiday; O listen to what thy companion is saying, do not weary of taking (?).'

Her companion and distant cousin Nub-Mehy is saying to the servant 'Give me eighteen cups of wine, I want to drink to drunkenness; my throat is as dry as straw.'[9]

Paheri's tomb provides us with details of his descent which is always traced through the female line; it is his mother, Kam, who is the child of Ahmose while his father, Itruri, was apparently tutor to Crown Prince Wadjmose, son of Tuthmosis I, a post which may also have been held by Paheri himself. Ahmose's father is recorded as Baba, son of Reant (his mother), and the maternal ancestors and cousins are recorded in preference to the paternal line. So striking is this preference for the female branch of the family that the tomb of Paheri was for a long time cited in support of the theory of a Theban matriarchal tradition. It is now accepted, however, that Paheri was simply following human nature, and claiming kinship with the highest-ranking members of his family, regardless of their sex.

To some modern observers – writing with the obvious benefit of hindsight – this sudden change in policy was a disaster waiting to happen, as a newly powerful queen would be unable to resist making an attempt on the throne itself:

The stubbornness and driving ambition of the queens could not help but precipitate a conflict with the males of the family, at least if the women persisted in grasping after what must have been the ultimate aspiration, viz. the crown. After five generations of rule this is precisely what happened.[10]

Perhaps a move from queen to king would seem an obvious promotion to a modern consort dissatisfied with her secondary function. However, it is doubtful whether an Egyptian queen, particularly one who held a secure and influential role of her own, would ever under normal circumstances consider such a dramatic step. The Egyptian abhorrence of change, the ingrained belief in a correct way of doing things which always included a divinely appointed male pharaoh on the throne, and the fact that the king was more than likely to be a close relation (brother, son or father) all make a female *coup*, under normal conditions, highly unlikely.

It can be no coincidence that the queen acquired her enhanced status at exactly the time that the king was throwing open the doors of the royal harem to welcome increased numbers of secondary wives and concubines into the shelter of his protecting arms. Indeed, it may well be that the queen needed her new titles and regalia simply to distinguish her, as the consort and mother of the future king, from all the other women who could now with some justification claim to be a wife of the king and even, given a bit of good luck, a future King's Mother. Polygamy had always been something of a royal tradition; it was an easily affordable luxury and in many ways it made sense to ensure that the king had as much opportunity as possible to father a male successor. However, the kings of the Old and Middle Kingdom seem to have been satisfied with one queen consort plus a rather discreet harem of concubines about whom we know very little, and it is only during the 13th Dynasty that we encounter the use of the title 'King's Chief Wife' which suggests the need to distinguish the queen consort from a host of other, lesser, wives. With the advent of the New Kingdom there came a dramatic increase in royal brides and, we must assume, a corresponding increase in the numbers of royal children, until the 19th Dynasty King Ramesses II was able to boast of fathering seventy-nine sons and fifty-nine daughters by his various wives who included his sister, three of his daughters and at least five foreign princesses.

These secondary wives should by no means be regarded as mere concubines, a term which has almost come to be synonymous with prostitute or harlot in our (theoretically) monogamous society. There was no disgrace in being included amongst the king's wives and, indeed, the occupants of the harem included high-bred Egyptian ladies and the daughters and sisters of Egyptian kings. These ladies could not all become queen consort, but they were all legally the wives or dependants of the king, and all were entitled to a recognized and respected position in Egyptian society. It would be fascinating to learn how the Egyptian harem women were selected – did they volunteer, were they donated by their parents, or were they press-ganged? It is probably fairly safe to assume that to introduce a daughter into the royal palace could bring a family nothing but good, particularly if she managed to attract and hold the attention of the king or crown prince. Parallels have often been drawn with the Chinese Han Dynasty harem, where kings and their high officials occasionally married their concubines and where it was not unknown for a concubine of non-royal birth to become both the wife and the mother of a king. A favourite concubine could use her influence for the good of her family, and for this reason Chinese nobles worked to get at least one daughter accepted into the royal harem.[11] However, non-royal Egyptian males seem curiously reluctant to acknowledge association with the palace through a woman, to the extent that Anen, brother of the commoner Queen Tiy, fails to mention this important link on any of his monuments. We have no record of any Egyptian donating his wife or daughter to the king, and no means of ascertaining how useful a daughter or sister in the royal harem could be.

A miracle brought to his Majesty Gilukhepa, daughter of the prince of Naharin, and the members of her entourage, some 317 women.[12]

By the time of Tuthmosis IV, the harem was also home to a number of important foreign princesses and their not-insubstantial retinues. These princesses, the daughters of strong political allies, travelled to Egypt with a rich dowry which was exchanged for a reciprocal bride price or tribute paid by the groom. They married the king, and sank into obscurity. Other, lesser, princesses were the daughters of vassal states sent as tribute to the Egyptian king; they remained in the royal harem providing an effective guarantee of their father's loyalty to the pharaoh:

Send your daughter to the king, your lord, and as presents send twenty healthy slaves, silver chariots and healthy horses.[13]

Yet other foreign women were sent in groups as gifts for the king. We must assume that these women rarely, if ever, saw their new husband/master. They appear to have lived their whole lives within the harem without the chance of either marriage or returning to their own lands; when they died they were buried in the nearby desert cemetery.

The women of Egypt have the character of being the most licentious in their feelings of all females who lay any claim to be considered as members of a civilised nation . . . Most of them are not considered safe unless under lock and key.[14]

While the queen consort seems to have enjoyed the luxury of her own palace and estates, the remaining royal wives and concubines, their young children, wet-nurses, nursemaids and attendants, lived together in the permanent women's palace or the harem. The word harem is today an unfortunate one; a word which instantly conjures up images of spoiled and scantily dressed eastern beauties reclining on silken cushions as they await the bidding of their lord and master. All too often our ideas of the Egyptian harem are based on what we imagine we know of the harem in other oriental monarchies, in particular the harem of the Grand Seraglio, the court of the Ottoman sultans at Istanbul, a harem which functioned from the Middle Ages until the First World War, when the Sultanate itself was deposed on the creation of the modern republic of Turkey. The secret world of the Turkish harem remained an impenetrable mystery for centuries, and rumours rather than facts about life in the Grand Seraglio have fed European notions about all harems. This, combined with a deep-seated belief in the innate decadence of ancient Egypt and its enviably abandoned women, has found expression in many forms of western culture. From Mozart to Mailer, the combination of exotic locations, hot sun and captive women kept for sexual delectation have been used to entertain and titillate supposedly sophisticated audiences.[15]

This vision is far from the truth. It would be far more correct to regard the Egyptian women's palace as a permanent dormitory used to house all the female dependants of the king, not just those tied to him for sexual purposes. These women, for reason of sheer numbers, could not be expected to travel with the king and his entourage. The harem was therefore home to a varied assortment of wives, daughters, sisters, infant sons, attendants, slaves and anyone else who could be legitimately found in the women's quarters of a private dwelling house. Included amongst the harem staff were a number of male administrators who found themselves responsible for the smooth running of a very large community. These officials bore titles ranging from 'Overseer of the Royal Harem' and 'Inspector of the Harem-Administration' to 'Gate-Keeper'; this last appears to have been employed to protect the harem and keep undesirable members of the community out rather than to keep the women in – as yet we have no evidence to suggest that free-born Egyptian women were ever forced to remain in the harem against their will. All the administrators appear to have been married men, and we find no direct evidence for that classic harem servant, and butt of many a tasteless joke, the eunuch. While there might have been obvious advantages in employing castrated men to work with a collection of attractive, isolated, bored and possibly frustrated women, this does not appear to have been standard practice in dynastic Egypt. There is no ancient Egyptian word which has been convincingly demonstrated to mean eunuch, and representations of harem scenes in the Amarna tombs of Ay and Tutu do not show any individuals with classic eunuchoidal appearance. We do have examples of mummified male bodies without testicles, but these seem to be the result of post-mortem damage during mummification itself, rather than a deliberate amputation. The mummified body of Tuthmosis III, known to be a father, was lacking both penis and testicles, while the hard-man military exploits of the Pharaoh Merenptah certainly suggest that he metaphorically possessed what his mummy now lacks.

The food was neither plain nor wholesome. As to the hours spent lolling in Turkish baths, naked and sleek, ladling perfumed water over each other, twisting pearls and peacock feathers in their long hair, nibbling sugary comfits, gossiping, idling away the hours, becalmed in the dreamy, steamy limbo-land . . .[16]

So Lesley Blanch describes daily life in the eighteenth-century harem of the Seraglio, a description which must owe a certain amount to imagination, as the harem was strictly out of bounds to all non-inmates, but which is probably correct in its assumption that the Turkish *odalisques* led a life of pampered luxury. Things were very different in Egypt, where the harem-palace itself was a self-contained and self-supporting unit, fully independent of the king's palace and deriving its income from its own endowments of land and the rents paid by tenant farmers. Many of the lesser harem women, far from idling away the hours, were expected to work for their keep; the harem itself must have required numerous cooks, washerwomen, nursemaids and general servants while *Mer-Wer*, a large harem-palace established by Tuthmosis III on the edge of the Faiyum, seems to have been home to a flourishing textile business. Here the finest Egyptian linen was produced under the supervision of the ladies of the harem.

The plans of surviving New Kingdom harem-palaces show groups of independent mud-brick buildings including living quarters, storerooms and a chapel or shrine, all surrounded by a high mud-brick wall. The living quarters took the form of enclosed structures focused inwards towards a central open area or courtyard which sometimes contained pools of water. This may be compared with the traditional modern Islamic harem of the early twentieth century, a large house built around a courtyard which might include a pool or fountain, and surrounded by high walls.[17] The physical setting of the more modern harem was very firmly focused inwards towards the central open space which became the scene of the daily activities of the harem-women. Here food was prepared, cosmetics were applied, and the days and evenings were spent singing, dancing and telling stories.

The dynastic Egyptian harem-palace served both as a nursery for the royal infants and as the 'Household of the Royal Children', the most prestigious school in the land. Here the young male royals, under the supervision of the 'Overseer of the Royal Harem' and the 'Teacher of the Royal Children', received the instruction which would prepare them for their future lives as some of the highest-ranking nobles in the land. The title 'Child of the Palace' (that is, a royal child, or one important enough to be brought up as one) is one often used by high officials from the Middle Kingdom onwards, the full reading in the New

Kingdom being 'Child of the Palace of the Royal Harem'. Important 18th Dynasty officials who chose to emphasize their childhood connection with the royal court include the Viziers Rekhmire, Ramose and Amenemope, the High Priest of Amen, Hapuseneb, and the Mayor of Thebes, Sennefer. Childhood networking in the royal harem must have been of crucial importance to those living in a state where everyone's career and status was dependent upon their relationship with the king.

At any time of civil unrest, given the high mortality rates amongst the male élite engaged in physical combat, we might expect to find the embattled monarchy placing a great reliance on the production of male children both to ensure the royal succession, be it father to son (for example, Sekenenre Tao to Kamose) or brother to brother (for example, Kamose to Ahmose) and to provide loyal subordinate military leaders. However, this does not appear to be the case at the start of the New Kingdom when the more minor male royal personages – the second sons and younger brothers of kings – take their turn at becoming invisible. With the younger males this is not so remarkable as both male and female royal children tended to be relatively obscure in infancy and childhood; their early invisibility did not necessarily prevent them from achieving fame later in their careers. However, the lack of adult princes is something of a puzzle, particularly at a time when the vast increase in numbers of royal wives might have led us to expect a dramatic increase in royal children.

In part, the invisibility of the royal sons must be a result of the selective preservation of the historical records, and in particular the royal monuments. The temples and funerary monuments of Thebes and the West Bank are covered with texts and scenes depicting various kings who are occasionally shown together with their queens and the royal princesses. However, the royal family only appear in these scenes as symbolic appendages of the king; they are not intended to be seen as independent individuals in their own right and indeed New Kingdom royal art is full of images of dependant royal woman who often appear as minuscule figures barely reaching to the knees of the colossal king who is their husband, father or both. The fact that sons are unlikely to appear as royal dependents in these scenes should therefore not be taken as an indication that they lacked importance, but rather as confirmation that they were expected to live a more independent existence. The princess was given respect as the daughter (or property?) of the king;

the prince had to earn his own respect. This in turn implies that while the position of King's Daughter was very much seen as a role in its own right, the role of King's Son was merely an accident of birth, not a full-time career. The crown prince was obviously an exception to this rule; as heir to the throne he was born with a clearly defined role and was often given the post of Great Army General to reinforce his status, just as the British heir to the throne is traditionally created Prince of Wales.

If royal sons are less likely to appear on royal monuments than their sisters then where, apart from their tombs, are we likely to find them? Even the location of their tombs poses a problem, as princely burials dating to the early 18th Dynasty are virtually unknown, although recent discoveries in the Valley of the Kings suggest that groups of princes may have been buried in batches in mass burial chambers. We do have examples of 18th Dynasty individuals classifying themselves as 'King's Son' but, for some reason, we have no one claiming to be a 'King's Brother'. This had led to the intriguing suggestion that royal princes may have in some way lost their royalty once the crown prince had produced an heir, thereby casting them outside the direct line of succession. This would have the effect of restricting the royal family to the king, his unmarried sisters, his spinster aunts, his mother and grandmother and his children; his brothers and uncles would no longer be regarded as fully royal, although they would still be entitled to a respected place in the community.[18] This automatic pruning of the royal family would have the advantage of reducing the number of individuals with a potential claim to the throne and would presumably keep the royal family securely exclusive. Whatever their official status, we can see that those princes who grew to adulthood before the death of their father received high-ranking appointments in the priesthood, the army and the civil service. The fate of their younger, orphaned brothers is less certain.

The best place to look for the missing 18th Dynasty princes is the workmen's village of Deir el-Medina. Here, throughout the 19th Dynasty and particularly during the reign of Ramesses II, the early 18th Dynasty royal family was regarded with great reverence. On a general level they were honoured as both the (theoretical) ancestors of the current kings and as excellent role models for military kingship, while on a more personal level the inhabitants of Deir el-Medina worshipped the Theban royal family as both the founders of their village and the initiators of the ultimate in job-creation schemes in the Valley of the Kings. The villagers had good reason to worship their partially deified patrons Amenhotep I and Ahmose Nefertari, and it is not surprising that these two demi-gods appear on many small monuments, sometimes standing alongside other Theban deities such as Hathor, Lady of the West. Occasionally, however, the inhabitants of Deir el-Medina chose to commemorate the lesser members of the Theban royal family, including some of the missing princes. The best-known example of this is found in the tomb of a man named Khabekhnet, where the north-eastern wall shows two rows of seated, named individuals who are identified as 'Lords of the West'. Included amongst these are some who are clearly the sons of kings who did not succeed their father to the throne. Unfortunately, beyond their names, we have little further information about these lost princes.

From the scanty records surviving from the beginning of the Eighteenth Dynasty, it emerges that a remarkable part was played in the history of the newly unified state by three ladies, Tetisheri and Ahhotpe . . . and Ahmose Nefertiry . . . There can be little doubt that their behaviour served as an inspiration to the leading women of the country (of whom Hatchepsut is the leading example) throughout the Eighteenth Dynasty.[19]

King Ahmose was blessed with not only a strong grandmother but with a forceful and politically active mother. Ahhotep I (or Ahhotpe, as above), consort and possibly sister of Sekenenre Tao II, exerted a profound and long-lasting influence on her son; on a stela recovered from Karnak, Ahmose encourages his people to pay homage to his mother as the 'one who has accomplished the rites and taken care of Egypt':

She has looked after her [that is, Egypt's] soldiers, she has guarded her, she has brought back her fugitives and collected together her deserters, she has pacified Upper Egypt and expelled her rebels.[20]

The precise meaning of this curious stela is now lost to us. However if, as it seems to maintain, Ahhotep herself had truly been able to thwart a rebellion by mustering the Egyptian troops, she must have been a woman capable of wielding real rather than ceremonial power. We may even deduce that Ahhotep had been called upon to act as regent following the untimely death of Kamose because we know that when Ahmose died at the end of his 25-year reign he was relatively young, possibly only in his early thirties. We know of no formal declaration of a regency, but there was certainly a well-established precedent for the dowager queen to act as regent for her young son; the 2nd Dynasty Queen Nemaathep had acted as regent for King Djoser and the 6th Dynasty Queen Ankhes-Merire had ruled on behalf of her six-year-old son Pepi II. Why the queen should be chosen to act as regent in preference to a male relation (perhaps father's brother) is now unclear, although we can speculate that it would be the mother above all who would safeguard her son's inheritance. If the theory of the royal princes losing their royalness on the assumption of their brother holds true, there would in any case be no close male member of the royal family available to take on the role.

There was certainly a clear divine precedent for a mother taking care of her son's inheritance. The story of Isis and Osiris tells how Osiris, rightful king of Egypt in the time of the gods, was murdered by his jealous brother Seth. Seth cut Osiris' body into many pieces which he scattered all over Egypt. Isis, his devoted wife and sister, toiled to collect the bits together and, with her magic powers, granted Osiris temporary life. So successful was her magic that nine months later their son Horus was born. The dead Osiris then became king of the Afterlife. Meanwhile the resourceful Isis hid Horus from his uncle in the marshes until he became a man, able to avenge his father's death. The women of Egypt were not routinely expected to display such initiative; they generally took a more passive role in society. However, decisive behaviour was acceptable and even to be encouraged in a female if that behaviour was intended to safeguard the rights of either a husband or child.

After her death Ahhotep was accorded a splendid burial on the West Bank at Thebes. Her mummy in its elaborate coffin was recovered in the mid nineteenth century, and is now housed in the Cairo Museum.

Although both Tetisheri and Ahhotep had been honoured by Ahmose it was his wife, Ahmose Nefertari, who first received the formal accolades which were to become the right of future queens of Egypt. Ahmose Nefertari, 'King's Daughter and King's Sister', 'Female Chieftain of Upper and Lower Egypt', wife and probably sister of Ahmose, mother of Amenhotep I, granddaughter of Tetisheri and possibly daughter of Kamose, was even more influential than her redoubtable mother-in-law. Unfortunately we have no text detailing her specific achievements, but we do know that Ahmose Nefertari was either given, or sold, the prestigious title of 'Second Prophet of Amen', a post which was intended to belong to the queen and her descendants for ever.

The queen later renounced this title for an even more prestigious position, the priestly office of 'God's Wife of Amen', an honour which came with its own endowment of goods and land plus a staff of male administrators and which, given the rising importance of the cult of Amen at this time, was a clear indication of the enhanced status of the queen. It is perhaps cynical to suggest that the position may have been deliberately contrived to allow the royal family some measure of control over the increasingly powerful and wealthy cult. Ahmose Nefertari obviously saw this as her most important role, and used the title of 'God's

Fig. 2.2 The god Osiris

Wife of Amen' in preference to any other. Contemporary illustrations show the queen dressed in a distinctive short wig and strangely archaic-looking clothes as she performs the religious duties associated with her new office. Unfortunately, we have little understanding of the precise function of the God's Wife; the title suggests that it should have been borne either by those queens who had coupled with Amen to produce a king (that is, by queen mothers), or by unmarried women who had dedicated themselves to the service of Amen, but a quick

Fig. 2.3   The god Horus

survey of the women who held the post shows that neither explanation can be correct. Hatchepsut, for example, was neither a virgin nor the mother of a king. It is possible, however, that the role related in some (theoretical) way to the sexual stimulation of the god which would ensure the renewal of the land: a second and less delicate title, 'God's Hand', which is occasionally used in conjunction with 'God's Wife', is an unmistakable reference to the masturbation which produced the first gods, Shu and Tefnut.

The role of 'God's Wife of Amen' was passed down from Ahmose Nefertari to her daughter Meritamen, and then to Hatchepsut who used it until she became king, when it was transferred to her daughter Neferure. The title fell into decline during the solo reign of Tuthmosis III – perhaps the new king had experienced enough powerful women – and died out completely after the reign of Tuthmosis IV, only to be revived during the Third Intermediate Period when, having merged with the position of 'Divine Adoratrice', it developed into a politically and economically highly significant post. The God's Wife of Amen now had theoretical control over the vast wealth of the estates of Amen.

Ahmose Nefertari fulfilled her wifely duties by presenting her husband–brother with at least four sons and five daughters, five of whom died in infancy or childhood. However, she was not content to restrict herself to breeding and abandoned the traditional shelter of the queen's palace:

To judge from the number of inscriptions, contemporary and later, in which that young queen's name appears, she obtained as celebrity almost without parallel in the history of Egypt.[21]

Setting a precedent now followed by modern royal couples, the queen accompanied her husband as he performed his many civic duties; we know that when Ahmose opened a new gallery at the Tura limestone quarry in his regnal Year 22, he was accompanied by his queen who stood modestly behind her husband in a typical wifely pose. The queen also seems to have assisted her husband in developing his building projects and, as we have already noted, Ahmose consulted his wife over his plans to honour their dead grandmother, Tetisheri. She was certainly active in the religious sphere; her piety, or perhaps her independent wealth, led her to dedicate far more religious offerings than any previous queen and offerings presented by Ahmose Nefertari have been found in temples as far apart as Karnak in the south and Serabit el-Khadim in the Sinai Peninsula.

Following the death of Ahmose, Ahmose Nefertari took on the role of regent for her young son, Amenhotep I, handing over the reins of state when her son became old enough to rule. Throughout his 21-year reign, Amenhotep I consolidated the successful foreign policies started by his father, uncle and grandfather. There was no further military action in Palestine, but the army expanded further south into Nubia where a viceroy was appointed to take care of Egypt's interests in the Upper Nubian Kingdom of Kush. The ubiquitous Ahmose, son of Ibana, was present to witness the new king's triumph:

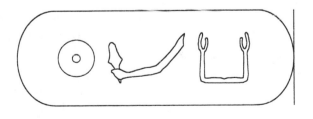

Fig. 2.4   The cartouche of King Amenhotep I

I transported the King of Upper and Lower Egypt Djeserkare [Amenhotep I], the justified, when he sailed south to Kush to make wider the borders of Egypt. His Majesty smote those Bowmen of Nubia in the midst of his army. They were brought away in a stranglehold, none escaping. The fleeing were laid low, as if they had never existed. I was at the head of the army and truly I fought. His Majesty saw my bravery. I brought away two hands to bring to his Majesty . . . Then I was rewarded with gold. I brought away two female captives as plunder, apart from those which I brought to his Majesty, and I was made 'Warrior of the Ruler'.[22]

Internally, there was an ambitious building programme encompassing several Upper Egyptian sites, and the arts and sciences flourished. Dying before his mother, Amenhotep I became the focus of a funerary cult at Deir el-Medina, where he was worshipped as 'Amenhotep of the Town', 'Amenhotep Beloved of Amen', or 'Amenhotep of the Forecourt'. When she, too, flew to heaven, Ahmose Nefertari was also deified and worshipped at Deir el-Medina as patron goddess of the Theban necropolis. She eventually became 'Mistress of the Sky' and 'Lady of the West' and her cult lasted throughout the New Kingdom.

Ahmose Nefertari's forceful personality completely eclipsed that of her son's consort and sister, Queen Meritamen. Although we are told that Meritamen also bore the title of 'God's Wife of Amen' we know little else about this lady, beyond the fact that she did not provide her husband with a living male successor. Amenhotep I was therefore followed as king by a man whom he himself had chosen, a middle-aged general who was to become King Tuthmosis I. As the early 18th Dynasty was a time when the ruling élite formed a close-knit and well-defined group almost invariably linked by marriage, the new heir to the throne may well have been a descendant of a collateral branch of the royal family.[23] Tuthmosis himself, however, makes no claim to royal blood. His father is never named and remains a man of mystery, although it seems safe to assume that had he been of noble or royal birth Tuthmosis would have been the first to acknowledge him, while his mother was a non-royal woman named Senisenb who was never a queen and who was always given the simple title of 'King's Mother'. Tuthmosis himself confirmed his mother's relatively humble origins when he required his loyal troops to swear an oath of loyalty on his accession 'by the name of His Majesty, life, health and strength, born of the Royal Mother Senisenb'. This choice of successor seems to have met with general approval and in the fullness of time Tuthmosis I became pharaoh of Egypt. The Tuthmoside era had begun.

There is some rather weak archaeological evidence to suggest that Amenhotep I may have associated himself in a co-regency with his intended successor. On the wall of the chapel of Amenhotep at Karnak, Tuthmosis I is shown dressed as a king, performing royal tasks and with his name written in the royal cartouche. If, as has been suggested, this scene was commissioned during the lifetime of Amenhotep I, there must have been two kings on the throne at the same time. Unfortunately, we have no means of knowing when the carving was made and, while it would certainly have made good sense for Amenhotep to associate himself formally with Tuthmosis, the case for a joint reign must rest unproven. It is, after all, equally possible that the building, started by Amenhotep, was finished after his death by Tuthmosis. The fact that Tuthmosis I started to count his regnal years from the death of his predecessor is of little help in determining whether or not the two shared a reign.

The tradition of the co-regency, a regular feature of 12th Dynasty reigns and one which reappears during the early 18th Dynasty, appears a strange one to those of us accustomed to seeing a single divinely appointed monarch on the throne. Joint rule must have posed many practical difficulties – how could the country be ruled by two kings at the same time? Were the royal duties performed in stereo or were they divided on some mutually agreed basis? Was there to be a 'junior' and a 'senior' king? And how was the joint reign to be dated? Egyptian

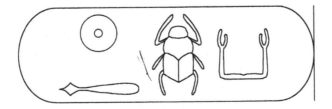

Fig. 2.5   The cartouche of King Tuthmosis I

theology decreed that the attributes of divine kingship were passed
from father to son, the son becoming the living Horus at the precise
moment that his dying father became the dead Osiris yet, as Gardiner
has pointed out, '. . . there is no hint that the Egyptians ever felt scruples
on this score. In matters of religion logic played no great part, and the
assimilation or duplication of deities doubtless added a mystic charm to
their theology.'[24]

The question of how such a joint reign was to be dated was no trivial
matter – the Egyptians always described their years with reference to
the current pharaoh. We now know that there were in fact two types of
co-regencies, each employing a different dating system. Where there
was clearly a 'senior' and a more 'junior' king, the joint reign was dated
by reference to the regnal years of the senior partner with the junior
king counting his own years only from the death of his senior. Such
unequal co-regencies leave very little evidence and are consequently
very hard for the historian to detect. Other co-regencies, where the
newest king started to count his regnal years from the beginning of the
co-regency while his co-ruler continued with his own regnal years,
may be viewed as a more equal partnership. However, this equality led
to a certain amount of chronological confusion as each year of such a
co-regency had two equally valid regnal dates, and indeed we occasionally find 'double-dated' texts and monuments giving the regnal years of
two contemporary kings, while the anniversaries of the succession of
each king created two New Year's days which were not necessarily
synchronized with the third New Year's day, that of the civil calendar.[25]
Given these not inconsiderable drawbacks, it is perhaps not surprising
to find that double-dated co-regencies were rare during the New
Kingdom.

In spite of the theological, political and dating problems posed by
joint reigns, they remained a feature of Egyptian kingship. There must,
therefore, have been enough compensating advantages to make a co-
regency appear worthwhile. Perhaps the main advantage was that the
co-regency made the intended succession absolutely clear; no one
could dispute the intentions of a king who had already announced his
successor. At times when the new king was not an obvious choice (for
example, when there was no legitimate male heir), the co-regency must
have seemed a sensible precaution which would deter any other
claimant to the throne and ensure continuity of rule in a land where so

much depended on the presence of a pharaoh on the throne. The additional benefit of allowing the new king to learn the art of government while the old king eased into a semi-retirement must have been appreciated by both monarchs.

King Tuthmosis I was married to a lady named Ahmose, a popular female name in New Kingdom Egypt. There is some disagreement over the origins of this lady, with some authorities classing her as a daughter of Amenhotep I and others placing her as the daughter of Ahmose and Ahmose Nefertari and therefore a full sister of Amenhotep I. Whatever her parentage, until recently all experts were in agreement that Ahmose must have been a princess of the royal blood, and that Tuthmosis must have married her in order to make his position as king even more secure. It is relatively common for a legally dubious claimant to a throne to seek to enhance his position by marrying a close female relative of his predecessor, a match which consolidates his claim while removing any potential challenge from the children or grandchildren of the previous king. In Egypt, such political matches appear to have been standard procedure; indeed, the first pharaoh of the Archaic Period, the victorious southern King Narmer, contracted a similar marriage when he married Neith-Hotep, a northern Princess. We should therefore not be too surprised to find that Tuthmosis appeared to follow this prudent plan.

However, Queen Ahmose, who bears the title of 'King's Sister' (*senet nesu*) is never accorded the more important title of 'King's Daughter' (*sat nesu*). The Egyptians were not generally shy of recording their ranks and achievements, and this unusual reticence may therefore be an indication that Ahmose was not the daughter of a king, and by extension that she could not be either the daughter or the sister of Amenhotep I. Instead, she may actually have been the sister or half-sister of Tuthmosis I. If this is the case, we may speculate that their brother–sister marriage must have occurred after Tuthmosis's promotion to heir apparent, as such incestuous marriages are extremely rare outside the immediate royal family. This would suggest that Hatchepsut, and indeed her full brothers and sister, may have been born after Tuthmosis had become co-regent, and that Hatchepsut may therefore have been little more than twelve years old when she married her half-brother to become queen consort.

The 18th Dynasty was to become remarkable for the number of times that the king was married to a close female relation, often his half- or full sister and occasionally even his daughter. Hatchepsut herself was married to her half-brother Tuthmosis II, bearing him at least one daughter who was herself almost certainly intended to marry her half-brother Tuthmosis III. Nor was this phenomenon confined to the early 18th Dynasty. A century after Hatchepsut's reign, King Amenhotep III married his daughter Sitamen and elevated her to the rank of King's Chief Wife alongside her mother, Queen Tiy. Amenhotep III was followed on the throne by his son Akhenaten who married at least one and possibly three of his six daughters, and he was followed in turn by the boy-king Tutankhamen who married his sister(?) Ankhesenamen who bore him at least two still-born children. It is clear that the tradition of fully consummated incestuous marriages was well established within the royal family, and we must not assume that these unions would have been considered in any way distasteful or even unusual by the parties concerned. Indeed, a Late Period papyrus now housed in the Cairo Museum tells the story of Prince Neneferkaptah and Princess Ahwere who had fallen head over heels in love with each other and who wished to marry despite the opposition of their father, who worried aloud about the situation:

If it so happens that I have only two children, is it right to marry one to the other? Should I not rather marry Neneferkaptah to the daughter of a general and Ahwere to the son of another general, so that our family may increase?[26]

The king was concerned about the match not because the bride and groom were brother and sister, but because it was an insular marriage which would not introduce new members into the royal family. Eventually he relented, gave his children his blessing and his daughter a dowry, and, as Ahwere frankly tells us:

I was taken as a wife to the house of Neneferkaptah . . . He slept with me that night and found me pleasing. He slept with me again and again and we loved each other.[27]

To egyptologists working in the nineteenth and early twentieth centuries, many of whom had developed their interest in egyptology as a

by-product of their primary interest in Biblical studies, these shame-
lessly incestuous unions appeared both unnatural and repugnant; 'a very
objectional custom' according to Sir J. Gardner Wilkinson,[28] speaking
for many of his contemporaries. Such marriages could only be explained as a necessity which could not be avoided. Already heavily
influenced by the erroneous theory of a matriarchal Theban royal
family, egyptologists now developed the so-called 'heiress theory'; a
theory which neatly explained the intra-family marriages by deducing
that the right to rule must be transmitted downwards through the generations via the royal women. It was not enough to be born a royal
prince or to be crowned king as it would be in a western-style monarchy – the true ruler of Egypt had to marry the royal heiress who was
always the daughter of a king and his consort and who carried the
essence of 'royalness' in her veins. The heiress then in turn became
queen, and mother of both the next king and the next royal heiress.

More recent research, and perhaps a greater willingness to accept the
realities of incestuous unions, shows that this heiress theory must be
incorrect. Many of the most successful kings of the 18th Dynasty, including Tuthmosis I, II and III, were clearly not the sons of royal
women and yet were fully accepted by their people. Conversely Tuthmosis III, Amenhotep I and Amenhotep III, and possibly Tuthmosis I,
had non-royal consorts who were treated with at least as much respect
as their better-born sisters. We must, therefore, seek some other explanation for the prevalence of incestuous royal marriages at this time.

The dynastic Egyptians, in contrast to most other peoples, ancient
and modern, were remarkably relaxed in their attitudes to marriage.
They do not seem to have felt the need to impose any state or religious
control over the choice of partners and, although the idea of the family
was always an important one, the impression given is that marriage – or,
more accurately, a sexual union – was of little interest to any but the
immediate families of the couple concerned. Co-habitation with slaves,
with foreigners, with brothers or sisters and even with relatively young
children were all legally permissible, as was polygamy and, it would
appear although we have no known examples, polyandry. Therefore, it
was possible for any Egyptian man to openly marry or sleep with his sister or
one or all of his unmarried daughters without incurring legal penalties.
Whether he would have been allowed to sleep with his mother – or indeed
whether he would have wished to – is another question.

Despite their legal validity, brother–sister unions are very rare until the Roman period when a complex system of inheritance laws forced families to favour brother–sister marriages in an attempt to keep their property intact. Unfortunately, the Egyptian habit of referring to wives and lovers as 'sisters' has caused a great deal of confusion in this area; the New Kingdom poet who sighed, 'My sister is come, my heart fills with joy as I open my arms to enfold her', was longing for his girlfriend, who was presumably not a close blood relation, and it would appear that most Egyptian males simply did not fancy their sisters and chose to look outside the nuclear family for a mate. We may suggest a variety of reasons for this: local custom, the wish to extend the basic family group, the wish to extend bonds with other families and perhaps a lack of sexual attraction between children raised together, may well have combined to make non-sibling marriage the preferred choice.

The royal family were, however, in an entirely different position. They were unique, exclusive, and had no desire to either increase in numbers or unite with other families. Indeed, they were even prepared to exclude brothers and sons from the immediate family in order to preserve their select status. Incestuous marriage was therefore a convenient means of ensuring the purity of the royal line and restricting the size of the royal family by concentrating 'royalness' within a small group of closely related individuals. As an added advantage, brother–sister marriage ensured that a suitable husband could always be found for the highest-ranking princesses who might otherwise have been unable to marry. Whether they were concerned that the husband of a princess might attempt to seize the throne for his own descendants, or whether they simply felt themselves to be superior to all others, the 18th Dynasty royal family was always very careful when it came to marrying off its daughters. Egyptian princesses never made diplomatic foreign marriages and when the King of Babylon, whose own daughter was married to Amenhotep III, inquired about an Egyptian bride for his own harem he was given short shrift: 'Since the days of old, no Egyptian king's daughter has been given to anyone.' Ankhesenamen, the young widow of Tutankhamen, broke with 18th Dynasty tradition when she wrote to Suppiluliuma, King of the Hittites, asking him to send a suitable prince: 'If you could send me one of your sons I would make him my husband.' Unfortunately, the bridegroom was murdered on the way to meet his bride, and it was not until the 21st

Dynasty that an Egyptian princess was sent as a bride to the Jewish King Solomon.

Brother–sister marriages were a useful means of reinforcing the links between the pharaoh and the gods while emphasizing the gulf between the immediate royal family and the rest of mankind. Isis and Osiris, Geb and Nut and Seth and Nephthys had all enjoyed brother–sister unions, although as these six existed at a time when there were no other eligible marriage partners this was perhaps less through choice than through necessity. Whatever the reasons, what had been good enough for the gods was good enough for pharaoh. For those who believed that their royal blood made them profoundly different from other mortals, a sister made the logical choice of spouse, while an Egyptian princess was surely the best possible mother for a future king of Egypt.

3

Queen of Egypt

𓅃𓇋𓏏𓂝𓆓

The king [Tuthmosis I] rested from life, going forth to heaven, having completed his years in gladness of heart. The hawk in the nest [appeared as] the King of Upper and Lower Egypt, Aakheperenre [Tuthmosis II], he became king of the Black Land and ruler of the Red Land, having taken possession of the Two Regions in triumph.[1]

The former general Tuthmosis I soon proved himself a worthy successor to the newly established tradition of the mighty Egyptian warrior-king, embarking on a series of flamboyant and highly successful foreign campaigns intended to impress Egyptian superiority on the traditional enemies of the south and north. In his second regnal year Egyptian troops marched southwards into Nubia where, as Ahmose, son of Ibana, tells us, they successfully 'destroyed insurrection throughout the lands and repelled the intruders from the desert region', advancing past the Third Cataract of the Nile, where Tuthmosis set up a stela to commemorate his great achievement, and reaching the island of Argo. The new king sailed home in triumph with the body of a Nubian bowman, a dreadful warning to others who might be tempted to rebel, draped 'head down over the bow of his majesty's ship, the *Falcon*'. He left behind him a subdued land controlled by a chain of Egyptian fortresses stretching across Nubia and the Sudan.

This was followed by an even more spectacular victory. After establishing new military headquarters at the old northern capital of Memphis, Tuthmosis pressed eastwards into Naharin, crossing the River Euphrates and entering the territory ruled by Egypt's new enemy, the King of Mitanni. Here, as the ever-present Ahmose records:

[His Majesty] went to Retenu to vent his wrath throughout foreign lands. His Majesty arrived at Naharin. His Majesty – life, prosperity and health be upon him – found that the enemy was gathering troops. Then his Majesty made a great heap of corpses among them. Countless were the living captives of his

Majesty from his victories. Lo, I was at the head of the army and his Majesty saw my bravery. I brought away a chariot, its horse, and the one who was upon it as a living captive to present to his Majesty. I was rewarded with gold yet again.[2]

After a great battle and with many of the enemy killed or taken prisoner, Tuthmosis laid down the foundations of what was later to develop into Egypt's Asian empire. Once again a commemorative stela was needed, this time to be set on the bank of the River Euphrates. On his journey home the victorious king paused for a celebratory elephant hunt in the swamps of Syria, thus establishing a family tradition which was to be followed some fifty years later by his grandson, Tuthmosis III, a prolific big-game hunter who was to boast of killing or maiming over a hundred elephants at the same hunting ground.

Tuthmosis I instigated an equally successful domestic policy and his reign saw extensive and innovative building programmes at all the major Theban sites. To Ineni, a high-ranking Theban official, Hereditary Prince, Overseer of Double Granary of Amen and possibly Mayor of Thebes, fell the responsibility for supervising what was to become the first phase of the 18th Dynasty embellishment of the Karnak temple complex. The original Middle Kingdom temple was now enclosed within a sandstone wall, the processional ways were extended, and two magnificent pylons or monumental gateways, complete with towers and flagpoles, were installed, the area between them being roofed over to form a pillared hall. Most impressive of all, two inscribed red-granite obelisks, each standing 19.5 m (64 ft) high and with a gold-leaf coated tip designed to mirror the sun's rays, were erected within the enclosure wall before the main entrance to the temple.

Ineni was evidently an experienced architect and overseer of building projects. He had previously worked on the construction of the gate of Amenhotep I at Karnak, and he was now to be entrusted with the quarrying of the king's secret tomb which was to be the first excavated in the remote Biban el-Muluk, the Valley of the Gates of the Kings, now better known simply as the Valley of the Kings, on the West Bank of the Nile, opposite Thebes. The autobiography preserved in his tomb tells how he:

. . . supervised the excavation of the cliff-tomb of His Majesty alone, no one seeing, no one hearing . . . I was vigilant in seeking that which is excellent. I

made fields of clay in order to plaster their tombs of the necropolis. It is work
such as the ancestors had not which I was obliged to do there.³

The tomb was to follow the new custom, established by Amenhotep
I, of physically separating the actual burial chamber from the mortuary temple. The theological move away from the cult of Re and
the associated pyramid form, and the development of mortuary
temples which were effectively temples of Amen, caused the architects some problems. It was neither practical nor desirable to site the
large and conspicuous mortuary temples in the steep Valley of the
Kings while, although the mortuary temple could be constructed on
the flatter and more accessible desert fringes, the burial chamber
could not be dug underneath the temple without incurring the risk
of flooding. Separation was inevitable, and brought a welcome side
effect; it was now possible to make a realistic attempt to hide the
entrance to the burial chamber from the thieves who were irresistibly
attracted by the sumptuous paraphernalia traditionally provided with
the burial of a king. The preservation of an intact tomb was vital,
not merely to provide storage for the grave goods which the deceased might need in the Afterlife, but to conserve the mummified
body itself. Egyptian theology decreed that the soul, or Ka, could not
survive if the body was destroyed and, as the prospect of 'dying the
second death' (that is, the destruction of the body and subsequent
death of the soul) seemed almost too horrific to contemplate, the
tradition of mummification was developed in a desperate attempt to
defeat nature and preserve the deceased for eternity. Unfortunately,
the custom of wrapping valuable items under the mummy bandages
meant that the bodies of dead kings, once discovered, were treated
with scant respect. By the beginning of the New Kingdom tomb-
robbery was a major problem, and it had become all too obvious that
a large monument placed in close proximity to a wealthy grave
simply served as a signpost to buried treasures.

Tuthmosis' hidden tomb, usually identified using the modern tomb-
numbering convention as KV38, was a relatively simple affair consisting
of a rectangular antechamber, a pillared burial chamber and small store-
room linked together by a series of narrow passages and steep stairways.
His associated mortuary chapel, *Khenmetankh* (literally 'United with
Life'), which was for a long time mis-identified as the shrine of Prince

Wadjmose, was situated a good hour's walk away from the Valley of the Kings, at a site later chosen for the mortuary temple of the 19th Dynasty King Ramesses II, now popularly known as the Ramesseum.

Tuthmosis had been a middle-aged man with a successful career behind him when he acceded to the throne and he had reigned for no more than ten to fifteen years before, aged about fifty, he 'rested from life'. Fifty years may seem a short life-span to modern readers accustomed to seeing relations living well into their seventies and eighties, but it would have been an eminently reasonable age for an active Egyptian soldier to achieve; throughout the New Kingdom, life expectancy at birth was considerably lower than twenty years, while those who survived the perils of birth and infancy to reach fourteen years of age might then expect to live for another fifteen years. This compares well with the average life expectancies normally found in pre-industrial societies, which tend to vary between twenty and forty years, and with the suggested average life expectancy of a Roman senator at birth of thirty years.[4] Those élite Egyptian males, who able to maintain higher standards of hygiene and nutrition than the less fortunate artisans and peasants, who performed little or no dangerous manual work, who were not faced with the dangers of childbirth and could afford the best medical attention, benefited from a slightly increased life expectancy, but no one could look forward with any confidence to a long old age. Although the Egyptians were famed throughout the ancient world for their medical expertise, there was relatively little that any doctor could do to help when faced with a seriously ill or wounded patient, and the average age for tomb owners (that is, the male élite) of the Dynastic Period has been calculated at between thirty and forty-five years.[5]

The high levels of infant and child mortality, combined with the low life expectancy, made it very difficult for the Egyptian royal family to maintain its exclusivity. In an ideal world, as we have already seen, the heir to the throne would be the son of the king and his consort who was usually herself a close blood relation, and often a half- or full sister of the king. The crown prince would, therefore, be of unblemished royal descent through both his father and his mother, and by marrying his sister he could maintain the tradition of family purity. However, no matter how many children were conceived by the royal couple, there could be no guarantee that any would live to become adults. Given the

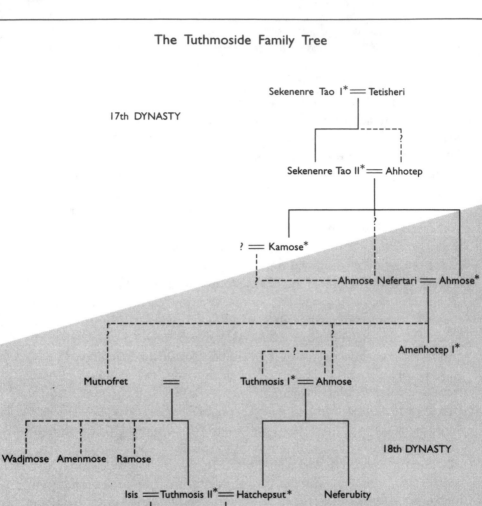

The Tuthmoside Family Tree

lack of effective contraceptives and often-expressed desire for large numbers of offspring, we might expect to find the nuclear royal family
expanding rapidly throughout the New Kingdom. This was not the
case. Instead, the Tuthmoside royal family was plagued by a dearth of
children, with sons being in particularly short supply and single daughters becoming the norm. Nor were they the only New Kingdom royal
family to suffer from this problem; King Ramesses II, perhaps exception-
ally unfortunate even by Egyptian standards, was eventually succeeded
by Prince Merenptah, his thirteenth son born to one of his many secondary wives. Although the Egyptian king always had the back-up of
his multiple wives and concubines, any of whom could in theory produce a legitimate king's son and heir, the succession of a lesser prince to
the throne was not regarded as ideal.

There is some confusion over the number of children actually born
to Tuthmosis I and his consort, Queen Ahmose. We know of two
daughters, Princess Hatchepsut and her sister Princess Akhbetneferu
(occasionally referred to as Neferubity) who died in infancy. We also
have firm historical evidence that Tuthmosis I fathered two sons, the
Princes Wadjmose and Amenmose, and possibly a third son, Prince
Ramose.[6] Princes Amenmose and Wadjmose survived into their late
teens but never acceded to the throne. As both boys had been raised in
the tradition of royal princes, and as Amenmose in particular seems to
have undertaken some of the duties of the heir to the throne, it appears
that both were regarded as potential kings who failed to inherit only
because they predeceased their father; both princes disappear before
the death of Tuthmosis I. Wadjmose, the elder brother, is the more
obscure. We know that he was taught by Itruri and possibly by Paheri,
grandson of Ahmose, son of Ibana; he is depicted in the tomb of Paheri
as a young boy sitting on his tutor's knee. He also appears in a prominent role in his father's badly damaged funerary chapel where a side-
room served as a family shrine for the mortuary cults of various family
members including the secondary Queen Mutnofret, the mysterious
Prince Ramose and Prince Wadjmose himself.

Amenmose, the younger but possibly longer-lived son, was accorded
the title of 'Great Army Commander', the role now traditionally allocated to the crown prince. Physical bravery had become an important
New Kingdom royal attribute and Amenmose was clearly expected to
enjoy the hearty lifestyle of the male élite. A broken stela tells us that,

Fig. 3.1   The infant Hatchepsut being suckled by the goddess Hathor

during his father's regnal Year 4, Amenmose was already hunting wild animals in the Giza desert near the Great Sphinx, a favourite playground of the royal princes. Big-game hunting was by now a major prestige sport recently made infinitely more exciting by the use of the composite bow and the swift and highly mobile horse-drawn chariot which allowed the pursuit of fast-moving creatures such as lions and ostriches. Middle Kingdom hunting had been a far more staid affair, with the brave huntsman standing still to fire arrows at a pre-herded and occasionally penned group of 'wild' animals.

Just how old could Amenmose have been when he was to be found chasing ostriches across the Giza desert? If Amenmose was the son of Ahmose and Tuthmosis, if Ahmose was the sister or half-sister of Tuthmosis, and if we therefore assume that the royal siblings embarked upon their incestuous marriage only after Tuthmosis became king, Amenmose must have been barely four years old during his father's Year 4; surely a little too young for even the most precocious of princes to be found training with the army or hunting wild animals. This reasoning is, of course, full of 'ifs', and it is entirely possible that a relatively young prince could have played a purely honorary role in the life of the army; Ramesses II, for example, allowed all his sons to travel with the army, and the five-year-old Prince Khaemwaset is known to have accompanied a military campaign in Lower Nubia. However, the apparent discrepancy in ages strongly suggests that Amenmose and Wadjmose, and perhaps the ephemeral Ramose, may not in fact have been the children of Ahmose but of an earlier wife, possibly the mysterious Lady Mutnofret who features alongside Wadjmose in his father's funerary chapel.

We know very little about Lady Mutnofret, but it is obvious that she was a person of rank, perhaps even of royal blood, who was held in the highest honour. This is confirmed by an inscription at Karnak where a lady named Mutnofret is described as 'King's Daughter'.[7] We have already seen that it is Mutnofret rather than Queen Ahmose who appears alongside Wadjmose and Ramose in the king's mortuary chapel; here her statue wears the royal uraeus and her name is written in a cartouche. Mutnofret is also known to have been the mother

Fig. 3.2   *A hippopotamus hunter*

of Tuthmosis' eventual successor, Tuthmosis II. The Princes Amenmose, Wadjmose, Ramose, and Tuthmosis II may therefore have been full brothers, possibly born before their father married Ahmose. This tangle of relationships would make more sense if we had confirmation that Tuthmosis was a widower at his accession – highly likely, given that he is likely to have been at least thirty-five years old – his first wife Mutnofret having borne him several sons before dying.

The Tuthmoside succession following the death of Tuthmosis I – the so-called 'Hatchepsut Problem' – is a subject which greatly perplexed late nineteenth- and early twentieth-century egyptologists, and the effects of their confusion still linger in some more recent publications. The names of the individual monarchs involved had been known for some time (Tuthmosis I, II and III, Hatchepsut), but the precise sequence of their reigns and their relationships with each other were not, although it was generally assumed that the three Tuthmoses followed each other in sequence with Hatchepsut appearing in some unknown capacity some time after Tuthmosis II. Unfortunately, the monumental evidence which might have been expected to help solve the mystery had been tampered with at some point in antiquity, the original cartouches[8] being re-cut to give the names of other phar-

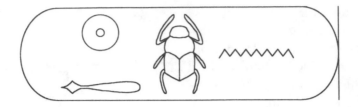

Fig. 3.3   The cartouche of King Tuthmosis II

aohs involved in the succession muddle. This deliberate defacement of the royal monuments was generally accepted as evidence of intense personal hatreds stemming from a desperate struggle for power within the royal family.

In 1896, the German egyptologist Kurt Sethe, basing his conclusions on a meticulous study of the erased cartouches, and on the erroneous assumption that the defaced cartouches must have been re-carved by the monarch whose name replaced the original, suggested that the succession of monarchs must have been as follows:[9]

1   Tuthmosis I. Deposed by –
2   Tuthmosis III
3   Hatchepsut and Tuthmosis III co-regents, Hatchepsut the senior king. Hatchepsut deposed by –
4   Tuthmosis III
5   Tuthmosis II and Tuthmosis I co-regents, until the death of Tuthmosis I
6   Tuthmosis II. Reigning until his death
7   Tuthmosis III and Hatchepsut co-regents until Hatchepsut's death
8   Tuthmosis III

It is perhaps all too easy for modern historians, blessed with the benefit of hindsight, to dismiss this over-elaborate sequence as a triumph of scholarly methodology over common sense. To those accustomed to studying the complex Ptolemaic succession, however, where parent succeeded child and brother succeeded sister in rapid and confusing sequence, it was not quite so far-fetched. The theory, accompanied by appropriate explanations of intra-family feuding to justify the rapid

1. The Temple of Amen at Karnak.

2. The Valley of the Kings.

3. (above) Hatchepsut as king offering before the barque of Amen.
4. (left) The God Amen.

5. (opposite) Seated statue of Hatchepsut from *Djeser-Djeseru* showing the king with a female body and male accessories.

6. (above) The near-identical figures for King Hatchepsut and King Tuthmosis III, Hatchepsut in front.

7. Scene showing the gods crowning King Hatchepsut, which had been attacked in antiquity.

8. Head of Hatchepsut.

9. Granite statue of Hatchepsut.

10. Red granite sphinx of Hatchepsut.

changes of ruler, became almost universally adopted despite a complete absence of corroborative evidence, and initially only the Swiss egyptologist Édouard Naville made a direct challenge to Sethe's suggested sequence of rulers, maintaining that the cartouches which replaced those of Hatchepsut should, equally erroneously, all be dated to the Ramesside period. Sethe and Naville, two illustrious contemporaries, were never to reach agreement over the fundamental aspects of Hatchepsut's reign and were, indeed, for a time reduced to open warfare over the subject; their famous scholarly arguments being conducted with dignity via the pages of learned journals. A well-known archaeological story tells of the time when the two found themselves to be near neighbours, Sethe occupying the 'German house' at Deir el-Bahri and M. and Mme Naville living close by in the newly built British expedition house. When the Navilles' kitchen collapsed into a tomb-pit, threatening the continuation of the British mission, Sethe generously invited his colleague to stay in the German house, on condition that the name of Hatchepsut would not be mentioned between them. The Navilles spent several peaceful weeks staying with Sethe before they returned to their house, their kitchen now restored, and the feud at once recommenced.[10]

While Naville was content with a flat denial of Sethe's conclusions, others struggled to incorporate the new scheme into their own work. Even those such as Flinders Petrie, who found themselves unable to accept the full complexities of the proposed succession, were heavily influenced by the underlying reasoning and unquestioningly accepted the principal of the Tuthmoside feud. Eventually, dissatisfaction with Sethe's scheme did start to gather momentum. In 1928 it was publicly repudiated by both Herbert Winlock and Eduard Meyer, working independently, and in 1933 William Edgerton[11] was able to highlight the fatal flaw in Sethe's argument: it was simply not safe to assume that those who defaced the cartouches of their predecessors invariably replaced the erased name with their own. Indeed, we now know that the name of Hatchepsut was often replaced by that of her predecessors, either Tuthmosis I or Tuthmosis II. Edgerton's work was confirmed by W. C. Hayes's study of the royal sarcophagi of the early 18th Dynasty which, by tracing the stylistic evolution of the sarcophagi, was able to suggest a more reasonable sequence of rulers.[12] Sethe's complex scheme was swept away, to be replaced by the far simpler succession of Tuthmosis I, Tuthmosis II, Tuthmosis III, with Hatchepsut taking power during the earlier part of the reign of Tuthmosis III.

Although Sethe's complex sequence of rulers was abandoned with some relief, the legacy of his work lingered, with many historians unable to shake off the idea of the Tuthmosides as a family at war with itself and the Tuthmoside court as a hot-bed of intrigue and plotting. The simplified order of succession now made it difficult to justify any hatred between either Tuthmosis I or Tuthmosis II and the other members of the family, but the legendary enmity between Tuthmosis III and Hatchepsut – bolstered by the undeniable fact that many of Hatchepsut's cartouches had indeed been attacked after her death – remained as an integral part of accepted early 18th Dynasty history, colouring many interpretations of their joint reign. Hatchepsut the hated stepmother, and Tuthmosis III the wronged and brooding king, had entered the historical imagination and could not easily be dislodged.

On the death of her father the young Hatchepsut, possibly only twelve years old, emerged from the obscurity of the women's palace to marry her half-brother and become queen consort of Egypt. Although we have very little information about Hatchepsut's life in the harem, we are fortunate enough to have a badly damaged sandstone statue which shows her as a miniature adult pharaoh sitting on the knee of her nurse Sitre, known as Inet, with her feet resting on the symbolic representation of the 'nine bows', the traditional means of depicting the military supremacy of the Egyptian king. Throughout the Dynastic age the position of royal wet-nurse was an honourable post of some influence and importance, often given as a reward to the mothers and wives of the élite courtiers. Hatchepsut clearly bore enough affection for the woman who had cared for her in infancy to commission a statue of Sitre to be placed in her Deir el-Bahri temple. Unfortunately, the statue inscription was so badly damaged as to be almost unreadable, but as Winlock himself records:

It seems that there has long been a flake of limestone in the Ambras Collection in Vienna . . . on which an ancient scribe had jotted down an inscription in vertical columns. Comparing this inscription with the one on the statue, I have little doubt that the ostracon gives the preliminary draft for the statue inscription, drawn up by the scribe who was directing the sculptor. On the statue the inscription is incomplete, and it gives us a curious feeling to find ourselves filling in the gaps from the original rough draft after a lapse of thirty-five hundred years.[13]

The text, so fortuitously preserved and identified, was translated by Winlock as follows:

May the king Maatkare [Hatchepsut] and Osiris, first of the Westerners, [the great god] Lord of Abydos, be gracious and give a mortuary offering [of cakes and beer, beef and fowl, and thousands of everything] good and pure, and the sweet breath of the north wind to the spirit of the chief nurse who suckled the Mistress of the Two Lands, Sit-Re, called Yen [Inet], justified.

During his 1903 season of excavations in the Valley of the Kings, Howard Carter opened a small tomb, now known by its number KV60, which housed two non-royal female burials, one of which was still lying in half a wooden coffin, together with a number of mummified geese and a mummified leg of beef. Carter was not interested in the tomb, which had suffered badly at the hands of tomb robbers, and he quickly sealed it up. However, the tomb was re-opened three years later and the body in the coffin was transported to the Cairo Museum. The second body was left where the robbers had abandoned it, lying on the floor of the tomb. The wooden coffin was inscribed with the name of In or Inet, and it would appear that Carter had stumbled across the burial of Hatchepsut's wet-nurse, who had been accorded the unprecedented privilege of interment in the Valley of the Kings.[14] The other body, that of an unusually fat woman with red-gold hair and worn teeth indicative of middle age, is so far unidentified.

Tuthmosis II and Hatchepsut buried their father and started to rule Egypt as a conventional New Kingdom king and queen consort, following the successful internal and foreign policies developed by Amenhotep I and Tuthmosis I. At home the now traditional building works at the Karnak temple of Amen continued, and the country prospered under the new regime. Unfortunately, the military achievements of Tuthmosis II have been almost entirely effaced by the more spectacular campaigns of both his father and his son, but there is evidence of at least two successful military strikes during his reign, even though it appears that Tuthmosis himself – possibly because the 'hawk in the nest' was too young – did not accompany his troops into battle. In Year 1 an army of foot-soldiers sailed southwards to crush an insurrection in Nubia, a triumph which was commemorated by a stela set up on the Aswan–Philae road which told the tale of the rebellion:

... one came to inform His Majesty that vile Cush had revolted and that those who were subjects of the Lord of the Two Lands had planned rebellion to plunder the people of Egypt . . .[15]

'Raging like a panther', Tuthmosis took swift action to defeat the rebels. Later there was a campaign in Palestine where, as Ahmose-Pennekheb records, Egypt's control of the region was reinforced and many prisoners were taken.

We are perhaps in some danger of underestimating Tuthmosis II's military prowess, and indeed of underestimating his entire personality. Winlock is not alone in seeing the new king as a somewhat negligible ruler:

The young King Tuthmosis II was a youth of no more than twenty, physically frail and mentally far from energetic, who let the country run itself. Old officials who had started their careers in the days of his grandfather – and even of his great-grandfather – occupied their places throughout his reign, and it was his father's generals who suppressed a rebellion which broke out in Nubia.[16]

It is all too easy to fall into the trap of seeing the Tuthmoside imperialism as a deliberate policy, with Tuthmosis I as the founder of a potentially mighty Asian empire which was, following the disappointingly peaceful reigns of Tuthmosis II and Hatchepsut, successfully consolidated by Tuthmosis III. This expansionist strategy – so obvious to modern students of Egyptian history – may not have been quite so apparent to either Tuthmosis II or Hatchepsut. By the time that Tuthmosis II came to the throne, Egypt had suffered the effects of a vicious war of liberation followed by a spate of foreign campaigns. Her traditional boundaries were now secure, an acceptable buffer zone had been

established between Egypt and her
nearest enemies, and Tuthmosis
may, with some justification, have
seen little need to engage in further unnecessary and expensive
military action.

It is also worth remembering
that battles often have little or no
impact on the archaeological
record while the texts and monuments which document military
campaigns are subject to the same
processes of random preservation
as other historical records. It is entirely possible that Tuthmosis II in-
dulged in more campaigns than
the historical record now gives
him credit for. Nor is it entirely
fair to criticize Tuthmosis II for

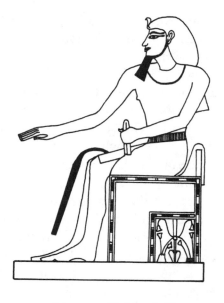

Fig. 3.4   Tuthmosis II

retaining the efficient bureaucracy of his predecessor. Indeed, it has
probably already become apparent to the reader that the same soldiers
and officials (for example, Ineni, Ahmose, son of Ibana, and Ahmose-
Pennekheb, to name but three) continued to serve under successive
kings, providing strong indirect evidence for the lack of any political
upheaval at the end of each reign.

The new consort was now accorded the conventional queen's titles
of King's Daughter, King's Sister and King's Great Wife, although her
preferred title was always God's Wife. She behaved in an exemplary
fashion throughout her husband's reign. A stela now housed in Berlin
(Ägyptisches Museum 15699) shows us the immediate royal family at
this time: Tuthmosis II stands to face the god Re while immediately
behind him stands the senior lady, the Dowager Queen Ahmose,
whose regal headdress of tall feathers and a uraeus worn on top of a
vulture crown indicates her importance. The Queen Consort Hatchepsut
stands modestly behind both her mother and her husband in approved
wifely fashion. She is dressed in a simple sheath dress and wearing a
rather understated crown, although her lack of tall feathers may owe as
much to a lack of space on the stela as it does to her more junior role.

There is no reason to suppose that Hatchepsut was anything other than content with her position at this time, and certainly no justification for the assertion that Tuthmosis II, 'knowing the temper of his ambitious consort', was forced to take measures to ensure that his son would eventually succeed to the throne.[17] Nor is there any proof to support the assumption that during the reign of the supposedly sickly Tuthmosis II it was Hatchepsut, the power behind the throne, who ruled Egypt: '. . . the experience which she gained in the time of her father was of the greatest use to her, and her natural ability made her to profit by it to the utmost.'[18]

Perhaps the clearest indication of Hatchepsut's acceptance of her subsidiary role is the excavation of her queen's tomb, which commenced some time towards the end of her husband's reign. At the beginning of the 18th Dynasty the Valley of the Queens had not yet come into operation and, in the absence of a formal queen's cemetery on the West Bank at Thebes, Hatchepsut selected a site in the Wadi Sikkat Taka ez–Zeida, a lonely and inaccessible ravine approximately one mile to the west of the site she was later to choose for her mortuary temple. Here the tomb was hidden high up in the face of the cliff, facing west, where there was a splendid view over the Nile Valley and where 'the setting October sun throws its last beams right into the mouth of the tomb'.[19] The tomb was well sited to deter tomb robbers, and almost inaccessible for its eventual excavator, Howard Carter:

The tomb was discovered full of rubbish . . . this rubbish having poured into it in torrents from the mountain above. When I wrested it from the plundering Arabs I found that they had burrowed into it like rabbits, as far as the sepulchral hall . . . I found that they had crept down a crack extending half way down the cleft, and there from a small ledge in the rock they had lowered themselves by a rope to the then hidden entrance of the tomb at the bottom of the cleft: a dangerous performance, but one which I myself had to imitate, though with better tackle . . . For anyone who suffers from vertigo it certainly was not pleasant, and though I soon overcame the sensation of the ascent I was obliged always to descend in a net.[20]

Having eventually gained entrance to the tomb, and cleared it of its accumulated debris, Carter discovered that internally the tomb was similar in plan to that which Tuthmosis II had been constructing

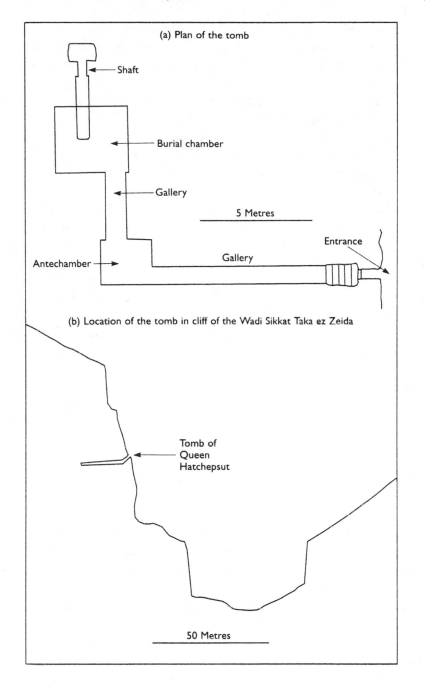

(a) Plan of the tomb

Shaft

Burial chamber

Gallery

5 Metres

Entrance

Antechamber

Gallery

(b) Location of the tomb in cliff of the Wadi Sikkat Taka ez Zeida

Tomb of
Queen
Hatchepsut

50 Metres

Fig. 3.5   Plan of Hatchepsut's first tomb

in the Valley of the Kings, with an entrance stairway descending to a doorway and leading in turn to a gallery, antechamber, second gallery and burial chamber. One of the descending galleries housed an impressive quartzite sarcophagus, a stone version of the massive rectangular wooden outer coffin provided for the burials of Queens Ahhotep and Ahmose Nefertari, measuring 1.99 m × 0.73 m × 0.73 m (6 ft 6 in × 2 ft 4 in × 2 ft 4 in). The lid, 0.17 m (6½ in) thick, was discovered propped against a corner of the sarcophagus. This, the first of the three magnificent sarcophagi which Hatchepsut was to commission, bore an inscription for 'The Great Princess, great in favour and grace, Mistress of All Lands, Royal Daughter and Royal Sister, Great Royal Wife, Mistress of the Two Lands, Hatchepsut'. On the lid was a prayer to the goddess Nut, adapted from the Old Kingdom *Pyramid Texts*:

Recitation: The King's Daughter, God's Wife, King's Great Wife, Lady of the Two Lands, Hatchepsut, says 'O my mother Nut, stretch thyself over me, that thou mayest place me among the imperishable stars which are in thee, and that I may not die.'[21]

The burial shaft, cut into the floor of the chamber, was unfinished. The tomb had been abandoned before the preliminary work had been completed, and it had clearly never been used by its intended owner.

Hatchepsut bore her brother one daughter, the Princess Neferure. For a long time it was believed that a second contemporary royal princess, Meritre-Hatchepsut (often referred to as Hatchepsut II), eventual consort of Tuthmosis III and mother of Amenhotep II, was the younger daughter of Hatchepsut and Tuthmosis II, but there is no foundation for this assumption which seems to be based on nothing more concrete than the coincidence that the two ladies shared the same name. Hatchepsut herself makes no mention of a second daughter on any of her monuments while Meritre-Hatchepsut is tantalizingly silent about her parentage although, given the fact that she became a God's Wife, Great Royal Wife and Mother of the king, it seems likely that she was born a member of the immediate royal family.

Neferure, undisputed daughter of Hatchepsut and Tuthmosis II, appears suitably invisible, as we might expect of a young royal child, throughout her father's reign. However, following the death of Tuthmosis II, she starts to play an unusually prominent part in court life, suddenly appearing in public alongside her mother, the king. The little princess is now far more conspicuous than her mother was at an equally early age, and it is difficult to escape the conclusion that, while Hatchepsut's childhood was overshadowed by that of her brothers, Neferure as an only child was being groomed from an early age to play an important role in the Egyptian royal family. However, there is a big difference between training a daughter to be queen consort – for it would have been almost a foregone conclusion, given her ancestry, that Neferure would marry the next pharaoh – and raising her to become king.

To hint, as some modern historians have done, that Hatchepsut intended from the outset that her daughter would become pharaoh is to imply one of two very different views of Hatchepsut's personality. The first, the simplest and in many ways the most acceptable scenario, is that Hatchepsut was being merely practical in her assumption that Neferure might eventually inherit the throne. If Hatchepsut had realized that she herself, as queen, would not bear a son, if Tuthmosis III had died in infancy and if the immediate royal family could offer no more suitable (that is, male) candidate for the crown, she may well have been proved correct. Historical precedent would certainly have been on 'King' Neferure's side, as the Middle Kingdom Queen Sobeknofru had successfully claimed the throne in the absence of any more suitable male heir. In this case, we might push our speculation further by suggesting that Tuthmosis III, the son and eventual heir of Tuthmosis II, was either not born until the very end of his father's reign, or that for some reason – perhaps because of his mother's lowly birth – he was not always considered an entirely suitable heir. It would certainly have been prudent, in an age where no child could be guaranteed to live to become an adult, to ensure that as many royal children as possible were educated as future kings.

Alternatively, it has been suggested by those historians belonging to the anti-Hatchepsut camp that Hatchepsut's treatment of Neferure was the outward sign of her own personal disappointment and thwarted ambition. Hatchepsut may have grown to see the position of queen consort and eventual queen mother as an unfulfilling and unacceptably subordinate role both for herself and her daughter. Herself the daughter and sister of a king, she had experienced years of being passed over in favour of male relations, and had no intention of seeing her much-loved daughter repeat her humiliation. She therefore planned that her daughter should upset the *status quo* and become a female pharaoh. In many respect this argument lacks conviction. We have no evidence to suggest that Hatchepsut was ever dissatisfied with her own role as consort during the reign of Tuthmosis II, although it could of course be argued that we are unlikely ever to find such evidence. More to the point, it seems unlikely that Hatchepsut, the product of a highly conservative society brought up to think in conventional gender stereo-types, would even dare to imagine that she had any chance of success-fully challenging *maat* without a valid and widely acceptable reason.

From infancy, the care of the royal princess was considered to be a matter of some importance, and successive high-ranking officials laid claim to the prestigious title of royal nurse or royal tutor. In his tomb at el-Kab, Ahmose-Pennekheb proudly recalls how 'the God's Wife re-peated favours for me, the great King's Wife Maatkare, justified; I edu-cated her eldest daughter, Neferure, justified, when she was a child at the breast'.[22] Later Senenmut, Hatchepsut's most influential courtier, became first Steward of Neferure and then royal tutor; Senenmut seems to have taken particular pride in his association with the young princess and we have several statues which show him holding Neferure in his arms, or sitting with her on his lap. When Senenmut eventually moved on to greater glories, the administrator Senimen took over the role of caring for the young princess. The extent to which Neferure was actu-ally educated by any of her tutors is hard for us to assess. It seems very probable that most kings of Egypt could read and write, particularly those who had been taught in the harem schools, but literacy was by no means a necessity as the king had access to armies of scribes who could read and write on his behalf. If Neferure was truly being raised to inherit the throne, we might expect that she was given the education appropriate to a crown prince. In general, however, royal women were less likely than their brothers to be literate but would find this less of a disadvantage than we might suppose, thanks to the ready availability of professional scribes who could be hired as often as needed.

Given her background as the daughter and half-sister of a king, it would seem almost certain that Neferure was the intended bride of Tuthmosis III. The heir to the throne would have been the only man royal enough to marry such a well-connected girl, and she in turn would have made the most suitable mother of the next king. However, we have no record of their ever marrying, and it was Meritre-Hatchepsut rather than Neferure who was to become the mother of the subsequent pharaoh of Egypt, Amenhotep II. It is therefore surprising to find that throughout her mother's reign Neferure bore the title of 'God's Wife', the title which her mother had preferred as both consort and regent, and one which was normally reserved for the principal queen or queen mother. Any 'normal' king would be accompanied in such scenes by his wife, and here we almost certainly have the true explanation of Neferure's prominence. Hatchepsut as king needed a God's Wife to participate in the ritual aspects of her role and to ensure the preservation of *maat*. As Hatchepsut could not act simultaneously as both God's Wife and King her own daughter, herself the daughter of a king (or rather two kings) and therefore an acknowledged royal heiress, was the ideal person to fill the role and act as her mother's consort. The dismantled blocks of the Chapelle Rouge at Karnak (discussed in further detail in Chapter 4) include three sets of scenes in which an unnamed God's Wife is shown performing her duties during the reign of King Hatchepsut. In the absence of a more suitable candidate for the position, it seems safe to assume that the anonymous lady must be Neferure. The groups of scenes make the importance of the God's Wife clear. This was not an honorary role and, in theory at least, the God's Wife had to be present during the temple rituals. In one scene the God's Wife is shown, together with a priest, performing a ritual to destroy by burning the name of Egypt's enemies. In the second tableau she stands, both arms raised, with three priests to watch Hatchepsut present the seventeen gods of Karnak with their dinner. The final ritual shows the God's Wife leading a group of male priests to the temple pool to be purified, and then following Hatchepsut into the sanctuary where the King performs rites in front of the statue of Amen.

Neferure fades out of the limelight towards the end of her mother's reign; she is mentioned in the first tomb of Senenmut built in regnal Year 7 and appears on a stela at Serabit el-Khadim in Year 11, but then vanishes. She is unmentioned in Senenmut's Tomb 353 dated to Year 16, and the lack of further references to the hitherto prominent princess strongly suggests that she had died and been buried in her tomb in the Wadi Sikkat Taka ez-Zeida, close to that being prepared for her mother. There is only one, inconclusive, shred of evidence which hints that Neferure may have outlived her mother and married Tuthmosis III.[23] It is possible, but by no means certain, that Neferure was originally depicted on a stela dated to the beginning of Tuthmosis III's solo reign. However, although Neferure's title of God's Wife is given, the associated name on the stela now reads 'Satioh'. We know that Satioh was the first principal wife of Tuthmosis III, and that she never bore the title God's Wife. Is it possible that the stela, originally designed to include Neferure as the chief wife of Tuthmosis III, could have been altered after her death to show a replacement chief wife?

There is a general consensus of opinion that Tuthmosis II was not a healthy man, and that throughout his reign he was 'hampered by a frail constitution which restricted his activities and shortened his life'.[24] His mummy, unwrapped by Maspero in 1886, was found to have been badly damaged by ancient tomb robbers. The left arm had become detached, the right arm was severed from the elbow downwards and the right leg had been completely amputated by a single axe-blow. Maspero was particularly struck by the unhealthy condition of the king's skin:

The mask on his coffin represents him with a smiling and amiable countenance, and with fine pathetic eyes which show his descent from the Pharaohs of the XVIIth dynasty . . . He resembles Tuthmosis I; but his features are not so marked, and are characterised by greater gentleness. He had scarcely reached the age of thirty when he fell victim to a disease of which the process of embalming could not remove the traces. The skin is scabrous in patches and covered with scars, while the upper part of the [scalp] is bald; the body is thin and somewhat shrunken, and appears to have lacked vigour and muscular power.[25]

Some years later Smith was also allowed access to the mummy, and noted that:

The skin of the thorax, shoulders and arms (excluding the hands), the whole of the back, the buttocks and legs (excluding the feet) is studded with raised macules varying in size from minute points to patches a centimetre in diameter.[26]

Smith concluded that the mottled patches of skin were unlikely to be the signs of disease, as similar blotches were also to be found, albeit to a lesser extent, on the mummified bodies of Tuthmosis III and Amenhotep II. He therefore decided that they must have been caused by preservative used in mummification.

Unfortunately, nothing in egyptology can ever be taken for granted, and it is by no means one hundred per cent certain that the body of a man in his early thirties found associated with the wooden coffin of Tuthmosis II is actually that of the young king. The body and coffin were discovered not lying in their original tomb but as part of a collection of New Kingdom royal mummies which is now known as the Deir el-Bahri cache. Although the new 18th Dynasty tradition of separating the hidden burial chamber from the highly conspicuous mortuary temple was, at least in part, intended to protect the royal burials from thieves, it had proved impossible to embark upon the excavation of substantial rock-cut chambers in secret, and it was widely known that the Valley of the Kings contained caches of untold wealth. The temptation proved irresistible, and the officials who controlled the necropolis were faced with the constant headache of guarding the royal burials, often needing to protect the sealed tombs from the very workmen who had worked on their 'secret' construction. Security occasionally failed, and the officials were then faced with the task of attempting to right the wrongs before resealing the tomb. A graffito from the tomb of Tuthmosis IV, dated to the reign of Horemheb and therefore written little more than seventy years after the original interment, tells how this desecrated tomb was restored on the orders of the king:

His Majesty, life, prosperity, health, ordered that it should be recommended to the fanbearer on the left of the King, the Royal Scribe, the Superintendent of the Treasury, the Superintendent of the Works in the Place of Eternity [i.e. the Valley of the Kings] . . . Maya . . . to renew the burial of Tuthmosis IV, justified in the Precious Habitation in Western Thebes.[27]

Towards the end of the New Kingdom, when Egypt was experiencing a period of economic instability with unprecedented poverty for the lower classes and sporadic bouts of civil unrest, it became increasingly obvious that necropolis security had completely broken down and that many of the tombs in the Valley of the Kings had been entered and looted. The royal burials were in a disgraceful condition; the bodies of the kings, stripped of their jewellery and often minus their wrappings, were simply lying where they had been flung. Urgent action was needed. During the Third Intermediate Period reign of Pinedjem II, the officials of the necropolis decided to conduct an inspection of all known tombs. Those that had already been desecrated were re-entered and the royal mummies and their remaining grave goods were removed, 'restored' at an official workplace, replaced in wooden coffins – either their own, or someone else's – and then transported to one of the royal caches. Most of the royal burials were transferred to the comparative safety of the rock-cut tomb of the Lady Inhapi (DB 320) while other, smaller, caches were established in the tombs of Amenhotep III (KV 35), Horemheb (KV 57) and Twosret/Sethnakht (KV 14).[28] Tomb DB 320, hidden in a crack behind the Deir el-Bahri cliff, had been specially prepared to receive the royal visitors. The burial chamber had been greatly enlarged so that behind the small doorway of the original tomb there was now a vast storage area. Unfortunately, the mummies, coffins and grave goods which eventually made their way to Deir el-Bahri were, in spite of the labels attached by the necropolis officials, hopelessly muddled; the mummy of the 19th Dynasty King Ramesses IX, for example, was discovered lying in the coffin of the Third Intermediate Period Lady Neskhons, the coffin of Queen Ahhotep I housed the body of Pinedjem I, and the coffin of Queen Ahmose Nefertari also contained the mummy of Ramesses III.

The Deir el-Bahri cache had been discovered in 1871 by the Abd el-Rassul family of Gurna, a village situated close to the royal tombs on the west bank of Thebes. Throughout the nineteenth and early twentieth centuries, the men of Gurna made their living by farming, by working for genuine archaeological excavations, and by the illicit selling of antiquities, both fake and real, to the tourists and antiquarians who were already flocking to Thebes in ever increasing numbers. In true Gurna tradition Ahmed Abd el-Rassul and his brothers kept their find to themselves, and started to sell off the more portable of the highly valuable contents of the tomb. Dealing in plundered antiquities was then, as it is now, a very serious offence and, after several years of lucrative trading, two of the brothers were arrested and the secret of the tomb was finally revealed. A party of officials led by Emile Brugsch, assistant to the director of the Egyptian Antiquities Service, was guided by Mohammed Abd el-Rassul along the steep mountain path behind the mortuary temple of Hatchepsut to the remote private tomb. Here Brugsch, the first to enter, was startled by the sight of corridors and rooms filled with a collection of mummies beyond his wildest expectations:

Their gold covering and their polished surfaces reflected my own excited visage that it seemed as though I was looking into the faces of my own ancestors. The gilt face on the coffin of the amiable Queen Nefertari seemed to smile upon me like an old acquaintance. I took in the situation quickly, with a gasp, and hurried to the open air lest I should be overcome and the glorious prize, still unrevealed, be lost to science.[29]

This collection of royal mummies and their grave goods included the bodies of at least forty kings, queens and chief priests dating to the 18th, 19th, 20th and 21st Dynasties, amongst whom were to be found Sekenenre Tao II, Ahmose, Amenhotep I, Ahmose Nefertari and Tuthmosis I(?), II and III. The shock of the discovery seems to have gone to Brugsch's head. He took the decision that, for reasons of security, the entire tomb was to be cleared and the precious antiquities sent at once by boat to Cairo. Three hundred workmen immediately set to work, and it is a matter of the deepest regret that no one felt it necessary to either photograph or plan the interior of the tomb before it was emptied. Brugsch's behaviour, all the more puzzling because he is known to have been a proficient and experienced photographer, has led to speculation that there may have been some sort of cover-up, and that perhaps Brugsch himself, or someone high-up in the government service, had actually been dealing in the pilfered antiquities. Brugsch seems not to have been particularly well suited to his position of responsibility, and 'he left behind him an evil reputation for his clandestine transactions with native antiquity-dealers, and for his intriguing and mischief-making habits'.[30]

Within a mere two days the precious wooden coffins had been removed from the tomb, wrapped in matting, sewn into sailcloth, and carried down to the river. Here, along the riverbank, huge crowds gathered to witness the final journey of the long-lost kings of Egypt. As the boat sailed by, the peasant women started to wail and tear their hair in the traditional Egyptian gesture of mourning. In Cairo, however, the situation quickly moved from the sublime to the ridiculous as a customs official, faced with the need to classify the bodies for tax purposes, decided that the mortal remains of some of Egypt's greatest pharaohs could best be described as *farseekh*, or 'dried fish'.

No tomb has been conclusively proved to be that of Tuthmosis II, although Tomb KV42 is the most likely contender. This tomb, anonymous, unadorned and with an uninscribed sarcophagus, is almost stark in its simplicity; it is matched by the relatively undistinguished mortuary temple set on the edge of the cultivation at Medinet Habu. This lack of elaborate funerary provision strongly suggests that the sudden death of the king had caught the royal stonemasons napping. Under normal circumstances a king would oversee the building of his own funerary monuments, with preparations for his death starting at the very commencement of the reign. In consequence, the size of a tomb and mortuary temple, and the magnificence of their decorations, are often directly related to the length rather than the success of their owner's rule. It may even be that Tuthmosis was never actually interred in his unfinished burial chamber;[31] a similar situation was to occur over 150 years later when the sudden death of Tutankhamen resulted in the abandonment of his intended royal tomb and his interment in the tomb of a nobleman, hastily decorated to make a suitable resting place for a king.

It is less likely that the simple tomb should be read as a sign of general indifference towards Tuthmosis II,[32] or indeed that Hatchepsut and/or Tuthmosis III would have neglected the burial of their predecessor as, under ancient Egyptian tradition, it was the burial of the old king which legitimized the accession of the new. Nor can we assume that Hatchepsut, bearing little affection for her late brother, was too preoccupied with her own plans to provide him with a decent funeral. She later dedicated at least one statue to her dead brother–husband, a likely indication that his early death was a genuine cause of sorrow to the widow–sister who still honoured his memory.

Tuthmosis II was succeeded on the throne by Tuthmosis III, his natural son by the Lady Isis (also known as Aset or Eset), a secondary

and somewhat obscure member of the harem whose origins are uncertain. Isis did not have the royal connections of her illustrious
predecessor Mutnofret, and her most prestigious title seems to have
been 'King's Mother'. Tuthmosis III was therefore only of royal descent on his father's side, and perhaps in consequence not entirely
acceptable as heir to the royal throne. This may be why in later
years, and despite the fact that he had started the numbering of his
regnal years from the death of his father, he was to suggest that he
had been associated with Tuthmosis II in a co-regency. In an inscription on the seventh pylon of the Karnak temple, Tuthmosis III tells
how as a young boy he had been serving as an acolyte in the temple
of Amen when, on an auspicious festival day, the great god himself
had selected him as a future king:

My father Amen-Re-Harakhti granted to me that I might appear upon the
Horus Throne of the Living . . . I having been appointed before him within [the
temple], there having been ordained for me the rulership of the Two Lands,
the thrones of Geb and the offices of Khepri *at the side of my father*, the Good
God, the King of Upper and Lower Egypt, Aakheperenre [Tuthmosis II], given
life forever.[33]

'At the side of' has been interpreted as meaning 'co-regent of my
father', although it seems equally likely to mean 'in the presence of' or
'before'; should the latter be the correct reading the proclamation
would represent Tuthmosis II's formal acknowledgement of his intended heir rather than the proclamation of a full co-regency. Tuthmosis III was only a child when his father died, and it would certainly
have been unusual for the still young Tuthmosis II to appoint an infant
co-ruler. However, the true importance of this inscription lies not in its
specific details, but in the fact that Tuthmosis, like Hatchepsut before
him, felt that he needed the support of an oracle of Amen to reinforce
his right to rule.

Tuthmosis III was obviously very pleased with this inscription. So
pleased, indeed, that he had it recarved over an earlier text which had
been commissioned by Hatchepsut on the northern side of the upper
portico of the Deir el-Bahri mortuary temple. However, this time the
text was adjusted so that it described the identical elevation of Tuthmosis I. Tuthmosis III clearly wished his people to understand that both

he and his grandfather had been personally appointed by Amen who used the same method of announcing his choice on both occasions. Snatches of the original text underlying the Tuthmosis III recarving suggest that Hatchepsut too had undergone the same divine selection process and, as hers is undeniably the earlier carving, it would appear that Tuthmosis had decided to borrow her experience for both himself and his grandfather.[34]

Even more dubious evidence for a Tuthmosis II and III co-regency has been left by a New Kingdom visitor to the Old Kingdom step-pyramid complex at Sakkara. The monuments of the most ancient pharaohs – already a thousand years old by the reign of Hatchepsut – were a constant source of interest to their New Kingdom descendants, who took day-trips to picnic at the pyramids just as modern British tourists flock to Stonehenge or the Tower of London. Here a graffito, scribbled in hieratic writing, gives the date as Year 20 of the joint reign of Hatchepsut and Tuthmosis (in that order), and goes on to explain that:

now his majesty was . . . king with [his?] father, exalted upon the Horus Throne of the Living . . .

If the 'majesty' in question is Tuthmosis III, and if the phrase '. . . king with his father' is not simply a meaningless expression, this graffito may well be considered valid evidence for a co-regency between Tuthmosis II and Tuthmosis III. However, it is equally likely that the king is Hatchepsut. In this case the graffito may be referring to Hatchepsut's 'coronation' or 'coming of age' which is discussed in more detail in Chapter 4.

At the time of his father's death Tuthmosis III was still a minor. His exact age at the time of his accession is unrecorded, but given that he reigned for over fifty years and that his mummy was not that of an elderly man, we can deduce that he was a young child or even a baby rather than a teenager. Hatchepsut herself was probably between fifteen and thirty years of age when she was widowed. To calculate her maximum age at this time, we must make the assumption that she was born after her father had acceded to the throne – this seems likely if we are correct in our assumption that Queen Ahmose was the sister or half-sister of Tuthmosis I. As her father reigned for approximately fifteen years, Hatchepsut can have been no more than fifteen years old when she married her brother and became consort. If Tuthmosis II then reigned for the maximum suggested period of fifteen years, she would have been thirty years old at his death. However, the only fixed facts that we have concerning the marriage of Hatchepsut and Tuthmosis II are that Tuthmosis I reigned for at least one year, and that Hatchepsut bore her brother at least one child. Given that puberty probably occurred at about fourteen years of age, Hatchepsut may have been no more than fifteen years old when her husband, reigning for only three years, died.[35]

The young dowager queen was called upon to act as regent on behalf of her even younger stepson. As we have already seen, this in itself was not an unusual situation, and it was accepted Egyptian practice that a widowed queen should rule for her minor son. Indeed, there had already been two highly successful 18th Dynasty regencies: Queen Ahhotep had acted as regent for King Ahmose, and later Ahmose Nefertari had ruled on behalf of her son Amenhotep I. No one, therefore, could have objected to Hatchepsut being appointed regent on the grounds of her sex and, as the daughter, sister and wife of a king, there was unlikely to be any member of the royal family more qualified to undertake the role. However, in one respect the situation was unprecedented: Hatchepsut was being called upon to act as regent for a boy who was not her son. To Naville, a fervent Hatchepsut supporter, this was clearly an intolerable situation:

It is the story of Sarah and Hagar as enacted in a royal family; but the queen was less happy than the Sarah of Scripture, for she was obliged to install Ishmael in the heritage of Abraham, to associate him with herself, and to give him her own daughter in marriage.[36]

Whatever her private feelings, Hatchepsut accepted her new role with good grace. Throughout the first couple of years of her stepson's rule she acted as a model queen regent, claiming only those titles to which she was entitled as the daughter and widow of a king and allowing herself to be depicted standing behind the new king in traditional queenly fashion. Her subordinate status at this time is confirmed by inscriptions at the Semna temple in Nubia, dated to Tuthmosis III Year 2, where Hatchepsut plays a very minor role in both the texts and the accompanying carved reliefs. Here, Tuthmosis III, as sole 'King of Upper and Lower Egypt and Lord of the Two Lands' is shown receiving the pharaoh's white crown from the hands of the ancient Nubian god Dedwen. However, only five years later there had been a profound political change. By the end of Year 7, Queen Hatchepsut had advanced from being the mere ruler of Egypt by default to becoming an acknowledged king.

4

King of Egypt

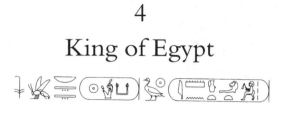

He [Tuthmosis II] went forth to heaven in triumph, having mingled with the gods. His son stood in his place as king of the Two Lands, having become ruler upon the throne of the one who begat him. His sister the Divine Consort, Hatchepsut, settled the affairs of the Two Lands by reason of her plans. Egypt was made to labour with bowed head for her, the excellent seed of the god, which came forth from him.[1]

During Year 7 of the reign of Tuthmosis III, the Steward of Amen, Senenmut, buried both his parents in a modest tomb cut into the hillside directly beneath the site which had already been selected for his own magnificent funerary monument on the West Bank at Thebes. Following the interment, the entrance to the tomb was closed, and it was subsequently completely covered by the rubble excavated during the construction of Senenmut's own tomb which started slightly later in the same year. The smaller tomb disappeared from view until it was rediscovered by accident during the 1935–6 season of work carried out by the Metropolitan Museum of Art, New York. The excavators, Ambrose Lansing and William Hayes, were the first to enter the burial chamber of Ramose and Hatnofer in over 3,000 years. Here they found a typical selection of grave goods, including several pottery jars or amphorae, one of which was dated to 'Year 7', one which bore the seal of the 'God's Wife Hatchepsut' and two which were stamped with the seal of 'The Good Goddess Maatkare'. Maatkare (literally, *maat* is the Ka of Re, or Truth is the Soul of the sun god Re) is the throne name of King Hatchepsut. The dating of the amphorae, sealed into the burial chamber by the debris from Senenmut's own tomb, is beyond question, therefore we know that, by Year 7 of her regency, Hatchepsut was acknowledged to be a king of Egypt. She was now the Female Horus of Fine Gold, King of Upper and Lower Egypt Maatkare Khnemet-Amen Hatchepsut (The One who is joined with Amen, the Foremost of Women).

The exact date of the new king's official elevation is, however,

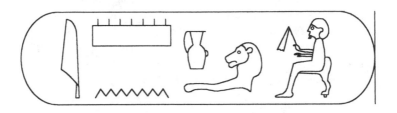

Fig. 4.1   The cartouche of King Maatkare Hatchepsut

unknown, and the subject is greatly complicated by the fact that Hatchepsut always used the same regnal years as Tuthmosis III, effectively dating her own reign from the time of her stepson's accession to the throne. Given her dominant role in the subsequent partnership, we might reasonably have expected to find that Hatchepsut had established her own independent regnal dates. As it seems unlikely that Hatchepsut ever considered herself to be junior to Tuthmosis III, the matching reign dates strongly suggest that she must have regarded herself as a king or co-regent from the moment of her husband's death. However, we know that this was not the case, and the contemporary evidence from the Semna temple already considered in Chapter 3 confirms that Hatchepsut was still, in theory at least, subordinate to Tuthmosis III during the earlier part of his regnal Year 2.

It would be entirely wrong to see Hatchepsut's usurpation of kingly powers as a sudden and unexpected *coup*. Hers was a gradual evolution, a carefully controlled political manoeuvre so insidious that it might not have been apparent to any but her closest contemporaries. The surviving monumental evidence, scanty though it is, allows us to track Hatchepsut's progress as she moves swiftly from the conventional wife of the Berlin stela, standing placidly in line behind her mother and her husband–brother, to become the most influential woman Egypt has ever known. Shortly before her coronation Hatchepsut is both regal enough to make offerings directly to the gods – hitherto the prerogative of the divine pharaoh – and wealthy enough to become the first non-king to commission a pair of obelisks. By now Hatchepsut is surely king of Egypt in all but name. However, no matter how gradual her assumption of power, there must have come a time when she crossed the line from queen to king and made her changed status public. There was a very great difference between being the person who actually ruled Egypt and becoming the acknowledged king, and her coronation and subsequent assumption of royal titles, albeit merely the formal acknowledgement of a *fait accompli*, must have had a definite date.

Contemporary documents and monumental inscriptions remain obstinately silent on this subject, while Hatchepsut herself chose to gloss over her periods as consort and regent, rewriting her own history so that she might invent a co-regency with Tuthmosis I which, together with the emphasis which was now to be placed on the myth of the divine birth of kings, would 'prove' beyond doubt her absolute right to rule. The legend of the miraculous birth of kings had always been an aspect of Egyptian kingship. The Westcar Papyrus, for example, a Middle Kingdom collection of fantastic stories about the 4th Dynasty royal court, tells us how during the Old Kingdom the Lady Reddjedet, assisted by the divine midwives Isis, Nephthys, Meskhenet and Heket, gave birth to the triplet sons of Re. The three baby boys delivered by the goddess were to become Userkaf, Sahure and Neferirkare, the first three kings of the 5th Dynasty:

Isis placed herself before her, Nephthys behind her, Heket hastened the birth. Isis said, 'Don't be so mighty in her womb, you whose name is Mighty.' The child slid into her arms, a child of one cubit, strong boned, his limbs overlaid with gold, his headdress of true lapis lazuli. They washed him, having cut his navel cord, and laid him on a pillow of cloth. Then Meskhenet approached him and said: 'A king who will assume the kingship in this whole land.' And Khnum gave health to his body.[2]

Hatchepsut was, however, the first pharaoh to make a feature of the story of her own divine conception and birth, ordering that the tale be told in a cartoon-like sequence of tasteful images and descriptive passages carved on the north side of the middle portico fronting her mortuary temple at Deir el-Bahri. Her filial relationship with Amen was always extremely important to Hatchepsut and throughout her reign she took every available opportunity to give due acknowledgement to her heavenly father as, by promoting the cult of Amen, she was effectively reinforcing her own position and promoting herself. It would be too simple to see the Deir el-Bahri birth story as merely another example of Hatchepsut's insecurity about her right to rule. The scenes themselves are by no means timid or apologetic; they are miraculous and joyful, and they convey above all a sense of Hatchepsut's pride in her own origins and achievements. It is perhaps no coincidence that the only other complete cycle of divine birth scenes comes from the Luxor temple of the later 18th Dynasty king Amenhotep III, a temple which was dedicated to the celebration of the royal Ka, or the divine royal identity. Amenhotep III, not generally regarded as an insecure monarch, was the first pharaoh to promote himself as a god in his own lifetime. His own birth scenes bear a striking similarity to those of Hatchepsut, and it would appear that, having admired his predecessors' work, he simply copied it wholesale, substituting the name of his own mother for that of Queen Ahmose.

Nor should the Deir el-Bahri scenes be regarded solely as a propaganda exercise as, from their position in the temple, it seems unlikely that they would have been seen by any but a handful of officiating priests who were already well aware of Hatchepsut's position. As we have already seen, Egyptian temples were not public buildings. They served as the home of the god and, as in any private home, the general public was kept outside the thick mud-brick enclosure walls. Only during the great festivals were the gates of the temple thrown open, and even then the public was only allowed access to the first court. The innermost sanctuary, where the king or the high priest worshipped on behalf of Egypt, was an intensely private place comparable to the master bedroom of a private home. The great temples of Egypt must have been oases of peace and tranquillity, a world apart from the bustling city life immediately outside their gates.

As Egyptian theology held that all kings were born the sons of Amen-Re, logic dictated that all queen mothers must have enjoyed sexual intercourse with Amen-Re. The Egyptians took a surprisingly practical approach to the subject of divine conception. Not for them the asexuality of an impersonal angelic annunciation. They knew that it took a man and a woman to make a baby and they recognized that their gods were capable of a variety of sexual feelings – rape, homosexuality and masturbation all played a part in heavenly life – so they developed the doctrine of theogamy, the physical union of a queen with a god. Amen-Re would come to Egypt and actually sleep with the mother of his future child. In order to preserve the reputation of the queen, for adultery was a heinous social crime, Amen cunningly disguised himself as the king.

At the Deir el-Bahri temple, the story of Hatchepsut's conception starts in heaven where Amen has assembled before him a group of twelve important divinities, including Isis, Osiris, Nephthys, Horus, Seth and Hathor, in order to make a momentous pronouncement. Amen has decided that the time has come to father a princess who will govern Egypt with a glorious reign: 'I will join for her the Two Lands . . . I will give her all lands and all countries.' The god of wisdom, Thoth, here acting Hermes-like as the messenger of Amen, proclaims the name of the chosen mother-to-be: it is Queen Ahmose, wife of Tuthmosis I, for 'she is more beautiful than any woman.'

We then move to Egypt. Queen Ahmose, sleeping alone in her boudoir, is visited by the god whom she believes to be her husband, and they sit face to face on her bed in a scene which represents one of the few occasions that a queen of Egypt is allowed to communicate directly with a deity. Amen tells Ahmose that she is to bear a daughter whom she will name Khnemet-Amen Hatchepsut (The One who is joined with Amen, the Foremost of Women). This daughter is destined to be the future ruler of Egypt. He then passes Ahmose the ankh, or sign of life and, in the tradition of the best romantic novels, we learn how:

She smiled at his majesty. He went to her immediately, his penis erect before her. He gave his heart to her . . . She was filled with joy at the sight of his beauty. His love passed into her limbs. The palace was flooded with the god's fragrance, and all his perfumes were from Punt.[3]

We return briefly to heaven to see the royal baby and her identical soul or Ka being fashioned on the potter's wheel by the ram-headed god Khnum. The creation of the royal Ka alongside the mortal body is of great importance; the royal Ka was understood to be the personification of the office of kingship and therefore its presence was incontrovertible proof of Hatchepsut's predestined right to rule. At the climax of her

coronation ceremony she would become united with the Ka which had been shared by all the kings of Egypt, and would lose her human identity to become one of a long line of divine office holders. Hatchepsut consistently placed considerable emphasis on the existence of her royal Ka, even including it in her throne name Maat-*ka*-re.

Meanwhile, as Amen watches anxiously, Khnum promises that the newly formed baby will be all that any father could desire:

I will shape for thee thy daughter [I will endow her with life, health, strength and all gifts]. I will make her appearance above the gods, because of her dignity as King of Upper and Lower Egypt.[4]

Fig. 4.2   The pregnant Queen Ahmose is led to the birthing bower

Khnum's work is finished and the frog-headed midwife Heket offers life to the two inert forms. At the same time, back in Egypt, Thoth appears before Queen Ahmose and tells her of the glories which await her unborn child.

Nine months later, the pregnant queen, wearing a vulture headdress and with a rather small 'bump' obvious beneath her straight shift dress, is led to the birth bower by Khnum and Heket. Here other deities wait to assist at the birth which, strictly a female–dominated rite of passage, is left to the imagination of the observer. When we next see Ahmose, she is sitting on a throne and holding the newborn Hatchepsut in her arms. Other deities surround the mother and child, while the goddess of childbirth Meskhenet sits in front of the throne. Meskhenet is to be the chief nurse and she seeks to reassure the royal infant: 'I am protecting thee behind thee like Re.' Finally Hathor, the royal wet-nurse, takes the newborn baby, and presents her to her father. Amen is over-whelmed with love for the infant. He takes her from Hathor, kisses her and speaks:

Come to me in peace, daughter of my loins, beloved Maatkare, thou art the king who takes possession of the diadem on the Throne of Horus of the Living, eternally.[5]

Hatchepsut is presented before the assembled gods, who also greet her with great joy. There is only one unusual note: the naked infant Hatchepsut is quite clearly shown as a boy. The message behind the scenes is quite clear. Hatchepsut has been shown to be the child of Amen, and therefore a legitimate pharaoh from the moment of her conception. As Amen is clearly unconcerned about the sex of his child, and indeed as he made clear his specific intention of fathering a girl-child, why should Egypt worry?

Fig. 4.3 *The infant Hatchepsut in the arms of a divine nurse*

The story now slowly starts to slide away from the heavenly towards the real world. Hatchepsut travels north to visit the ancient shrines of the principal gods of Egypt accompanied by her earthly father, Tuthmosis I. This is followed by a coronation before the gods and then by a subsequent earthly coronation by Tuthmosis I who presents his daughter to the court and formally nominates her as his co-regent and intended successor:

Said to her by His Majesty: 'Come, thou blessed one. I will take thee in my arms that thou mayest see thy directions [carried out] in the palace; thy precious images were made, thou hast received the investiture of the double

crown, thou art blessed . . . When thou risest in the palace, thy brow is adorned
with the double crown united on thy head, for thou art my heir, to whom I
have given birth . . . This is my daughter Khnemet-Amen Hatchepsut, living, I
put her in my place.[6]

The news is received with universal joy, and the people start to
celebrate with gusto. The priests confer to decide on Hatchepsut's
royal titulary, and finally her coronation takes place on an unspecified
New Year's day; a practical choice of dates which would allow her
regnal years and the civil calendar to coincide. Unfortunately, this
part of the story is, as far as we can tell, a complete fiction. While it
is entirely possible that some public ceremony did occur during
Hatchepsut's childhood – perhaps a coming-of-age celebration which
involved Hatchepsut being officially presented before the court? –
there is absolutely no evidence to show that Tuthmosis I ever regarded Hatchepsut as his formal successor, or that he had the intention of passing over both his son and his grandson in order to
honour his daughter. The unchallenged succession of Tuthmosis II,
and her own conventional behaviour as queen–consort, confirms that,
at the time of her father's death, Hatchepsut did not expect to
become king of Egypt.[7]

A slightly different contemporary tale is potentially far more useful in
our search for Hatchepsut's coronation date. This text, inscribed on
what was once the outside wall of Hatchepsut's Chapelle Rouge at
Karnak, hints that the political situation may have already undergone a
profound change by the end of Year 2 of the joint reign while stopping
short of providing any absolute proof of this.[8] The Red Chapel, now
known more commonly by its French name of Chapelle Rouge, was a
large sanctuary of red quartzite endowed by Hatchepsut to house the
all-important barque of Amen. Amen's barque, or barge, known as
Userhat-Amen (Mighty of Prow is Amen), was a small-scale gilded
wooden boat bearing the enclosed shrine which was used to protect the
statue of the god from public gaze. When Amen, on the holy days
which were also public holidays, left the privacy of his sanctuary to
process through the streets of Thebes, he sailed in style concealed
within the cabin of his boat-shrine which was carried, supported by
wooden poles, on the shoulders of his priests. When Amen was not
travelling the barque rested in its own sanctuary or shrine. The sacred

barque had always played a minor role in Egyptian religious ritual, but during the early New Kingdom it had become an increasingly important part of theology, and most temples now gave great prominence to the barque sanctuary. Unfortunately, Hatchepsut's shrine was dismantled during the reign of Tuthmosis III and subsequently used as filling for other building projects. Although many of the blocks were rediscovered in the 1950s, the chapel has never been re-assembled, and over three hundred blocks from the Chapelle Rouge are now displayed in the form of a gigantic jigsaw puzzle in the Open-Air Museum at Karnak.

Carved on block 287 of the Chapelle Rouge is part of an important text, narrated by Hatchepsut herself, in which she describes a religious procession associated with the festival of Amen, held at the nearby Luxor temple during

Fig. 4.4   Hatchepsut and Amen on a block from the Chapelle Rouge

Year 2 of an unspecified king's reign. The Luxor temple, approximately two miles to the south of the Karnak temple and connected to it by a processional route which Hatchepsut herself embellished with a series of barque-shrines, was dedicated to both Amen in the form of the ithyphallic god Min, and to the celebration of the divine royal soul, or Ka.[9] It played an important role in the cult of the deified king and was the place where, during the celebration of the annual Opet festival, the king re-affirmed his unity with the royal Ka which gave him the right to rule. The Luxor temple was therefore an eminently suitable place for the god to make a pronouncement concerning a future ruler and it was here, during the later 18th Dynasty, that Amen was to recognize General Horemheb as a King of Egypt. During the ceremony described by

Hatchepsut, and in the presence of the anonymous king, the oracle makes the momentous announcement that Hatchepsut herself is to become pharaoh:

. . . very great oracle in the presence of this good god, proclaiming for me the kingship of the two lands, Upper and Lower Egypt being under the fear of me . . . Year 2, 2 *peret* 29 [that is, Year 2, the 2nd month of Spring, day 29], the third day of the festival of Amen . . . being the ordination of the Two Lands for me in the broad hall of the Southern Opet [Luxor], while His Majesty [Amen] delivered an oracle in the presence of this good god. My father appeared in his beautiful festival: Amen, chief of the gods.[10]

The oracle had been developed during the New Kingdom as a channel of communication between the gods and the common people, and had proved particularly popular as a means of solving the day-to-day petty crimes that baffled the police who were forced to operate without the benefit of divine omniscience. Consulting the oracle provided a quick, cheap and easily accessible alternative to the formal courts. As the statue of the god processed through the streets on his ceremonial boat, it was possible for anyone to step forward and challenge him with a simple yes/no-type question, such as 'Did Isis steal my washing?' or 'Did Hathor kill my duck?' The god would consider the evidence and then answer by causing his barque-bearers to move either forwards or backwards – a legal system which to modern eyes at least seems to have been open to a great deal of abuse, but one which nevertheless satisfied the ancient Egyptian desire for immediate and public justice. More involved variations on this theme existed; it was, for example, possible to write different options on separate ostraca, lay them before the god, and see whether the god gravitated towards a particular solution, while in more complicated cases a list of suspects could be read out and the god would cause his attendants to move at the mention of the name of the guilty party.

However, those oracles who took the trouble to communicate with the ordinary people were invariably the lesser local gods; the deified Ahmose and Amenhotep I both served as oracles and the judgements of Amenhotep I were particularly well-regarded at Deir el-Medina. The oracles who spoke to kings were the major state gods. Amen, king of the gods, was particularly keen on conveying his wishes via an oracle which could only be translated by the high priest or king, and we should perhaps not be too surprised to find that Amen's commands often coincided exactly with the interests of his interpreter.[11]

Argument has raged amongst egyptologists as to who the unnamed king of Chapelle Rouge block 287 might be. Some feel that he must be Tuthmosis I and that the text therefore represents Hatchepsut's recollection – presumably fictitious – of a time during her father's reign when the god acknowledged her as the true heir to the crown. If this is the case, the block can be of little help in determining the date when Hatchepsut actually proclaimed herself king and the entire scene must be classified as a further example of Hatchepsut's compulsion to justify her own reign. However, it is always possible that the mystery monarch is Tuthmosis III and that the block is therefore a record of the actual date when Hatchepsut decided to make public her right to the throne. Indeed, it is not beyond the bounds of possibility that Hatchepsut, a resourceful lady, organized a highly public pronouncement by the oracle at exactly the moment she was proposing to make her plans known.

Unfortunately, block 287 merely describes an oracle, it does not go on to record a coronation. However, details of Hatchepsut's coronation at Karnak are actually included in a third-person narrative carved on several blocks which, from the direction of their hieroglyphs, must have originally formed part of the opposite outside wall of the Chapelle Rouge. The coronation must, therefore, have occurred much later in the text, and presumably much later in time, than the events described on block 287. The coronation inscription is unfortunately undated but, as it is highly unlikely that Hatchepsut would have allowed the date of such a momentous occasion to go unrecorded, there is always the possibility that one of the missing blocks from the Chapelle Rouge will one day reappear to solve the mystery.

If we do not have a specific date for Hatchepsut's coronation, we do at least have a date for her jubilee, or *sed*-festival, which is recorded on the walls of both the Karnak and Deir el-Bahri temples. The celebration of the *heb-sed*, a tradition stretching back over a thousand years to the dawn of the dynastic age and perhaps even beyond, was a public ritual of rebirth and renewal intended to revivify the ageing king and increase public confidence in his reign.[12] It marked the start of a new cycle in the monarch's life and was, of course, the excuse for a nationwide celebration; the ancient Egyptians were never ones to deny themselves a good party. Tradition dictated that the jubilee would be proclaimed from Memphis on the first day of spring – the season of rejuvenation – and that there would follow five days of festival culminating in a grand procession of the state and local gods. The more solemn rituals of the *heb-sed* included a reenactment of the dual coronation, where the monarch was reanointed first with the white crown of the King of the South and then with the red crown of the North, and a ceremonial run where the king, carrying traditional emblems, was required to race four times around a specially prepared arena or pavilion in order to prove his (or in this case her) physical fitness to rule.

In theory, a king was entitled to celebrate his first jubilee thirty years after his coronation and thereafter as frequently as he desired. Hatchepsut, atypical as always, announced her jubilee during regnal Year 15. This was by no means the first royal tradition to be broken by Hatchepsut, and indeed Hatchepsut was not the first king to bend the *heb-sed* rules; it is possible that her father had erected his obelisks to mark his own jubilee although he is unlikely to have ruled for more than fifteen years, while five kings later Amenhotep IV, before he became Akhenaten, celebrated a jubilee after a mere four years on the throne. There is no doubt that a national celebration relatively early in her reign would have been a sound political move, boosting national morale and providing a good omen for the future prosperity of the regime, and perhaps Hatchepsut felt that, after fifteen years as ruler of Egypt, she was in need of renewal. However, it remains possible that Year 15 was chosen as a special year because it marked an important thirtieth anniversary. If Hatchepsut had only been fifteen years old at the death of Tuthmosis II, this may well have been her own thirtieth year or, given that she frequently portrayed herself as the immediate successor to Tuthmosis I, it may well have been thirty years since the death of her father. It may even have been, given that Hatchepsut also described herself as her father's co-regent, thirty years since the accession of Tuthmosis I.

jubilee must, of course, in theory have also been Tuth-
⌐, and indeed the young king does appear to enjoy his own
⌐d celebrations at this time. On the walls of the Deir el-Bahri
te⌐ ⌐e see both kings making parallel offerings of milk and water;
Hatchepsut offers to the south, Tuthmosis to the north. The northern
colonnade of the middle terrace shows Amen embracing Tuthmosis
who wears the double crown and carries the ankh or life sign, and a
mace, while in the northwest offering hall Tuthmosis presents a table of
offerings to Amen who blesses him accordingly:

I give to you the celebrating of millions of *sed*-festivals on the throne of Horus
and that you direct all the living like Re, forever.[13]

However, the occasion appears to have belonged almost entirely to
Hatchepsut and she takes pride of place in every scene. Tuthmosis III
later celebrated his own independent jubilees on a far grander scale
during Years 30 (the correct year for such a celebration), 34 and 37.

We shall probably never know what event precipitated Hatchepsut into
proclaiming herself king. It is, of course, possible that she had always
intended to seize power, and that following the death of Tuthmosis II
she had merely been biding her time, waiting for the politically oppor-
tune moment to strike. Hayes is perhaps the most persuasive proponent
of this theory:

. . . at the time of his [Tuthmosis II] death, her every waking thought must have
been taken up with the stabilization of the government and the consolidation
of her own position . . .[14]

It is, indeed, clear that the longer the move was postponed the more difficult it
would have become to accomplish; for Tuthmosis III was all the while
growing older, forming his own party and consolidating his own position.[15]

However biased his interpretation of Hatchepsut's character, Hayes
must be correct in his assumption that such an unconventional move
would need to be made sooner rather than later. Not only was Tuthmosis growing up and attracting his own supporters, there was also the
possibility that he might die in infancy, lessening Hatchepsut's own

claim to the throne by precipitating a dynastic crisis in which the position of the dowager queen might have been compromised by the introduction of a rival male claimant. Why then did Hatchepsut wait for between two and seven years before implementing her plan? Was she too young and inexperienced to act sooner? Or was she simply using the time to gather the support that she would need for her unorthodox actions?

The once popular image of the queen as a scheming and power-hungry woman owes more to the now-discredited theory of the feuding Tuthmosides than to concrete historical evidence. All that we know of her previous life, first as queen consort and then as queen regent, shows Hatchepsut to have been an unexceptional and indeed almost boringly conformist wife and mother paying due honour to both her husband and her stepson, loving her young daughter and contenting herself with the traditional role allotted to royal women. Although abnormal behaviour in a royal princess is unlikely to have been recorded for posterity, it is equally unlikely that an obviously egocentric megalomaniac would have been allowed to rise to the dizzy heights of consort, God's Wife and regent. Tuthmosis II was not compelled by either law or tradition to accept his sister as his chief wife and, even though Hatchepsut was a princess of the royal blood, a speedy banishment to the security of the harem-palace would have left Tuthmosis free to select a more amenable queen and a more suitable guardian for his infant son.

Hatchepsut's subsequent lengthy reign, characterized by its economic prosperity, monumental building and foreign exploration, seems to confirm her competence and mental stability. This was not, as far as we can tell some three and a half thousand years later, the rule of a semi-deranged obsessive but a carefully calculated period of political manoeuvring which allowed an unconventional pharaoh to become accepted on the throne and which brought peace and prosperity to her people. In all ways bar one, it was a conventional and successful New Kingdom reign. But, if the image of Hatchepsut as a woman motivated purely by ambition and greed is to be toned down or even entirely discarded, what possible explanation could there be for her usurpation of power? And what made her action acceptable to the Egyptian élite? Was there some unrecorded crisis which demanded a swift response and the establishment of a strong pharaoh on the throne? A sudden threat to the security of the immediate royal family, such as an insurrection in the royal harem, might well have prompted Hatchepsut to take drastic action to safeguard her stepson's position.[16] In any such emergency Hatchepsut would have been a natural choice as co-regent as she, already regent and 'only' a woman, would not necessarily have been perceived as posing the threat to the authority of the true king.

Hatchepsut's treatment of the young Tuthmosis III indicates that she never regarded his existence as a serious problem even though, as an intelligent woman, she must have realized that every passing year would strengthen his claim to rule alone. She never attempted to establish a solo reign and, instead of hiding the boy-king away or even having him killed, she was careful to accord him all the respect due to a fellow monarch. Indeed, Tuthmosis was even encouraged to spend part of his youth training with the army, the now traditional education of the crown prince but possibly a dangerous decision for one in Hatchepsut's increasingly vulnerable position, as the support of those who controlled the New Kingdom army was vital to the survival of the pharaoh. Although he was represented less often than Hatchepsut, and although he was undoubtedly the junior partner in the co-regency, 'leading as shadowy an existence as a Japanese Mikado under the Shogunate',[17] Tuthmosis never entirely disappeared from view. He even had a few monuments of his own, although these are almost invariably to be found outside Egypt's borders, either in Nubia or Sinai. Within Egypt, Hatchepsut was careful never to appear subordinate to Tuthmosis; her image or her cartouche preceded that of her co-ruler on all but one of their shared monuments, and even the private monuments of the time recognized that Hatchepsut was the dominant king:

. . . by the favour of the Good Goddess, Mistress of the Two Lands [Maatkare], may she live and endure forever like Re – and of her brother, the Good God, master of the ritual Menkheperre [Tuthmosis III] given life like Re forever.[18]

A consideration of the character and behaviour of Tuthmosis himself must play an important part in any analysis of Hatchepsut's actions. If we ignore speculation and stick to known facts we see that, whatever his private thoughts, Tuthmosis publicly accepted his aunt as co-regent. Initially, as an infant with a politically insignificant mother and no influential male relations, he can have had little choice in the matter. However, he would have been of an age to challenge Hatchepsut for at least five years prior to her death, and his training in the army would have made a successful military *coup* a virtual certainty. Reigning alone, Tuthmosis was to prove himself one of the most able warrior-pharaohs that Egypt has ever experienced. It is almost impossible to equate the hero of no fewer than seventeen aggressive Asian campaigns with the image of the impotent wimp who resented his co-regent for twenty years but who was never able to assert his right to rule. Similarly, it is difficult to envisage the two co-rulers remaining locked in deadly enmity for almost a quarter of a century; surely one or other would have taken steps to remove their rival? It has been argued that Hatchepsut felt unable to dispose of Tuthmosis as he was her passport to the kingship although, if she was so secure in her rule that Tuthmosis was unable to challenge her position, it is unlikely that his death would have dislodged her. There is certainly no obvious reason why Tuthmosis should not have attempted discreetly to remove Hatchepsut.[19]

Yet, as far as we are aware, Tuthmosis made no such challenge to his stepmother's authority. He seems to have been content to allow the situation to take its course and, again lacking any evidence to the contrary, we must assume that he was relatively happy to accept the coregency. Perhaps, having grown up under Hatchepsut's guidance, he could not easily envisage removing her from power. Indeed, as we have already seen, it is even possible that Tuthmosis did not regard his own right to the throne as automatic. His need to cite an oracle of Amen in support of his kingship is certainly unusual; the true king generally had no need of such obvious divine support. In any case, Tuthmosis must have realized that the situation could not last indefinitely. All previous co-regencies had ended peacefully, not with an abdication but with a death. Tuthmosis himself, accustomed to the tradition of the co-regency and with no particular political axe to grind, may have found his position easier to accept than the modern observers who today grow angry and indignant on his behalf.

If Tuthmosis was unable or unwilling to take action against his aunt during her lifetime, how did he treat her when she was dead? We know that, following Hatchepsut's death, somebody masterminded a determined attempt to delete the memory of the female pharaoh from the

Egyptian historical record. To this end her monuments were desecrated and her name and images were erased, variously being replaced by the name or image of Tuthmosis I, II or III. Initially these attacks were regarded as firm proof of a personal vendetta on the part of Tuthmosis III, and it was assumed that the new king – overcome by his long-suppressed hatred against the usurper who had denied him his rights for so long – must have ordered his henchmen to take action against Hatchepsut's monuments at the very beginning of his solo rule. However, new evidence has started to indicate that the proscription of Hatchepsut's memory did not occur until the very end of Tuthmosis' reign, or perhaps even later in the New Kingdom. This makes it less easy to attribute the attacks to personal spite; if Tuthmosis was really filled with such an uncontrollable hatred, why wait for over twenty years to act? Instead of impulsive actions they start to look like well-calculated political moves, and it would seem that it is no longer safe to cite the attacks on Hatchepsut's memory as proof of Tuthmosis' hatred of his aunt.[20]

The vast majority of the Egyptian people, the peasants and lower classes, would have been ignorant of any struggle for power within the palace. As long as there was a pharaoh on the throne, and as long as the state continued to function correctly (that is, paying out rations), the people remained remarkably content with their lot. However, no pharaoh could hope to rule without the support of the relatively small circle of male élite who headed the army, the civil service and the priesthood. These were the men who effectively controlled the country and kept the king in power. Again, we must assume that these influential men found their new monarch acceptable even if they did not positively welcome a woman at the helm. Why was she so acceptable? Was her assumption of power so gradual that it went unnoticed until it was too late to act, or was there no one else more suitable? Perhaps Gibbon has provided us with the best explanation for this uncharacteristic departure from years of tradition when he observes that:

In every age and every country, the wiser, or at least the stronger, of the two sexes has usurped the powers of the State, and confined the other to the cares and pleasures of domestic life. In hereditary monarchies, however . . . the gallant spirit of chivalry, and the law of succession, have accustomed us to allow a singular exception; and a woman is often acknowledged the absolute sovereign of a great kingdom, in which she would be deemed incapable of exercising the smallest employment, civil or military.[21]

Hatchepsut, the singular exception, had inherited a cabinet of tried and trusted advisers from her brother, many of whom had previously worked under her father and all of whom seem to have been happy to switch their allegiance to the new regime. The two old faithfuls Ahmose-Pennekheb and Ineni were still serving the crown, and Ineni in particular seems to have been especially favoured by the new king:

Her Majesty praised me and loved me. She recognised my worth at court, she presented me with things, she magnified me, she filled my house with silver and gold, with all beautiful stuffs of the royal house . . . I increased beyond everything.[22]

Although Ineni was obviously deeply impressed by Hatchepsut's rule, indeed so impressed that he failed to record the name of the 'real king', Tuthmosis III, in his tomb, he never specifically refers to his mistress by her regal name of Maatkare, and it would appear that he died just before she reached the height of her powers. In contrast, Ahmose-Pennekheb omits Hatchepsut from the list of kings whom he has served and offers an unusual combination of her queenly and kingly titles: 'the God's Wife repeated favours for me, the Great King's Wife Maatkare, Justi-fied', which would indicate that his autobiography too might have been composed at a time when there was some confusion over Hatchepsut's official title.

Gradually, as her reign progressed, Hatchepsut started to appoint new advisers, many of whom were men of relatively humble birth such as Senenmut, steward of the queen and tutor to Neferure. By selecting officials with a personal loyalty to herself, Hatchepsut was able to ensure that she was surrounded by the most devoted of courtiers; those whose careers were inextricably linked to her own. However, by no means all the new appointees were self-made men and some, like Hapuseneb, High Priest of Amen and builder of the royal tomb, already had close links with the royal family. Hapuseneb may have actually been a distant relation of Hatchepsut; we know that his grandfather Imhotep had been vizier to Tuthmosis I. Other important characters at Hatchepsut's court included Chancellor Neshi, leader of the expedition to Punt, the

Treasurer Tuthmosis, Useramen the Vizier, Amenhotep the Chief Steward and Inebni, who replaced Seni as Viceroy of Kush. After Hatchepsut's death, some of her most effective courtiers continued to work for Tuthmosis III, and there is no sign that they suffered in any way from having been linked with the previous regime.

From the day that Hatchepsut acceded to the throne, she started to use the five 'Great Names' which comprised the full titulary of a king of Egypt and which reflected some of the divine attributes of kingship. To the ancient Egyptians each of these names had its own significance. The Horus name represented the king as the earthly embodiment of Horus; the Two Ladies or *nebty* name indicated the special relationship between the king and the goddesses of Upper and Lower Egypt; the golden Horus name had a somewhat obscure origin and meaning; the *prenomen*, which always followed the title 'he who belongs to the sedge and the bee' (generally translated as 'King of Upper and Lower Egypt'), was the first name to be enclosed within a cartouche; the *nomen*, also written within a cartouche and preceded by the epithet 'Son of Re', was usually the personal name of the king before he or she acceded to the throne. The *prenomen* was always the more important name, and this was either used by itself, or with the *nomen*. Thus we often find contemporary texts referring to the new king simply as Maatkare (*maat* is the Ka of Re), although her full title was Horus 'Powerful-of-Kas', Two Ladies 'Flourishing-of-Years', Female Horus of Fine Gold 'Divine-of-Diadems', King of Upper and Lower Egypt 'Maatkare', Daughter of Re, 'Khenmet-Amen Hatchepsut'. Similarly Tuthmosis III, often accorded only his *prenomen* of Menkheperre (The Being of Re is Established), was more properly named Horus 'Strong-bull-arising-in-Thebes', Two Ladies 'Enduring-of-kingship-like-Re-in-Heaven', Golden Horus 'Powerful-of-strength, holy-of-diadems', King of Upper and Lower Egypt 'Menkheperre', Son of Re 'Tuthmosis Beautiful-of-Forms'.

Throughout her reign, Hatchepsut sought to honour her earthly father, Tuthmosis I, in every way possible, while virtually ignoring the existence of her dead husband–brother, Tuthmosis II. It is not particularly unusual to find that a young girl brought up in a female-dominated environment feels a strong desire to emulate and impress her absent father, particularly when he is acknowledged to be the most powerful and glamorous man in the land. However, to some observers this hero-worship went far beyond the natural affection that a young woman might be expected to feel for her dead father:

This [devotion to a dominant father] is a trait which prominent females some-times show. Anna Freud turned herself into Sigmund's intellectual heir, Benazir Bhutto makes a political platform out of her father's memory, and one is reminded of a recent British prime minister whose entry in *Who's Who* in-cluded a father but no mother. Did Tuthmosis I ever call his daughter 'the best man in the dynasty', and is this why Hatchepsut shows no identification with other women?[23]

Perhaps the most important point here is that all these women lacked an acceptable female role-model and therefore, once they had made the decision to commit themselves to a career in the public eye, had little choice but to follow their fathers rather than their mothers, sisters, cousins or aunts into what had become the family business. Hatchepsut, as king, had no other woman to identify with. She had already spent at least fifteen years emulating her mother as queen and now wanted to advance to king. Of all the women named above, Mrs Bhutto, a lady who is not afraid to use the name and reputation of her father to enhance her own cause, is perhaps the closest parallel to Hatchepsut. More telling might be a comparison with Queen Elizabeth I of Eng-land, a woman who inherited her throne against all odds at a time of dynastic difficulty when the royal family was suffering from a shortage of sons, and who deliberately stressed her relationship with her vigorous and effective father in order to lessen the effect of her own femininity and make her own reign more acceptable to her people: 'And though I be a woman, yet I have as good a courage, answerable to my place, as ever my father had.'

Citing Tuthmosis as the inspiration for Hatchepsut's actions is, how-ever, in many ways putting the chariot before the horse. Tuthmosis I was Hatchepsut's reason to rule, not her motivation, as Egyptian tradi-tion decreed that son should follow father on the throne. Given Hat-chepsut's unusual circumstances, she needed to stress her links with her father more than most other kings. Therefore, in order to establish herself as her father's heir – and thereby justify her claim to the throne – Hatchepsut was forced to edit her own past so that her husband–brother, also a child of Tuthmosis I, disappeared from the scene and she became the sole Horus to her father's Osiris. To this end she redesigned her father's tomb in the Valley of the Kings, emulated his habit of erecting obelisks, built him a new mortuary chapel associated with her own at Deir el-Bahri and allowed him prominence on many of her inscriptions.

Nor was Hatchepsut the only 18th Dynasty monarch to revere the memory of Tuthmosis I; Tuthmosis III also sought to link himself with the grandfather whom he almost certainly never met while virtually ignoring the existence of his own less impressive father. As a sign of respect Tuthmosis III, somewhat confusingly, occasionally refers to himself as the son rather than grandson of Tuthmosis I. Fortunately, the autobiography of Ineni specifically tells us that Tuthmosis II was succeeded by 'the son he had begotten', removing any doubt as to the actual paternity of Tuthmosis III. The terms 'father' and 'son' need not be taken literally in these circumstances; 'father' was often used by the ancient Egyptians as a respectful form of address for a variety of older men and could therefore be used in a reference to an adoptive father or stepfather, patron or even ancestor. That Tuthmosis I should be regarded as an heroic figure by his descendants is not too surprising. Not only had he proved himself a highly successful monarch, he was also the founder of the immediate royal family. His predecessor Amenhotep I, although officially classified as belonging to the same dynasty, was in fact no blood relation of either Hatchepsut or Tuthmosis III.

As a king of Egypt, Hatchepsut was entitled to a suitably splendid monarch's tomb. Therefore, soon after her accession, work on the rather understated tomb in the Wadi Sikkat Taka ez-Zeida ceased and the excavation of a far more regal monument commenced in the Valley of the Kings. Following recent 18th Dynasty tradition, this tomb was to have two distinct components: a burial chamber hidden away in the Valley (now known as Tomb KV20) and a highly visible mortuary temple, in this case *Djeser-Djeseru* or 'Holy of the Holies', a magnificent temple nestling in a natural bay in the Theban mountain at Deir el-Bahri.[24] Two architects were appointed to oversee the essentially separate building projects, and Hapuseneb was placed in charge of work at KV20 while Senenmut is generally credited with the work at Deir el-Bahri. However, it is possible that the two elements of the tomb were originally intended to be linked via hidden underground passages, and

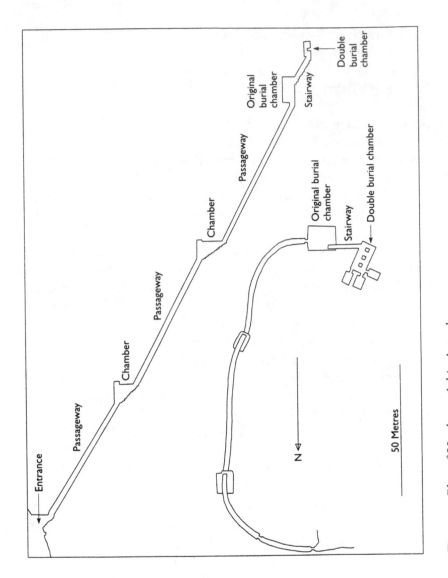

Fig. 4.5   Plan of Hatchepsut's king's tomb

an unusually long and deep series of tunnels leading straight from the Valley of the Kings to the burial chamber may have been designed to allow the chamber itself to lie directly beneath the mortuary temple. Deir el-Bahri is separated from the Valley of the Kings by a steep outcrop of the Theban mountain. Today it takes a good half an hour to walk between the two, following the steep mountain trail which had been named 'Agatha Christie's path' on the grounds that it plays an important part in her ancient Egyptian detective mystery *Death Comes as the End*.[25] However, the two sites are actually less than a quarter of a mile apart as the mole tunnels. It would therefore have been perfectly feasible for Hatchepsut to be buried below her mortuary temple while enjoying the security of a tomb entrance hidden in the Valley. Unfortunately, the unstable nature of the rock in the Valley of the Kings seems to have thwarted this plan and, in order to avoid a localized patch of dangerously crumbling rock, the straight passages were forced to curve in on themselves, creating a bent bow shape. The finished tomb, if straightened out, would in any case have been approximately one hundred metres too short to reach the temple.

For many years egyptologists have assumed that Tuthmosis I was, by the beginning of Hatchepsut's reign, peacefully resting in Tomb KV 38, which had been built for him in secret 'no one seeing, no one hearing' by his loyal architect Ineni. It therefore made sense for his devoted daughter to select a nearby site for her own tomb, KV 20. However, a recent re-examination of the architecture and contents of KV 38 has made it clear that, while this tomb was definitely built for Tuthmosis I, it is unlikely to have been started before the reign of his grandson, Tuthmosis III. This means that, wherever Hatchepsut and Tuthmosis II buried their father, it could not have been in Tomb KV 38. Where then had Tuthmosis I been interred?

It could be that the original tomb of Tuthmosis I has yet to be discovered; his would not be the first tomb to be 'lost' in the Valley of the Kings. However, it seems far more likely that Hatchepsut, rather than build herself a completely new tomb, had taken the unusual decision to extend the tomb already occupied by her father by adding a further stairway leading downwards to an extra chamber. This extension would make the tomb eminently suitable for a double father–daughter burial. The proportions of the burial chamber of KV 20, and the unusually small stairway which leads to this chamber, certainly hint that this section may be a late addition, while its architectural style has indicated a direct link with the Deir el-Bahri mortuary temple which is not suggested by the remainder of the tomb.[26] The inspiration for the double-burial may have been the simple filial love that Hatchepsut felt for her father, or it may have been a more practical move designed to associate Hatchepsut permanently with her ever-popular father's mortuary cult: Winlock has suggested that Hatchepsut needed to use her father's remains to enhance the sanctity of her own burial just as 'in the Middle Ages the bodies of the saints were translated from the Holy Land to Europe to enhance the sanctity of the new cathedrals'.[27]

The new plan means that Tuthmosis I was actually interred twice in Tomb KV 20, firstly during his funeral when he was placed in a traditional wooden sarcophagus (now lost) in the original burial chamber, and later, during Hatchepsut's reign, when he was provided with a splendid quartzite sarcophagus and moved downwards to the new chamber. This would, of course, cast doubt upon the hitherto accepted theory that the tomb was designed to run directly beneath *Djeser-Djeseru*; the unusual length of the passageways may instead represent a fruitless search for the layers of hard rock which would permit the carving of decorations on the tomb walls.

The location of Tomb KV 20 – if not of its original owner – had been known since the Napoleonic Expedition of 1799; in 1804 a gentleman named Ch. H. Gordon had left his mark on the entrance door-jamb; in 1817 Giovanni Battista Belzoni had recorded the tomb on his map of the Valley of the Kings; in 1824 James Burton had gained access to an upper chamber; and in 1844 Karl Richard Lepsius had partially explored the upper passage. However, all the passageways had become blocked by a solidified mass of rubble, small stones and other rubbish which had been carried into the tomb by floodwaters. It was not until 1903–4 that Howard Carter, after two seasons of strenuous work, was able to clear the corridors and make his way along the long and winding passageways to the double burial chamber. This he found to be filled with debris from a collapsed ceiling, and he embarked on a further month's clearance work, labouring under the most trying of conditions:

. . . the air had become so bad, and the heat so great, that the candles carried by the workmen melted, and would not give enough light to enable them to continue their work; consequently we were compelled to install electric lights, in the form of hand wires . . . As soon as we got down about 50 metres, the air became so foul that the men could not work. In addition to this, the bats of centuries had built innumerable nests on the ceilings of the corridors and chambers, and their excrement had become so dry that the least stir of the air filled the corridors with a fluffy black stuff, which choked the noses and mouths of the men, rendering it most difficult for them to breathe.[28]

All the rubbish extracted had to be carried in baskets along almost 200 m (656 ft) of narrow, curving passageways and steep stairways to the surface 100 m (328 ft) above. Overcoming these obstacles with the aid of an air suction pump installed by the excavation's American sponsor, Mr Theodore M. Davis, the intrepid Carter discovered that the tomb followed a fairly simple plan, with four descending stepped passages linked by three rectangular chambers leading to a rectangular burial chamber measuring 11 m × 5.5 m × 3 m (36 ft × 18 ft × 10 ft). The ceiling of the burial chamber was originally supported by a row of three central columns, and there were three very small store rooms opening off the main chamber. Here Carter found not one but two yellow quartzite sarcophagi and Hatchepsut's matching quartzite canopic box. Unfortunately, the tomb had been robbed in antiquity, and the once-magnificent grave goods were reduced to piles of broken sherds, fragments of stone vessels and 'some burnt pieces of wooden coffins and boxes; a part of the face and foot of a large wooden statue covered in bitumen'.[29] It does not seem beyond the bounds of possibility that the burned wooden fragments might be the remains of the original coffins and sarcophagus of Tuthmosis I. Fifteen polished limestone slabs inscribed in red and black ink with chapters from the *Amduat*, a book of royal funerary literature provided during the New Kingdom for the use of the dead king, and here obviously intended to line the burial chamber, were lying on the floor where the builders had abandoned them.

Included amongst the debris of broken pottery and shattered stone vessels recovered from the burial chamber and lower passages were the remains of two vases made for Queen Ahmose Nefertari. These vessels seem to have been regarded as Tuthmoside family heirlooms, and as such were a part of the original funerary equipment of Tuthmosis I. One of the vases gives the name and titles of the deceased queen 'long may she live', plus a later inscription which tells us that Tuthmosis

*Fig. 4.6   The goddess Isis from the
sarcophagus of Hatchepsut*

II '[made it] as his monument to his father'. Other vessels, this time bearing the name and titles of Tuthmosis I, had also been inscribed by Tuthmosis II and were presumably also a part of the original funerary equipment of Tuthmosis I placed in his tomb by his son. The tomb also contained fragments of stone vessels made for Hatchepsut before she became king – possibly transferred from her previous tomb – and vessels bearing the name of Maatkare Hatchepsut which must have been made after she acceded to the throne.

The magnificent sarcophagus of King Hatchepsut was discovered open, with no sign of a body, and with the lid lying discarded on the floor. It is now housed in Cairo Museum along with its matching quartzite canopic chest. Carved from a single block of yellow quartzite, the sarcophagus has a cartouche-shaped plan-form with a rounded head end and a flat foot end, and it has been inscribed, polished and painted. The second sarcophagus, found lying on its side with its almost-undamaged lid propped against the wall nearby, was eventually presented to Mr Davis as a gesture of appreciation for his generous financial support. Mr Davis in turn presented the sarcophagus to the Museum of Fine Arts, Boston. This second sarcophagus had originally been engraved with the name of 'the King of Upper and Lower Egypt, Maatkare Hatchepsut'; incontrovertible evidence that it had been intended for the use of the female king. However, just as the sarcophagus was virtually complete, there had been a change of plan. A new sarcophagus was commissioned for Hatchepsut, and the rejected sarcophagus was transferred to Tuthmosis I. The stonemasons made the best that they could of the situation, restoring the surface of the quartzite so that it could be re-carved with the name and titles of its new owner. In an attempt to erase the original carvings several centimetres of the outer surface were lost and the sarcophagus was reduced by 6 cm (2½ in) in width and 1.5 cm (½ in) in length, while the lid was made good by the judicious use of painted plaster. Finally, the sarcophagus was re-carved with the name of Tuthmosis I. A dedication text makes Hatchepsut's generosity clear:

... long live the Female Horus ... The king of Upper and Lower Egypt, Maatkare, the son of Re, Hatchepsut-Khnemet-Amun! May she live forever! She made it as her monument to her father whom she loved, the Good God, Lord of the Two Lands, Aakheperkare, the son of Re, Tuthmosis the justified.[30]

The sarcophagus finally measured 222.5 cm (7 ft) long × 89 cm (3 ft) wide with walls 13 cm (5 in) thick, and would therefore have been too short to have held the anthropoid coffin of Tuthmosis I which, recovered from the Deir el-Bahri mummy cache, measures 232 cm (7 ft 6 in) long by 72 cm (2 ft 3 in) wide at the elbows and 70 cm (2 ft 3 in) high at the face. The feet, normally the deepest part of the coffin, had been destroyed in antiquity. The 18th Dynasty workmen, realizing that the reconditioned sarcophagus might prove too small for its intended occupant, had attempted to enlarge the cavity by hacking away at the inner surfaces of the end walls. However, even when the inner space had been enlarged twice, it still only measured 210 cm × 64 cm × 64.5 cm (6 ft 10 in × 2ft × 2ft); it would have easily accommodated a mummified body, but not one encased in a nest of two or three wooden coffins. Presumably, when the time came to inter the king, his coffin(s) would have been discarded.

At around 155 cm tall (approximately 5 ft) Tuthmosis would certainly not have been considered a giant amongst the ancient Egyptians, but nor would he have been unnaturally short for a New Kingdom man; an average male height of approximately 166 cm (5 ft 5 in) is suggested by the available human remains.[31] The Tuthmosides evidently had a family tendency towards shortness; Tuthmosis II was 169 cm (5 ft 6 in) tall and Tuthmosis III, at 161 cm (5 ft 3 in), has often been likened to an ancient Egyptian Napoleon Bonaparte (or, less frequently, to Alexander the Great and even to Horatio Nelson) on account of both his military prowess and his stocky build. As Hatchepsut's sarcophagus was too short for Tuthmosis I we must assume that she was less tall than her father; presumably her body, wrapped in bandages and encased within at least one wooden coffin, would have fitted into her smallest sarcophagus, that recovered from the Wadi Sikkat Taka ez-Zeida, which would have taken a coffin up to 181 cm (5 ft 11 in) in length.

Tuthmosis I was not, however, destined to lie alongside his daughter as, sometime after the death of Hatchepsut, Tuthmosis III decided to re-inter his grandfather in an even more magnificent tomb. To some modern observers this seems a very natural reaction:

That . . . upon finding himself supreme master of Egypt he should have per-mitted the body of his revered ancestor and predecessor on the throne to lie buried in the tomb – in the very sarcophagus – of the accursed usurper is, to the mind of the writer, incredible . . . One would expect him to have striven to surpass his former co-regent in lavishness and to have scorned the shoddy expedient of 'doing over' a second-half [sic] monument or of failing to pro-vide one at all.[32]

The new tomb (KV 38) contained yet another yellow quartzite sar-cophagus dedicated to Tuthmosis I and inscribed by his loving grand-son: 'It was his son who caused his name to live in making excellent the monument of [his] father for all eternity.'[33] This time the workmen made sure that the sarcophagus was exactly the right size to accom-modate Tuthmosis' new cedarwood anthropoid coffin; one of a series of three coffins thoughtfully provided by Tuthmosis III.

Unfortunately, Tuthmosis was once again to be denied his eternal rest. During the late 20th Dynasty his new tomb was plundered, the sarcophagus lid was broken, the body was stripped of its precious jewel-lery and the valuable grave goods were stolen. One of the coffins pre-pared for Tuthmosis I by Tuthmosis III eventually came to light as part of the Deir el-Bahri mummy cache. As might be expected, this coffin was obviously an early 18th Dynasty artifact and bore the name of Tuthmosis. However the coffin had been 'borrowed' by a later king; it had been re-gilded and re-inlaid for use by the Theban ruler Pinedjem I, a monarch who ruled southern Egypt over 400 years after the death of Tuthmosis I. The gold foil carefully applied for Pinedjem's inter-ment had itself been subsequently removed, possibly by the necropolis officials who stored the coffins in the cache, allowing the original name of Tuthmosis to be seen once again.

It is obvious that Tuthmosis' body must have been separated from its coffin before Pinedjem was buried. This must cast serious doubt upon the mummy tentatively identified as that of Tuthmosis I at the end of the nineteenth century. Maspero had found this mummy resting, Russian doll-style, in a nest of two coffins, the inner one a Third Intermediate Period coffin originally intended for Pinedjem and the outer coffin that of Tuthmosis I but adapted for the use of Pinedjem. This unlabelled body seemed of the correct size and age to be Tuthmosis I although, like many of the other mummies in the cache, it had been 'restored' in antiquity and was now wrapped in late New Kingdom cloth. When the newer wrappings were removed, it was revealed that the original mummy, that of a man with a wrinkled face apparently in his mid-fifties, was badly decomposed and that the hands of the body had been torn away by thieves searching for precious jewellery. The head, however, as described by Maspero 'presents a striking resemblance to those of Tuthmosis II and III' while the rather long narrow face displayed 'refined features . . . the mouth still bears an expression of shrewdness and cunning'.[34]

Maspero took this physical similarity to the other Tuthmoside kings as confirmation of the mummy's royal identity and suggested that the body must have been restored to its original coffin by the officials responsible for packing the Deir el-Bahri cache. This, of course, suggests that Pinedjem's body had also become separated from its coffins in antiquity, and indeed Pinedjem later turned up inside the coffin of Queen Ahhotep II. X-ray analysis of the 'Tuthmosis I' body, however, indicates that it may in fact be the body of a man in his late teens or early twenties. While there are many problems with the ages suggested by the X-ray analysis of mummies, this does leave us with the tantalizing possibility that the body, if it is not that of Tuthmosis I, may be that of a young male member of the royal family, possibly even one of Hatchepsut's elder brothers, Amenmose or Wadjmose.[35]

Tuthmosis III furnished his grandfather with his third mortuary chapel, a part of his own cult temple, *Henketankh*, which was situated halfway between the original mortuary temple of Tuthmosis I and the point where the Deir el-Bahri temple causeway reaches the desert's edge. The mortuary chapel which Hatchepsut had built to honour her father within *Djeser-Djeseru* was abandoned, while Tuthmosis' original mortuary temple, *Khenmetankh*, was left to become a generalized Tuthmoside family chapel; a scene showing Tuthmosis I seated in front of the enigmatic Prince Wadjmose and receiving an offering from Tuthmosis III suggests that Tuthmosis III may have actually restored this chapel as a cult temple dedicated to the memory of his grandfather.[36]

5

War and Peace

$$⟨ \! \! ⟩ \! \! \backsim \! \! \frown \! \! \smile \! \! \square \! \! ⟨⟨⟨ ° | \! \! ⎰⎱$$

To look upon her was more beautiful than anything; her splendour and her form were divine; she was a maiden, beautiful and blooming.[1]

Hatchepsut lived before the full-length looking glass had been invented. She could examine her features in the highly polished metal 'see-face' which, carried in a special mirror-bag designed to be slung over the shoulder, was an essential accessory for every upper-class matron, but she was forced to turn to others for confirmation of her overall beauty. We should perhaps not be too surprised to find that her loyal and prudent courtiers dutifully praised their new king as the most attractive woman in Egypt. Her own words, quoted above, betray a rather touching pride in her own appearance – clearly these things mattered to even the highest-ranking Egyptian female – while incidental finds of her most intimate possessions, such as an alabaster eye make-up container, with integral bronze applicator, engraved with Hatchepsut's early title of 'God's Wife', or a pair of golden bracelets engraved with Hatchepsut's name but recovered from the tomb of a concubine of Tuthmosis III, serve as a reminder that Hatchepsut, the semi-divine king of Egypt, was also a real flesh-and-blood woman.

We have no contemporary, unbiased, description or illustration of Hatchepsut, although we can assume that, in common with most upper-class Egyptian women of her time, she was relatively petite with a light brown skin, a relatively narrow skull, dark brown eyes and wavy dark brown or black hair. She may, in fact, have chosen to be completely bald. Throughout the New Kingdom it was common for both the male and the female élite to shave their heads; this was a practical response to the heat and dust of the Egyptian climate, and the false-hair industry flourished as elaborate wigs were *de rigueur* for more formal occasions. The king's smooth golden body was perfumed with all the exotic oils of Egypt:

His majesty herself put with her own hands oil of ani on all her limbs. Her fragrance was like a divine breath, her scent reached as far as the land of Punt; her skin is made of gold, it shines like the stars . . .²

Hatchepsut's surviving statues, although always highly idealized, provide us with a more specific set of clues to her actual appearance. The new king evidently had a slender build with an attractive oval face, a high forehead, almond-shaped eyes, a delicate pointed chin – which in some instances is almost a receding chin – and a rather prominent nose which adds character to her otherwise rather bland expression. Towards the beginning of her reign her features show a certain feminine softness, a possible indication of her youth; later statues show her sterner, somehow harder, and more the embodiment of the traditional pharaoh. To some sympathetic observers her face betrays outward signs of her inner struggle: '. . . worn, strong, thoughtful and masculine but with something moving and pathetic in the expression'.³ To Hayes, describing a red granite statue from Deir el-Bahri, the king displays '. . . a handsome face, but not one distinguished by the qualities of honesty and generosity'.⁴ There is a general family resemblance between the statuary of Hatchepsut and Tuthmosis III – large noses obviously ran in the Tuthmoside family – which is not necessarily the result of both kings being sculpted by the same workshop. This can present problems for the unwary student of egyptology, and entire learned papers have been devoted to the question of exactly which monarch is represented by a particular statue.

From the time of her coronation onwards Hatchepsut no longer wished to be recognized as a beautiful or indeed even a conventional woman. She chose instead to abandon the customary woman's sheath dress and queen's crown and be depicted wearing the traditional royal regalia of short kilt, crown or head-cloth, broad collar and false beard. Very occasionally, towards the beginning of her reign, she took the form of a woman dressed in king's clothing; two seated limestone statues recovered from Deir el-Bahri show her wearing the typical king's headcloth and kilt, but with a rounded, almost girlish face, no false beard and a slight, obviously feminine body with an indented waist and unmistakable breasts (see, for example, Plate 5).⁵ More often, however, she was shown not only with male clothing and accessories but performing male actions and with the body of a man (Plates 8, 9 and

Fig. 5.1   Hatchepsut as a man

10). When depicted as a child at the Deir el-Bahri temple, she was presented as a naked boy with unmistakable male genitalia. Her soul, or Ka, was an equally obvious naked boy. To any observer unfamiliar with Egyptian art-history and unable to read hieroglyphic inscriptions, the female queen had successfully transformed herself into a male king. At first sight the explanation for this transvestism seems simple:

The Egyptians were averse to the throne being occupied by a woman, otherwise Hatchepsut would not have been obliged to assume the garb of a man; she would not have disguised her sex under male attire, not omitting the beard . . . How strong this feeling was in Hatchepsut's own time is shown by the fact that she never dared to disregard it in her sculptures, where she never appears as a woman.[6]

To dismiss Hatchepsut's new appearance as a naive attempt to pose or pass herself off as a man[7] in order to fool her subjects is, however, to underestimate both the intelligence of the new king and her supporters and the sophistication of Egyptian artistic thought. It is perfectly possible that the vast majority of the population, illiterate, uneducated and politically unaware, were indeed confused over the gender of their new ruler, and Hatchepsut may well have wished to encourage their confusion; if her people felt more secure under a male king, then so be it. However, the lower classes were to a large extent unimportant. There was no Egyptian tradition of popular political activity and the peasants had absolutely no say in the government of their country. Indeed, Egypt was never regarded as 'their country'; everyone knew that the entire land belonged to the king and the gods. Those who did matter were the male élite and the gods, and both of these were already fully aware of Hatchepsut's sex.

Hatchepsut, former God's Wife and mother of the Princess Neferure, was widely known to be a woman. There is absolutely no evidence to suggest that she suddenly came out as a transsexual, a transvestite or a lesbian, and the fact that she retained her female name and continued to use feminine word forms in many of her inscriptions suggests that she did not see herself as wholly, or even partially, male. Although we have absolutely no idea how the new king dressed in private, we should not necessarily assume that she invariably wore a man's kilt and false beard.

Accusations of 'deviant personality and behaviour . . . [and] abnormal psychology',[8] levelled by those who have attempted to psychoanalyse Hatchepsut long after her death, are generally lacking any supporting evidence. At least one modern medical expert has attempted to link this perceived 'deviant' behaviour with Hatchepsut's devotion to her father:

. . . Hatchepsut, from her early years, as exemplified by her apparent identification with her father, had a strong 'masculine protest' (to use Adler's term), with a pathological drive towards actual male impersonation . . . The difficulty with her marriage partners [sic] might indicate a maladjustment in hetero-sexuality. The fact that she had children [sic] does not obviate such a maladjustment.[9]

However, such analyses, based on the scanty surviving evidence, betray a profound lack of understanding of the nature of Egyptian kingship.

Similarly, it would be wrong to dismiss these male images as mere propaganda. They were, of course, intended to convey a message, but so were all the other Egyptian royal portraits from the start of the Old

Kingdom onwards. None of the images of the pharaohs was entirely faithful to their original, but nor were they intended to be. They were designed instead to convey selected aspects of kingship popular at a particular time. Therefore we find that the kings of the Old Kingdom are generally shown as the remote embodiment of semi-divine author- ity, the rulers of the Middle Kingdom appear more careworn as they struggle with the burdens of office and the pharaohs of the New Kingdom have acquired a new confidence and security in their role. Conformity was always very important and physical imperfections were generally ignored, to the extent that the 19th Dynasty King Siptah is consistently portrayed as a healthy young man even though we know from his mummified body that he had a deformed foot. The same rule of conformity applied to queens, so we find that the unfortunately buck-toothed Queens Tetisheri and Ahmose Nefertari are never de- picted as anything other than conventionally beautiful. If a royal statue or painted portrait happened to look like its subject, so much the better. If not, the all-important engraving of the name would prevent any confusion as the name defined the image. Indeed, it was always possible to alter the subject of a portrait or statue by leaving the features un- touched and simply changing its inscription.

Hatchepsut's assumption of power had left her with several unique problems. There was no established Egyptian precedent for a female king or queen regnant and, although there was no specific law prohib- iting female rulers – indeed Manetho preserves the name of a King Binothris of the 2nd Dynasty during whose reign 'it was decided that women might hold kingly office' – this was purely a theoretical conces- sion. It was generally acknowledged that all pharaohs would be men. This was in full agreement with the Egyptian artistic convention of the pale woman as the private or indoor worker, the bronzed man as the more prominent public figure. Hatchepsut, as a female king, therefore had to make her own rules. She knew that in order to maintain her hold on the throne she needed to present herself before her gods and her present and future subjects as a true Egyptian king in all respects. Furthermore, she needed to make a sharp and immediately obvious distinction between her former position as queen regent and her new role as pharaoh. The change of dress was a clear sign of her altered state. When Marina Warner writes of Joan of Arc, history's best recognized cross-dresser, she could well be describing Hatchepsut:

Through her transvestism, she abrogated the destiny of womankind. She could thereby transcend her sex; she could set herself apart and usurp the privileges of the male and his claims to superiority. At the same time, by never pretending to be other than a woman and a maid, she was usurping a man's function but shaking off the trammels of his sex altogether to occupy a different third order, neither male nor female, but unearthly . . .'[10]

Both these women chose to shun conventional female dress in order to challenge the way that their societies perceived them. However, there are clear differences between the two cases. Joan wished to be seen as neither a woman nor a man, but as an androgynous virgin. By taking the (surely unnecessary) decision to adopt male garb at all times, not just on the field of battle where it could be justified on the grounds of practicality, she was making a less than subtle statement about the subordinate role assigned to those who wore female dress. Unfortunately, in choosing to make this statement she was not only flouting convention but laying herself open to the charges of unseemly, unfeminine behaviour which were eventually to lead to her death. Her cropped hair and her transvestism horrified her contemporaries. Cross-dressing, generally perceived as a threat to ordered society, was in fact specifically prohibited by the Old Testament:

The woman shall not wear that which pertaineth unto a man, neither shall a man put on a woman's garment; for all that do so are abomination unto the Lord.[11]

Hatchepsut, living in a far more relaxed society, had a far more focused need. The queen, however well-born, would always be seen as a mere woman who was occasionally permitted to rule Egypt on a temporary basis. The king was male (an irrelevance to Hatchepsut), divine, and able to communicate with the gods. Hatchepsut did not want to be seen as a mere queen who ruled: she wanted to be a king.

To emphasize her changed status, Hatchepsut made full use of the concept of the divine duality of kings. Theology decreed that the king of Egypt should be a god, the son of Amen, who received his divinity on the death of his predecessor. At the same time, however, it was obvious that the king of Egypt was a mere human being born to mortal parents and incapable of performing even the most minor of divine acts in his own lifetime. This duality of existence resulted in the recognition of an important distinction between the office and the person. The office holder (pharaoh) who enjoyed a particular status because of his office was recognized as being a completely separate entity from the human being (Hatchepsut) who was that office holder. It was this concept which helped men from outside the immediate royal family, such as Tuthmosis I, to become accepted as the true pharaoh: the coronation confirmed the divinity of the new king, and from that point on he was truly royal. Throughout her reign Hatchepsut strove to emphasize the conventional aspects of the role of pharaoh, a role which she felt she could fill regardless of gender. By so doing, however, she effectively eliminated herself from the archaeological record as an individual in her own right.

Why, then, was it so necessary for Hatchepsut to become a king rather than a queen? To modern observers there may appear to be little difference, if any, between the roles of king and queen regnant. If Queen Elizabeth II were suddenly to announce that she wished to be known as King Elizabeth her decision would be viewed as eccentric, but not as a fundamental change of function. It would be a mere playing with words. Hatchepsut was not, however, playing with words. To the ancient Egyptians, a vast and almost unbridgeable gulf separated the king from the rest of humanity, including the closest members of his own family. There was, in fact, no formal Egyptian word for 'queen', and all the ladies of the royal household were titled by reference to their lord and master: the consort of the king was either a 'King's Wife' or a 'King's Great Wife', the dowager queen was usually a 'King's Mother' and a princess was a 'King's Daughter'. An Egyptian queen regnant simply had to be known as 'king'; she had no other title.

The correct presentation of the king was clearly a matter of great importance to the ancient Egyptians, to the extent that those who invaded and conquered Egypt almost invariably adopted the traditional pharaonic regalia as a means of reinforcing their rule. We therefore find non-Egyptians, such as the Asiatic Hyksos rulers of the Second Intermediate Period or the Greek Ptolemies of the post-Dynastic Period, all dressing as conventional native pharaohs. It may be that the obvious combination of female characteristics and male accessories shown at the start of her reign should be interpreted as a short-lived attempt to present a new image of the pharaoh as an asexual mixture of male and female strengths.[12] If this is the case, the experiment surely failed, as Hatchepsut soon reverted to the all-male appearance of the conventional Egyptian king. These early statues do not suggest a blend of sexual characteristics in the way that the later statuary of Akhenaten does – it is always possible to tell whether Hatchepsut intended to be depicted in the body of a woman or a man – and this may be an indication that they in fact belong to a transitional period when either Hatchepsut or her sculptors was uncertain of the image which the new king wished to project.

The only king who dared to go against established tradition, consistently allowing himself to be depicted as far removed from the accepted idealized stereotype, was the later 18th Dynasty Pharaoh Akhenaten. This unconventional monarch was apparently happy to see himself presented as a virtual hermaphrodite with a narrow feminine face, drooping breasts, a sagging stomach and wide hips, although even he retained the conventional crown, false beard and crook and flail which symbolized his authority. These representations have cast a doubt over the sexuality of Akhenaten, although he is known to have had at least two wives and to have fathered at least six daughters, which is entirely absent from images of Hatchepsut. Many early egyptologists believed, on the basis of his portraits, that the heretic king was a woman, while Manetho's second 18th Dynasty queen regnant, Akhenkheres daughter of Oros (Amenhotep III), is now thought to be Akhenaten.

Hatchepsut's bold decision to throw off the feminine appearance which would for ever classify her as a queen (and therefore by definition as not divine and vastly inferior to the king) was an eminently sensible one which solved several constitutional problems at a stroke. She could now be seen to be the equal of any pharaoh, she could ensure the continuance of the established traditions which were vital to the maintenance of *maat*, she could become the living embodiment of Horus, a male god and, last but certainly not least, she could replace Tuthmosis III in the religious and state rituals which only a king could perform. It may be that a more secure female monarch would have had the confidence to adapt the traditional masculine garments and accessories to produce a more feminine version for her own use, and indeed the previous queen regnant Sobeknofru had not found it necessary to alter her way of dress when she ascended to the throne, but Hatchepsut clearly felt that it was important to be seen to be as 'normal' a king as possible. Sobeknofru in any case does not present an exact parallel to Hatchepsut. She came to the throne at a time when there was no obvious male heir, and therefore she had no need to justify or excuse her rule. She also reigned for less than four years; hardly enough time to construct the impressive monuments and statues which would present her with the opportunity to display large-scale images of herself as king.

Throughout the dynastic period the image was viewed as a powerful force which could, if required, provide a substitute for the person or thing depicted. The image could also be used to reinforce an idea so that, by causing herself to be depicted as a traditional pharaoh in the most regal and heroic form, Hatchepsut was making sure that this is precisely what she would become. Egyptian art is notoriously difficult for modern observers to understand on anything other than a superficial level; it needs a willingness to abandon ingrained ideas of perspective, scale and accuracy of depiction as well as an understanding of contemporary symbolism. However, Hatchepsut's regal scenes must be regarded as highly successful in that they effectively convey a comparatively simple message: here is the legitimate king of her land. Just as Queen Elizabeth I of England, as an old woman in the last decade of her 45-year reign, could be celebrated and painted as 'Queen of Love and Beauty' – an ever-young maiden with flowing hair and a smooth complexion and wearing the crescent moon of Cynthia, goddess of the Moon[13] – so Hatchepsut, a widow and mother, could command her artists and sculptors to depict her as a traditional Egyptian pharaoh, complete with beard.

The god knows it of me, Amen, Lord of the Thrones of the Two Lands. He gave me sovereignty over the Black Land and the Red Land as a reward. None rebels against me in all lands. All foreign lands are my subjects. He made my boundary at the limits of heaven. All that the sun encompasses works for me . . .[14]

Hatchepsut chose to re-invent herself not merely as a king, but as a traditional warrior-king, conqueror of the whole world. To many modern historians this was nothing but a giant fraud. Her reign was perceived as being disappointingly 'barren of any military enterprise except an unimportant raid into Nubia',[15] and it therefore followed that 'the power of Egypt in Syria was much shaken during the regency of Hatchepsut'.[16] This deliberate non-aggressive stance was in marked contrast to the expansionist policies of Tuthmosis I, Amenhotep I and the great warrior Ahmose, and was to put Tuthmosis III at a severe disadvantage when, at the beginning of his solo reign, he was required to quell uprisings amongst the Egyptian client states in Palestine and Syria. The unfortunate tendency towards pacifism was generally considered to be the direct result of Hatchepsut's gender. As a woman, it was reasoned, she was not only unlikely to wish to indulge in wars, but she would also have been physically incapable of leading the army into battle:

Hatchepsut was neither an Agrippina nor an Amazon. As far as we know, violence and bloodshed had no place in her make-up. Hers was a rule dominated by an architect, and the Hapusenebs, Neshis and Djehutys in her following were priests and administrators rather than soldiers.[17]

Hatchepsut stands out as one of the great monarchs of Egypt. Though no wars or conquests are recorded in her reign, her triumphs were as great as those of the warrior-kings of Egypt, but they were the triumphs of peace, not war. Her records, as might be expected from a woman, are more intimate and personal than those of a king . . . This was no conqueror, joying in the lusts of battle, but a strong-souled noble-hearted woman, ruling her country wisely and well.[18]

Few historians working in the pre-politically correct 1950s and 1960s, faced with the apparent pacifism of Hatchepsut's reign and the well-documented military activities of Tuthmosis III, were able to resist drawing sweeping conclusions. The two kings, already deadly enemies, were now to be seen as the leaders of two opposing political factions. Hatchepsut the female, with her interest in internal works and foreign trade, belonged to what could be classed as the party of peace. She was supported in her ideas by a party of self-made bureaucrats. Tuthmosis, supported by the traditional male élite including the priesthood of Amen, belonged to the more radical 'war' party, his vigorous programme of conquests and expansion being interpreted as a sign that Egypt was attempting to shake off her insular past and become a major world power:

Our theory then is that there was a choice to be made and that two different parties chose differently, Hatchepsut's faction in terms of the lesser effort of

earlier times and Tuthmosis III's faction in terms of a new and major international venture.[19]

Old-fashioned egyptologists are not the only ones to have assumed
that a woman's natural sensitivity, physical frailty and ability to gen-
erate life would naturally lead her to shy away from bloodshed. For a
long time this, in a slightly altered form, has been the sincerely held
belief of many feminist theorists and historians who view extreme
violence and aggression as a purely male phenomenon and who associate the peace movement, now seen as a strength rather than a
weakness, with women and motherhood. Woman's ability to create
life is often seen as incompatible with the wish to order the death of
another human being. Various theories have been put forward to
explain the phenomenon of male aggression, ranging from the simple
biological (the higher testosterone levels found in men) to the complex psychological (men's need for compensation for their inability to
bear children), while Freud suggested that male aggression was the
natural result of the sexual rivalry between father and son competing
for the love of the mother. Freud went on to deduce from this that
men had developed civilizations as a means of compensating for the
suppression of their childhood sexual instincts, while the feminist
theorist Naomi Wolf, discussing the 'beauty myth' which she sees as
ensnaring modern women, has developed this argument a stage further by suggesting that as 'Freud believed that the repression of the
libido made civilization; civilization depends at the moment on the
repression of the female libido . . .'[20]

However, the idea that a woman would automatically be less aggressive than a man may appear strange to those who have lived under some
of the world's most recent female rulers. Neither Mrs Golda Meir nor
Mrs Indira Gandhi was known for her soft and passive femininity while
the track record of the 'Iron Lady', Margaret Thatcher, speaks for itself.
Mrs Thatcher, following a tradition established by Hatchepsut and continued by Elizabeth I, even dressed as a soldier during an official visit to
Northern Ireland, a gesture which was presumably intended to express
solidarity with the troops as she herself had no intention of taking up
arms and fighting on the streets of Belfast. It could almost be argued on
this admittedly very small sample that modern women who obtain
positions of power normally reserved for men are more and not less

likely to resort to military action, particularly if they feel that they still
have something to prove. There is certainly nothing in Hatchepsut's
character to suggest that she would be frightened of taking the military
initiative as and when necessary.

A quick survey of the prominent women of history tends to confirm that being female is not necessarily a bar to taking decisive
military action. Societies in general may have prevented their women
from fighting but there have been some notable exceptions. Hip-
polyta, Penthesilea and the other single-breasted warrior Amazons
may be dismissed as a legend invented to frighten men but Boadicea,
Zenobia of Palmyra and Joan of Arc, real women living in societies
which would not traditionally allow females to enlist, all donned masculine battle dress to lead their male soldiers into action. Other
queens, including Elizabeth I as she rallied the English fleet at
Tilbury, wore the battle dress to show their commitment to the cause
but commanded from afar, while Cleopatra, who participated periph-
erally in the battle of Actium before fleeing 'true to her nature as a
woman and an Egyptian'[21] never, as far as we are aware, dressed as an
Egyptian soldier. All these women seem to have been instinctively
aware that the very presence of a fragile woman on the field of battle,
far from discouraging the troops, may actually bring out feelings of
latent gallantry and thereby inspire their soldiers to greater effort.
Antonia Fraser, who dubs this type of woman a 'Warrior Queen',
notes that:

. . . a Warrior Queen – or female ruler – has often provided the focus for what
a country afterwards perceived to have been its golden age; beyond the obvious example (to the English) of Queen Elizabeth I, one might cite the
twelfth-century Queen Tamara of Georgia, or the fifteenth-century Isabella of
Spain.[22]

The woman who takes up arms on behalf of her country, such as
Marianne of France, is often seen as the ultimate patriot. At the same
time the enemy who is forced to fight against a woman may be
shamed by his unchivalrous actions. He is caught in a classic 'no-win'
situation; he can never achieve a great victory by defeating a mere
woman, while a lost battle could lead to open ridicule by his male
contemporaries.

Evidence is now growing to suggest that Hatchepsut's military prowess has been seriously underestimated due to the selective nature of the archaeological evidence which has been compounded by preconceived notions of feminine pacifism. Egyptologists have assumed that Hatchepsut did not fight, and have become blind to the evidence that, in fact, she did. As has already been noted, ancient battles do not necessarily have a great impact on their immediate environment, and we are dependent upon the preservation of monumental or textual evidence for confirmation that any skirmish took place. Occasionally we may learn of a great battle by chance from a single inscription, and it will already have been noticed that Ahmose's war of liberation, which freed Egypt from Hyksos rule, is only actually recorded in its full detail in the tomb of Ahmose, son of Ibana. As so many of Hatchepsut's texts were defaced, amended or erased after her death, it is entirely possible that her war record is incomplete. Furthermore, Hatchepsut's reign, falling between the reigns of two of the greatest generals Egypt was ever to know (Tuthmosis I and Tuthmosis III), is bound to suffer in any immediate comparison. A more realistic comparison, say with the reign of Tuthmosis II, shows that Hatchepsut's reign was not at all unusual. It is almost certainly a mistake based on hindsight to see the Asiatic empire as a master-plan devised by Tuthmosis I, hindered by Tuthmosis II (who may be excused on the grounds of ill-health) and Hatchepsut and finally brought to fruition by Tuthmosis III.

The Deir el-Bahri mortuary temple, *Djeser-Djeseru*, provides us with evidence for defensive military activity during Hatchepsut's reign. By the late nineteenth century Naville had uncovered enough references to battles to convince him that Hatchepsut had embarked on the now customary series of campaigns against her vassals to the south and east. These subjects, the traditional enemies of Egypt, almost invariably viewed any change of pharaoh as an opportunity to rebel against their overlords, while the pharaohs themselves seem to have almost welcomed these minor insurrections as a means of proving their military might:

The fragments and inscriptions found in the course of the excavations at Deir el-Bahri show that during Hatchepsut's reign wars were waged against the Ethiopians, and probably also against the Asiatics. Among these wars which the queen considered the most glorious, and which she desired to be recorded on the walls of the temple erected as a monument to her high deeds, was the campaign against the nations of the Upper Nile.[23]

Blocks originally sited on the eastern colonnade show the Nubian god Dedwen leading a series of captive southern towns towards the victorious Hatchepsut, each town being represented by a name written in a crenellated cartouche and topped by an obviously African head. The towns all belong to the land of Cush (Nubia). Elsewhere in the temple, Hatchepsut is portrayed as a sphinx, a human-headed crouching lion crushing the traditional enemies of Egypt. There is also a written, but unfortunately badly damaged, description of a Nubian campaign in which Hatchepsut appears to be claiming to have emulated the deeds of her revered father:

. . . as was done by her victorious father, the King of Upper and Lower Egypt, Aakheperkare [Tuthmosis I] who seized all lands . . . a slaughter was made among them, the number [of dead] being unknown; their hands were cut off . . . she overthrew [gap in text] the gods [gap in text] . . .[24]

The evidence from the Deir el-Bahri temple is a mixture of official pronouncements and conventional scenes, and it is therefore possible that the Nubian campaigns may be battles which Hatchepsut has 'borrowed' from earlier pharaohs, possibly her father. Such borrowing or usurping, disgraceful cheating to modern eyes, would have been entirely in keeping with Egyptian tradition which stated that the pharaoh had to be seen to defeat the enemies of Egypt; those who did not actually fight simply invented or borrowed victories which, as they depicted them, became real through the power of art and the written word. This means that a formal inscription carved by a king of Egypt and unsupported by independent collaborative evidence can never be taken as the historical truth. However, an unofficial graffito recovered from the Upper Egyptian island of Sehel (Aswan), and written on behalf of a man named Ti who served under both Hatchepsut and Tuthmosis III, confirms that there was indeed some fighting in the south during Hatchepsut's reign:

The Hereditary Prince and Governor, Treasurer of the King of Lower Egypt, the Sole Friend, Chief Treasurer, the one concerned with the booty, Ti. He says: 'I followed the good god, the King of Upper and Lower Egypt Maatkare, may she live! I saw him [i.e. Hatchepsut] overthrowing the Nubian nomads, their chiefs being brought to him as prisoners. I saw him destroying the land of Nubia while I was in the following of His Majesty . . .'[25]

Ti goes further than the Deir el-Bahri evidence in suggesting that Hatchepsut was actually present during the fighting in Nubia. He himself was present at the battle not as a soldier, but as a bureaucrat. Further confirmatory evidence for at least one Nubian campaign comes from the tomb of Senenmut, where a badly damaged and disjointed series of inscriptions read 'I seized . . .' and later 'the land of Nubia', and from the stela of a man named Djehuty, a witness to the southern fighting, who tells us that he actually saw Hatchepsut on the field of battle, collecting the spoils of war.

There is less direct evidence for military campaigning to the north-east of Egypt, although again the Deir el-Bahri temple does hint at some skirmishes; in at least one inscription it is said of Hatchepsut that 'her arrow is amongst the northerners'. However, it is a consideration of the subsequent conquests of Tuthmosis III which provides the best evidence for the maintenance of firm military control over the north-eastern territories. When Tuthmosis III eventually became sole ruler of Egypt, the client states in Syria and Palestine seized the traditional opportunity to rebel, a reaction which suggests that the death of Hatchepsut may have been viewed as a potential weakening rather than strengthening of Egypt's power in the Levant. The Egyptian army, however, had been properly maintained, the soldiers were ready, the correct administration was in place, and Tuthmosis was able to launch an immediate and successful counter-attack. Tuthmosis, in his role as head of the army throughout the latter part of the co-regency, had already conducted at least one successful campaign in Palestine, during which he had captured the strategically important town of Gaza; by Year 23, the first year of Tuthmosis' solo reign, Gaza is described as 'the town which the ruler had taken'. Tuthmosis went on to become one of Egypt's most successful generals, pushing back the eastern and southern boundaries of the Egyptian Empire until Egypt became without doubt the dominant force in the Mediterranean world. Would his career have been so brilliant had it not been preceded by the reign of Hatchepsut?[26]

Hatchepsut's military policy is perhaps best described as one of unobtrusive control; active defence rather than deliberate offence. While either unwilling or unable to actually expand Egypt's sphere of influence in the near east, she was certainly prepared to fight to maintain the borders of her country. Her military record is in fact stronger than that of Tuthmosis II, who did not lead his campaigns in person, and far more impressive than that of Akhenaten, a male king who showed an extreme reluctance to protect his own interests even though he received a stream of increasingly desperate letters from his Levantine vassals begging him for military assistance. It would certainly be very unfair to draw a direct comparison between the campaigns of Tuthmosis I, Tuthmosis III and Hatchepsut, and then criticize the latter for not adopting a more aggressive stance. It is, in fact, Tuthmosis III who is unusual in this line-up; all the other 18th Dynasty pharaohs embarked on the customary campaigns towards the beginning of their reigns, but only Tuthmosis III made fighting his life's work. After all, although a good military record was a desirable aspect of kingship, not all kings could be lucky enough to participate in a decisive military campaign. The fact that Hatchepsut did not need to fight may actually be taken as an indication of strength rather than weakness. The most successful 18th Dynasty monarch, Amenhotep III, a king who ruled over Egypt at a time of unprecedented prosperity, certainly had a less than impressive war record. This was not through personal cowardice or adherence to a deliberate policy of peace; Amenhotep III did not fight because he did not need to. Throughout his rule Egypt remained the greatest power in the Mediterranean world and, rather than rebel, Egypt's vassals and neighbours stood in awe.

We have ample evidence to show that Hatchepsut's wider foreign policy should be classed as one of adventurous trade and exploration. Her famous expedition to Punt, clearly one of the highlights of her reign, should not be seen as an isolated event but as the climax of a series of trading missions which included visits to Phoenicia to collect the wood which Egypt so badly needed to build her ships, and the exploitation of the copper and turquoise mines in Sinai which is attested by stelae and inscriptions at the Wadi Maghara and Serabit el-Khadim. All of these missions were standard indications of a successful rule, comparable to the exploits of the great pharaohs of the past, and as such were recorded with pride on the walls of the Speos Artemidos temple, Middle Egypt:

Roshawet [Sinai] and Iuu [now unknown] have not remained hidden from my august person, and Punt overflows for me on the fields, its trees bearing fresh myrrh. The roads that were blocked on both sides are now trodden. My army, which was unequipped, has become possessed of riches since I arose as king.[27]

Trade, throughout the 18th Dynasty, was a matter of obtaining luxurious imports rather than, as in the modern western world, the problem of finding markets for exported Egyptian surpluses. The mysterious and exotic Punt, the 'land of the god', had been known since Old Kingdom times as a source of such desirable commodities as myrrh, incense, ebony, ivory, gold and even dancing pygmies, who were particularly prized at the Egyptian court:

You said in your dispatch that you have bought a dwarf of the god's dances . . . like the dwarf whom the god's treasurer Bawerded brought from Punt in the time of King Isesi . . . Come northward to the residence at once! Hurry, and bring with you this dwarf . . . If he goes down into a boat with you, choose trusty men to be beside him on both sides of the boat in case he falls overboard into the water. If he lies down to sleep at night, choose trusty men to be beside him in his tent. Inspect him ten times during the night. My Majesty longs to see this dwarf more than the spoils of the mining country and of Punt.[28]

Expeditions to Punt had been a feature of several Middle Kingdom reigns, and the trading missions of Mentuhotep III, Senwosret I and Amenemhat II had all successfully navigated their way to and from this fabulous land. The exact location of Punt is now a mystery, although the flora and fauna depicted in the reliefs indicate that it must have been an African country, probably situated somewhere along the Eritrean/Ethiopian coast between latitudes 17°N and 12°N. Punt could therefore be reached via the Red Sea port of Quseir which lay at the end of an arduous trek along the desert road from Coptos. The Egyptians, well accustomed to sailing up and down the Nile, were not particularly well versed in the hazards of sea travel, and the long voyage to Punt must have seemed something akin to a journey to the moon for present-day explorers. However, the rewards of such a journey clearly outweighed the risks, and missions to Punt continued during the reigns of Tuthmosis III and Amenhotep III. The tradition of trading with Punt died out during the 20th Dynasty, and by the end of the dynastic period Punt had become an unreal and fabulous land of myths and legends.

We are told that it was actually Amen, not Hatchepsut, who took the decision to send an expedition to Punt during regnal Year 9, and that the king of the gods gave his personal guarantee that the mission would be successful:

Said by Amen, the Lord of the Thrones of the Two Lands: 'Come, come in peace my daughter, the graceful, who art in my heart, King Maatkare . . . I will give thee Punt, the whole of it . . . I will lead [your soldiers] by land and by water, on mysterious shores which join the harbours of incense, the sacred territory of the divine land, my abode of pleasure . . . They will take incense as much as they like. They will load their ships to the satisfaction of their hearts with trees of green [that is, fresh] incense, and all the good things of the land.[29]

The fact that her expedition proved itself able to emulate the glories of former pharaohs, returning in triumph from Punt with ships bursting with wondrous goods, presented the new king with a marvellous propaganda *coup* and an irresistible opportunity to advertise the glories of her reign. The undeniable success of the mission must have made it obvious to even the most hardened of sceptics that the gods were not offended by the female monarch, and that *maat* was indeed present throughout the land. It is therefore no surprise that Hatchepsut deemed the story worthy of inclusion in her mortuary temple. Here the record of the expedition to Punt is preserved in a series of delightful vignettes and brief texts first carved and then painted on the southern half of the middle portico. The prominence of this position (the story of Hatchepsut's divine conception and birth was carved on the opposite side of the same colonnade) gives some indication of the importance which Hatchepsut attached to the tale.

Most unusually, the story of the expedition does not take the form of a sequence of static, lifeless and rather dull images; instead the artists have attempted a realism which is rarely found in monumental Egyptian art. The native people, their animals and even their trees are vibrant with life, providing the viewer with a genuine flavour of this strange foreign land and making it difficult to imagine that the artists who carved the fat queen of Punt or her curious home had not actually left

Egypt's boundaries. Unfortunately, the charm and fine workmanship of the individual scenes has attracted the inevitable treasure hunters, and the story is now to a certain extent spoiled by the gaps which mark the position of stolen blocks. The loss of the blocks depicting the remarkable queen of Punt is particularly to be deplored although fortunately one of these blocks, now safely housed in the Cairo Museum, has been replaced in the temple wall by an exact plaster replica.

Throughout the text Hatchepsut maintains the fiction that her envoy, the Chancellor Neshi, has travelled to Punt in order to extract tribute from the natives who admit their allegiance to the distant King Maatkare. In fact the expedition was a simple trading mission to a land which, occupied by a curious mixture of races, seems to have been a well-established trading post. The Puntites traded not only in their own produce of incense, ebony and short-horned cattle, but in goods from other African states including gold, ivory and animal skins. In return for a vast selection of luxury items, Neshi is to offer a rather feeble selection of beads and weapons; as Naville, a man of his time, commented in 1898, he offers the men of Punt '. . . trinkets like those which are used at the present day in trading with the negroes of Central Africa':[30]

The necklaces brought to Punt are in great number; they perhaps had only a slight value; but they pleased the Africans, as they now please the Negros, to whom articles of ornament which are in themselves things of no intrinsic value, or cheap stuffs with showy colours, or cowries are often given in exchange, things valueless in themselves, but much in request amongst these African peoples.[31]

Naville forgets to mention that the fact that Neshi was accompanied by at least five shiploads of marines may have encouraged the Puntites to participate in this rather one-sided trade.

Punt had many desirable treasures, but was particularly rich in the precious resins (myrrh, *Commiphora myrrha*, and frankincense, *Boswellia carterii*) which Egypt needed for the manufacture of incense. Incense could be made from either a single aromatic tree gum or a mixture of them; a favourite Egyptian incense known as *kyphi* was said to contain as many as sixteen different ingredients, but the recipe is now unfortunately lost. Incense was burned in great quantities in the daily temple rituals, and employed in the formulation of perfumes, the fumigation of houses, the mummification of the dead and even in medical prescriptions, where those suffering from sour breath – women in particular – were advised to chew little balls of myrrh to relieve their symptoms. This might explain why the odour of Amen, in the legend of the divine birth of kings, is reported to smell like the odours of Punt. The Punt brands of incense were highly prized, but could not be found in any great quantity within Egypt's borders where trees of any kind were rare. Therefore Neshi was dispatched to obtain not only supplies of the incense itself, but living trees complete with roots which could be re-planted in the gardens of the temple of Amen. The thirty or so trees or parts of tree depicted in the Deir el-Bahri scenes seem to represent either two different species or the same tree at different seasons, as one type is covered in foliage while the other remains bare. The trees have been tentatively identified as representing frankincense and myrrh, although it is unfortunate that different experts cannot agree which type of tree is which.

Fig. 5.2   Tree being transported from Punt

Five Egyptian sailing ships
equipped with oars are shown arriving at Punt where the sailors dis-
embark into small boats, unload
their cargo and make for the
shore. Here they find a village set
in a forest of ebony, incense and
palm trees, its houses curious con-
ical structures resembling large
beehives made of plaited palm
fronds and set on poles above the
ground so that their only means of
access is by ladder. The inhabitants
of the village are a curiously
mixed bunch, some being depicted as black or brown Africans
while others are physically very
similar to the Egyptian visitors.
However, the animals shown are
clearly African in origin. There

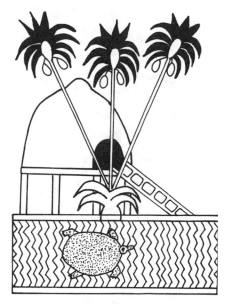

Fig. 5.3   House on stilts, Punt

are both long- and short-horned cattle, long-eared domesticated dogs,
panthers or leopards, a badly damaged representation of a creature
which might possibly be a rhinoceros and tall giraffes, which were
considered so extraordinary that they were led to the ships and taken
back to Egypt. The tree-tops are full of playful monkeys and there are
nesting birds, a clear indication that it is spring.

The Egyptian envoy Neshi, unarmed but carrying a staff of office and
escorted by eight armed soldiers and their captain, is greeted in a
friendly manner by the chief of Punt who is himself accompanied by
his immediate family of one wife, one daughter and two sons. The
slender chief is obviously not of Negro extraction; his skin is painted a
light shade of red, he has fine Egyptian-style facial features and an
aquiline nose. It is his long thin goatee beard, and the series of bracelets
adorning his left leg, which mark him out as a foreigner. However his
grotesquely fat wife, with her wobbling, blancmange-like folds of flab
and enormous thighs emphasized by her see-through costume, presents
a marked contrast to the stereotyped image of the upper-class Egyptian
woman as a slender and serene beauty. Her appearance must have seemed

extraordinary to the ancient Egyptians and even Naville, normally the most courteous of commentators, found the portrait of the queen and her already plump young daughter highly unnerving:

> Their stoutness and deformity might be supposed at first sight to be the result of disease, if we did not know from the narratives of travellers of our own time that this kind of figure is the ideal type of female beauty among the savage tribes of inner Africa. We can thus trace to a very high antiquity this barbarous taste, which was adopted by the Punites [sic], although they were probably not native Africans.[32]

Fig. 5.4   The obese queen of Punt

We can only wonder how the queen of Punt, who is evidently too fat to walk and is therefore carried everywhere by a disproportionately small donkey, ever managed to ascend the ladder which led to her home.

The Egyptians present the natives with a small pile of trivia; amongst the trinkets shown we can distinguish beads, bracelets, an axe and a single dagger in its sheath. The Puntites appear to receive these less than impressive offerings with delight, and cordial relations are so well established that Neshi orders that the appropriate preparations be made to entertain the chief of Punt in his tent:

> The preparing of the tent for the royal messenger and his soldiers, in the harbours of frankincense of Punt, on the shore of the sea, in order to receive the chiefs of this land, and to present them with bread, beer, wine, meat, fruits and all the good things of the land of Egypt, as has been ordered by the sovereign [life, strength, health].[33]

It is possible that the expedition spent several weeks travelling westwards to the interior of Punt escorted by Puntite guides and collecting both ebony and incense. It would almost certainly have been necessary for the ships to wait for the reversal of the winds which would carry them back to Egypt. However, when next we see the expedition the ships are being loaded for the return journey. Egyptians and Puntites labour side by side as baskets of myrrh and frankincense, bags of gold and incense, ebony, elephant tusks, panther skins and a troop of over-exuberant monkeys are all taken aboard. Truly, 'Never were brought such things to any king, since the world was.'[34]

The return journey is left to the imagination, presumably because it would not have added to our appreciation of the vast treasure being carried to Egypt. Instead, we skip directly to the unloading of the ships in the presence of Hatchepsut herself. We are told that this momentous event occurred at Thebes although, given that the River Nile was not yet connected to the Red Sea, it seems unlikely that the ships were able to sail directly from Punt to Thebes. There is, however, some evidence to suggest that sea-going ships, originally constructed in the Nile Valley, were dismantled and carried in kit-form overland both to and from the Red Sea port of Quseir. The

Fig. 5.5   Ape from Punt

final leg of the sea–land–river return journey, the voyage from Coptos to
Thebes, could therefore indeed have been by boat. Papyrus Harris I, a
contemporary text detailing the reign of the 20th Dynasty King Ramesses
III, includes an explicit description of a return from Punt:

They arrived safely at the desert-country of Coptos: they moored in peace,
carrying the goods they had brought. They [the goods] were loaded, in travelling overland, upon asses and upon men, being re-loaded into vessels on the
river at the harbour of Coptos. They [the goods and the Puntites] were sent
forward downstream, arriving in festivity, bringing tribute into the royal
presence.[35]

*Fig. 5.6   Tuthmosis III offers before
the barque of Amen*

The Red Sea coastal area, with
its desert conditions, lack of fresh
water and great distance from the
known security of the Nile Valley,
was not considered a suitable place
to live, and no fixed ports were
maintained along its length.
Quseir, the traditional departure
point for voyages south, did not in
any case have the satisfactory harbour facilities which would war-
rant the establishment of a permanent port.

Whichever the port of arrival,
we once again see the parade of
luxury goods as the expedition disembarks. In fact, more space is devoted to the loading and unloading of the vessels than is given
to the mysteries of the land of
Punt itself. Egyptian sailors
struggle under the weight of incense trees temporarily planted in
baskets and slung between two carrying poles while behind them
come men carrying ebony and

boomerangs, amphorae filled with precious unguents and curiously shaped blocks of resin. Yet other sailors drive the herds of cattle and one even leads a cynocephalus ape, highly valued as the sacred animal of Thoth, god of wisdom. The precious silver, gold, lapis lazuli and malachite are carefully weighed in the scales of Thoth while a motley collection of foreigners, both Puntites and Nubians, disembarks and kneels before the King.

Hatchepsut, the ever-dutiful daughter, dedicates the best of the goods to her father Amen:

The King himself, King of Upper and Lower Egypt, Maatkare, takes the good things of Punt, and the valuables of the divine land, presenting the gifts of the southern countries, the tributes of the vile Kush, the boxes [of gold and precious stones] of the land of the negroes to Amen-Re, the Lord of the Throne of the Two Lands. The King Maatkare, she is living, she lasts, she is full of joy, she rules over the land like Re eternally.[36]

Hatchepsut stands proud before the god himself. Senenmut, the king's favourite, prominent in his role of Overseer of the Granaries of Amen, stands with Neshi to praise the king on the success of her mission; all three figures and much of the accompanying text have been hacked off the wall in antiquity. Meanwhile, in the background of just one scene, the figure of Tuthmosis III appears, wearing the regal blue crown and holding out two tubs of incense to the sacred barque of Amen.

6

Propaganda in Stone

𓊪𓏏𓇳𓈖𓂝𓅓𓏏𓆇𓊹

*I am his daughter in very truth, who works for him and knows what he
desires. My reward from my father is life, stability, dominion upon the
Horus Throne of all the Living, like Re, for ever.*[1]

King Hatchepsut embarked at once upon an ambitious programme of
public works, restoring the monuments of past pharaohs and establishing new temples for the glory of the gods. The benefits of this
policy were to be felt up and down the Nile, but it is for the monumental work in and around Thebes that her reign is now best remembered. Such a programme was of threefold importance. At its most
obvious level it impressed upon the people the economic prosperity of
the new regime. Although Hatchepsut, as absolute ruler, had no need to
pay for land, labour or materials, she did need to feed her workforce,
and only the more affluent pharaohs could afford to dispense the daily
rations of bread, beer and grain which were given in lieu of wages.
Similarly, only a well-established and well-organized monarch could
boast the efficient and far-sighted bureaucracy necessary to implement
such labour-intensive plans. The massive stone buildings now starting
to rise amidst the mud-brick houses of Thebes and the other major
centres of population served as a constant reminder that there was a
powerful pharaoh on the throne. They were, as Winlock has remarked,
'everlasting propaganda in stone'.[2]

At the same time the new buildings, literally intended to last as
'mansions of millions of years' (temples) or 'houses of eternity' (rock-
cut tombs), would ensure that the name of their founder would live
with them for ever. The preservation of the personal name, always an
important consideration for upper-class Egyptians, was particularly important to Hatchepsut, who seems to have understood that she would
need to provide constant justifications of her own atypical reign. If her
monuments could be larger and more impressive than those of her

predecessors, then so much the better; a flattering comparison with the past was often a useful means of stressing the achievements of the present. Finally, the new temples would serve as perhaps the greatest offering that a king could make to the gods; they would be a tangible and permanent proof of the king's extreme piety, and would ensure that the gods would cooperate in maintaining the success of the reign.

The larger-scale stone buildings possessed one very useful feature which was quickly recognized and exploited. Their walls provided the new monarch with an enormous, obvious and permanent billboard upon which to speak directly to both her present and future subjects. Indeed, there was no other effective means of conveying general propaganda to the people. Word of mouth was doubtless used on a daily basis to communicate more specific and ephemeral matters, but spoken messages would surely perish with time, while the writings preserved on fragile papyri and ostraca would never reach a wide audience. Hatchepsut, never one to miss an opportunity, soon became adept at using the walls of her own buildings to proclaim her own glories and justify her own reign.

In the deserts of Middle Egypt, approximately one mile to the southeast of Beni Hassan, Hatchepsut endowed two temples dedicated to the obscure deity Pakhet, 'She who Scratches', a fierce lion-headed goddess of the desert, worshipped locally. Much later the Greeks equated Pakhet with their own goddess Artemis, and her larger temple, cut into a small, steep-sided valley, is now widely known by its classical name of Speos Artemidos, or the 'Grotto of Artemis'. Its local name is the Istabl Antar (the stable of Antar; Antar was a pre-Islamic warrior poet), while the neighbouring smaller temple of Pakhet is known as the Speos Batn el-Bakarah. The Speos Artemidos survived the reigns of both Tuthmosis III and Akhenaten virtually intact, but was unfortunately 'restored' by Seti I who added his own texts to the previously unadorned sanctuary. The Speos Batn el-Bakarah was badly defaced during the reign of Tuthmosis III.

The Speos Artemidos consisted of two chambers: an outer pillared vestibule or hall which led via a short passage to an inner sanctuary cut into the living rock. A niche set into the back wall of the sanctuary, intended to house the cult statue of Pakhet, formed the religious focus of the shrine. The internal walls bore few decorations, although a series of texts and scenes carved on the south wall of the vestibule, around the

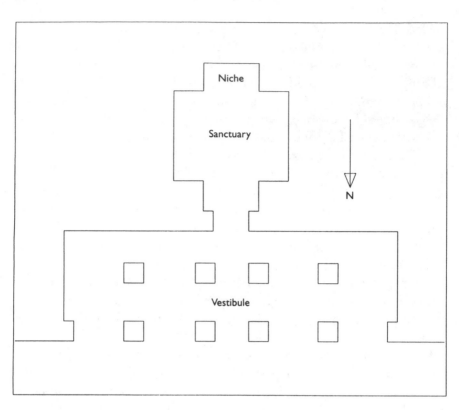

Fig. 6.1   Plan of the Speos Artemidos

doorway to the sanctuary, were intended to re-emphasize Hatchepsut's filial bond with Amen, the father who had chosen her as ruler of Egypt. Here we can read Amen's words as he proclaims Hatchepsut's kingship:

Utterance by Amen-Re, Lord of the Thrones of the Two Lands . . ., 'O my beloved daughter Maatkare, I am thy beloved father. I establish for thee thy rank in the kingship of the Two Lands. I have fixed thy titulary.'[3]

The accompanying scene shows Hatchepsut kneeling before the seated Amen, while the fierce Pakhet extends her left arm and pledges her support for the new king: 'my fiery breath being as a fire against thine enemies . . .' Thoth then announces the accession of Hatchepsut before the assembly of gods. Finally we see Hatchepsut offering incense

and libations to Pakhet who again extends her rather bloodthirsty blessing: 'I give thee all strength, all might, all lands and every hill country
crushed beneath thy sandals like Re.'

However, it is the lengthy text carved high above the pillars across the
front of the temple which is of great interest to students of Egyptian
history. Here Hatchepsut makes a bold pronouncement of the policy of
her reign; a policy of renewal and restoration. She wishes her readers to
understand that, from the very moment of her creation she, Hatchepsut,
was destined to restore the purity of the Egyptian temples to their
former glories:

I have done these things by the device of my heart. I have never slumbered as
one forgetful, but have made strong what was decayed. I have raised up what
was dismembered, even from the first time when the Asiatics were in Avaris of
the North Land, with roving hordes in the midst of them overthrowing what
had been made; they ruled without Re . . . I have banished the abominations of
the gods, and the earth has removed their footprints.[4]

Here Hatchepsut is deliberately invoking the legend of the dreadful
maat-less Second Intermediate Period – a much exaggerated version
of real events – in order to underline the peace and stability of her
own reign. Indeed, she is the first of the post-Ahmose pharaohs to
express a loathing of the Hyksos, establishing a useful tradition of
hostility and hatred which many later rulers were to copy. Hatchepsut was not a woman to allow a few factual inaccuracies to hinder
her from writing a revised version of history, and she now claims
credit for both ridding the land of the detested foreigners and for
restoring the monuments and indeed the religion of her ancestors,
pious acts which would have met with approval from gods and mortals alike. There can be no truth at all in her boast that she rid Egypt
of the Asiatics; Hyksos rule had ended many years before Hatchepsut
came to the throne. Similarly, her claim that the Hyksos heathens
'ruled without Re' is also untrue; as we have already seen, the
Hyksos rulers adapted their own religion to that of their adopted
country and several Hyksos kings actually bore names compounded
with that of Re. However, in Hatchepsut's eyes, these exaggerations
would not have been lies. The role of pharaoh was a permanent one
which passed from individual to individual and, as the current office-

holder, Hatchepsut was quite entitled to use the achievements of
previous pharaohs when and as she saw fit.

There is, however, more than a grain of truth in Hatchepsut's boast
that she undertook the restoration of the monuments of her forebears,
particularly those of Middle Egypt which had suffered badly during the
Second Intermediate Period. Earlier in the inscription we are given
specific details of Hatchepsut's repairs to the temple of Hathor at Cusae,
a building which had fallen into such disuse that 'the earth had swal-
lowed up its noble sanctuary, and children danced upon its roof'. Cusae,
an Upper Egyptian town approximately forty miles to the south of the
Speos Artemidos, had been at the very limit of the Hyksos sphere of
influence and had suffered badly during the late 17th Dynasty wars of
liberation.

The tradition of preserving or restoring the monuments of the ancestors was one dear to the heart of all Egyptians; the Middle Kingdom
text 'The Instruction for Merykare' makes the position absolutely clear:

Do not destroy the monuments of another! . . . Do not build your tomb by
demolishing what was already made in order to use it for that which you wish
to make . . . A blow will be repaid in kind.[5]

A king who respects the monuments of his ancestors will in turn have
his own buildings respected; a king who deliberately demolishes an
earlier monument is storing up trouble for himself. It is not even acceptable to plunder ancient ruins in order to salvage building materials for
the erection of a magnificent new edifice; decayed older buildings
should be left alone, and fresh building supplies sought for the new.
However, it seems to be enough to merely respect an ancient monument. The king has no particular duty to restore any such ruin although, if he does, this will undoubtedly be interpreted as an act of filial
piety pleasing to both the gods and the ancestors. Restoration of a
monument, the bringing of order to chaos and the remembrance of the
name of a past king, could all be seen as a small echo of the role of the
pharaoh as the upholder of *maat*. The principle that monuments should
be preserved was never in doubt. Hatchepsut, however, did not always
practise what she preached. At Karnak she demolished a gateway built
by Tuthmosis II, and she ruined her father's hypostyle hall by removing
its wooden roof and erecting a pair of obelisks in the now-open space,

although she claims in mitigation that Tuthmosis I himself ordered her to make this alteration. Potentially more serious was the fact that her workmen dismantled a sanctuary of Amenhotep I and Ahmose Nefertari which stood in the path of the processional way leading to her mortuary temple at Deir el-Bahri.

Hatchepsut had started her regal building programme early, anticipating her elevation to the throne by ordering a pair of obelisks from the Aswan granite quarry while still queen regent. By the time these had been cut she was an acknowledged king, and her newly acquired royal titles could be engraved on their tips. Obelisks – New Kingdom cult objects intended to be a stone representation of the first beams of light to illuminate the world – were tall, thin, square stone shafts tapering to a pyramid-shaped peak. Traditionally erected in pairs before the entrance to the temple, their twin tips were sheathed in gold foil so that they sparkled and shimmered in the rays of the fierce Egyptian sun. Obelisks were dedicated to the god by the king, and their shafts contained columns of hieroglyphs giving details of their erection and dedication. However, they were also regarded as living beings; obelisks were given personal names, and offerings were made to them.

In continuing the newly established obelisk tradition, Hatchepsut was once again emulating the deeds of her esteemed father who, with the help of Ineni, had been the first monarch to erect a pair of obelisks before the entrance to the Karnak temple. Indeed, Hatchepsut tells us how Tuthmosis himself had urged his daughter to follow his precedent: 'It is your father, the King of Upper and Lower Egypt Aakheperkare [Tuthmosis I], who gave you the instruction to raise obelisks.'[6] To Senenmut fell the responsibility of overseeing operations and, in an inscription carved at the Aswan granite quarry, we see him standing to present his work to his mistress who is still only a 'King's Great Wife':

... the Hereditary Prince, Count, great favourite of the God's Wife ... the Treasurer of the King of Lower Egypt, Chief Steward of the Princess Neferure, may she live, Senenmut, in order to inspect the work on the two great obelisks of Heh. It happened just as it was commanded that everything be done; it happened because of the power of Her Majesty.[7]

The successful planning, cutting, transportation and erection of a pair of obelisks was a remarkable feat of engineering for a society totally reliant

on man–power, river transport and human ingenuity. Some successful
New Kingdom examples reached over 30 m (98 ft) in height and
weighed over 450 tons (457,221 kg) while Hatchepsut's 'unfinished
obelisk', abandoned in the Aswan quarry after it developed a fatal crack,
would have stood over 41 m (134 ft) tall and weighed an estimated
1,000 tons (1,016,046 kg).[8] The work in the granite quarry was physically demanding, labour intensive and mind–numbingly repetitive. After
a suitable band of rock had been identified, a series of small fires was lit
and doused with water to crack the surface of the granite which could
then be worked with relative ease. Once the uppermost face had been
prepared the sides were cut not by saw – the granite was far too hard –
but by teams of men rhythmically bouncing balls of dolerite (an even
harder rock) against the granite surface. The underside was then prepared in the same way until the obelisk was lying supported by isolated
spurs of the mother-rock and a large quantity of packing stones. The
supporting spurs were then knocked away, the packing carefully removed, and the obelisk was ready to be dragged to the canal where it
would be loaded on a barge and towed first to the River Nile and
thence to Thebes. The classical historian Pliny, fascinated by the techniques developed to load the unwieldy obelisks on the barges during
the Roman Period, noted how:

A canal was dug from the river Nile to the spot where the obelisk lay and
two broad vessels, loaded with blocks of similar stone a foot square – the
cargo of each amounting to double the size and consequently double the
weight of the obelisks – was put beneath it. The extremities of the obelisk
remaining supported by the opposite sides of the canal. The blocks of stone
were removed and the vessels, being thus gradually lightened, received their
burden.[9]

Hatchepsut included Senenmut's work amongst the major achievements of her reign, recording the transportation of the obelisks both in
a series of illustrations on blocks from the Chapelle Rouge at Karnak
and on the lower southern portico of her Deir el-Bahri mortuary
temple. Here we are shown the two obelisks lying lashed to sledges as
they are towed on a sycamore wood barge towards Thebes by a fleet of
twenty-seven smaller boats powered by over 850 straining oarsmen.
Fortunately, the flow of the river helps the barge on its way. The

transport of the obelisks is an important civil and religious event, and the great barge is accompanied by three escort ships whose priests appear to be blessing the proceedings. The two obelisks are not shown as we might expect, lying side by side, but are lying base-to-base, their tips pointing up and down stream respectively. To transport the obelisks in this way would have required an enormously long barge (over 61 m, or 200 ft), and the difficulties in handling such a long vessel would have been daunting even for the Egyptians, who were accomplished boat-men. It seems highly likely that this artistic convention intended to stress the fact that there were actually two obelisks rather than one, and that the obelisks were in fact transported side by side. Upon their arrival in Thebes there is a public celebration. A bull is killed, and further offerings are made to the gods. Of course, it is Hatchepsut, not Senen-mut, who takes full credit for the achievement, and on the displaced blocks of the Chapelle Rouge we see the new king presenting the obelisks to her father Amen. The bases of these two obelisks may still be seen at the eastern end of the Amen temple at Karnak; their shafts have long been destroyed.

Hatchepsut's second pair of granite obelisks was commissioned to mark her *sed*-jubilee in Year 15. This time the granite came from the island of Schel at Aswan, and the work was under the control of the steward Amenhotep:

The real confidant of the King, his beloved, the director of the works on the two big obelisks, the chief priest of Khnum, Satis and Anukis, Amenhotep.[10]

The new obelisks were erected in the hypostyle hall of Tuthmosis I – its roof and pillars being removed for the occasion – and here one still stands. It is now, at 29.5 m (96 ft 9 in) high, the tallest standing obelisk in Egypt. The inscriptions carved on the shaft and base once again follow the same old themes, stressing Hatchepsut's relationship with both her earthly and her heavenly father and emphasizing her right to rule, but we are also provided with some original details concerning the commis-sioning of the monument:

My majesty commissioned the work on it in Year 15, day 1 of the 2nd month of winter, ending in Year 16, the last day of the 4th month of summer, making seven months from the commissioning in the quarry. I did this for him

[Amen] with affection as a king does for a god. It was my wish to make it for him, gilded with electrum . . . My mouth is effective in what it speaks; I do not go back on what I have said. I gave the finest electrum for it, which I measured in gallons like sacks of grain. My Majesty called up this quantity beyond which the Two Lands had ever seen. The ignorant know this as well as the wise.[11]

While Hatchepsut's first pair of obelisks was entirely covered in gold foil, 'two great obelisks, their height 108 cubits, wrought in their entirety with gold, filling the two lands [with] their rays',[12] the second pair had gold leaf applied only to their upper parts.

The erection of the obelisks was perhaps the most spectacular of the improvements which Hatchepsut made to *Ipet-Issut*, or 'The Most Select of Places', now better known as the Karnak temple complex. The Karnak temple had retained its same basic 12th Dynasty form throughout both the Second Intermediate Period and the reigns of Kamose and Ahmose. However, during the time of Amenhotep I, when the war of liberation was completed and the sandstone and limestone quarries had been re-opened, serious building works commenced. From this reign onwards, each succeeding New Kingdom king attempted to outdo his predecessors in the scale of his or her embellishments, and the temple slowly grew from a relatively simple collection of mud-brick chapels and shrines linked by processional ways to become the vast religious complex whose magnificent ruins may be seen today.

Although the Great Temple of Amen remained the focus of the site, and the Theban Triad (Amen, Mut and Khonsu) were always its principal gods, a variety of other deities was worshipped at Karnak and there were eventually chapels dedicated to Montu, Ptah, Sekhmet, Osiris, Opet and Maat. There was a substantial temple dedicated to Amen's spouse, Mut, which stood within its own enclosure wall and which was linked to the Great Temple by a paved processional way, and a much smaller temple of their moon-god son Khonsu situated close to that of his father, Amen. The Karnak temple was connected to the nearby temple of Amen–Min at Luxor by a processional way lined by sphinxes, and was linked to the River Nile by a system of canals.

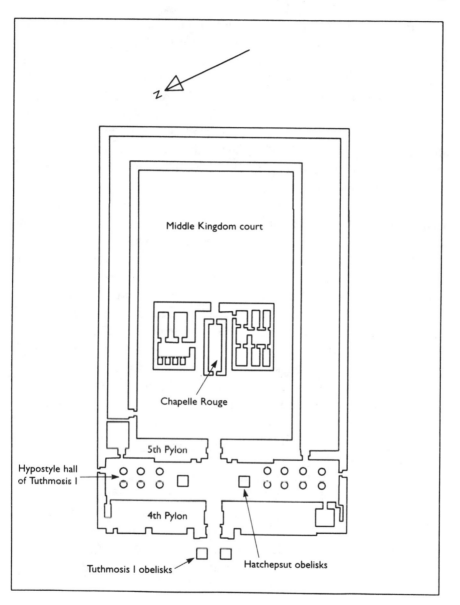

Fig. 6.2   Reconstruction of the Amen temple at Karnak during the reign of Hatchepsut

Within the grounds of the temple complex was a small mud-brick palace which, lacking any sleeping quarters, was used during the celebration of some of the religious rituals associated with kingship, particularly the coronation. We know that during Hatchepsut's reign this palace was situated on the north side of the temple façade, but unfortunately no trace of it now remains. The larger, fully equipped palace where the King and her retinue stayed while visiting Thebes is also lost; almost certainly built on lower ground (the Karnak temple was on the raised mound of the old township), this palace is probably now below the level of the ground water.

Amenhotep I had started the Karnak embellishment ball rolling by adding an alabaster kiosk or barque shrine, a monumental gateway, a limestone replica of the White Chapel of Senwosret I and a cluster of smaller shrines or chapels. Tuthmosis I made far more extensive improvements; in addition to his famous pair of obelisks, he built two white stone pylons or gateways (pylons IV and V) which were connected by the hypostyle entrance hall where Hatchepsut later placed her obelisks, and he extended the processional ways. Even the short-lived Tuthmosis II undertook some improvements to the temple, although a few re-used blocks are now all that remain of his efforts.

Hatchepsut's main contribution to the Temple of Amen was her Chapelle Rouge, the red quartzite barque sanctuary of Amen which has already been discussed in some detail in Chapter 4. The Chapelle stood on a raised platform immediately in front of the original mud-brick and limestone Middle Kingdom temple, flanked to the north and south by groups of smaller sandstone cult shrines, the so-called 'Hatchepsut Suite' whose decorations show the king making offerings before a variety of gods. At the same time improvements were made to the processional way which linked the temple of Amen to the temple of his consort Mut, and a series of wayside kiosks was built to provide resting places for the barque of Amen as it travelled from temple to temple within the Karnak complex. A new pylon (pylon VIII), a magnificent monumental gateway passing between two tall towers each topped by a gold-tipped flagpole, was the first such gateway to be built on the southern axis of the temple. This pylon was originally decorated with images of Hatchepsut as king, but suffered at the hands of later 'restorers', so that Tuthmosis III and Seti I are now shown on the reliefs and Tuthmosis III and Tuthmosis II (who replaces Hatchepsut) appear on the doorway.

The tourists who annually swarm into Thebes seldom depart from the ancient city of Amen without visiting the magnificent natural amphitheatre of Deir el-Bahri, where the hills of the Libyan range present their most imposing aspect. Leaving the plain by a narrow gorge, whose walls of naked rock are honey-combed with tombs, the traveller emerges into a wide open space bounded at its furthest end by a semi-circular wall of cliffs. These cliffs of white limestone, which time and sun have coloured rosy yellow, form an absolutely vertical barrier. They are accessible only from the north by a steep and difficult path leading to the summit of the ridge that divides Deir el-Bahri from the wild and desolate Valley of the Tombs of the Kings. Built against these cliffs, and even as it were rooted into their sides by subterranean chambers, is the temple of which Mariette said that 'it is an exception and an accident in the architectural life of Egypt'.[13]

Hatchepsut's mortuary temple, *Djeser-Djeseru* or 'Holiest of the Holy', was set in a natural bay in the Theban cliffs on the West Bank of the Nile close to the ruined mortuary temple of the 11th Dynasty King Mentuhotep II and almost directly opposite the Karnak temple complex. Later Tuthmosis III was to choose a nearby site for his own West Bank temple dedicated to Amen, *Djeser-Akhet* or 'Holy Horizon'. The name Deir el-Bahri, which literally means 'Monastery of the North', and which is now often used to refer both to the general area and more specifically to Hatchepsut's mortuary temple, is a reference to the mud-brick Coptic monastery established at the site during the fifth century AD.

The Deir el-Bahri bay had for a long time been revered as a holy place associated with the cult of the mother-goddess Hathor in her role as Goddess of the West or Chieftainess of Thebes. For this reason it had been chosen as the location of the mortuary temple of Nebhepetre Mentuhotep II, the Theban founder of the Middle Kingdom. Mentuhotep II had been the epitome of a successful Egyptian king. He had united Egypt at the end of the First Intermediate Period, instigated success-ful campaigns against the traditional enemies to the north and south, established a new capital at Thebes and, throughout his 51-year reign, undertaken prolific building works, including the restoration of ancient monuments and the construction of new buildings. The parallel be-tween his glorious reign and that of Tuthmosis I must have been obvious and it is not surprising that Hatchepsut, ever prone to hero-worship Tuthmosis I, held her 'father Mentuhotep II'[14] in special regard.

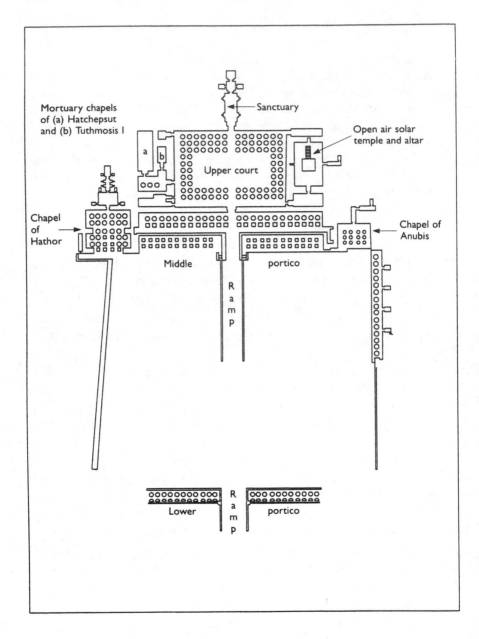

Mortuary chapels
of (a) Hatchepsut
and (b) Tuthmosis I

Sanctuary

Open air solar
temple and altar

a   b

Upper court

Chapel
of
Hathor

Chapel of
Anubis

Middle   portico

R
a
m
p

Lower   portico

R
a
m
p

Fig. 6.3   Plan of Djeser-Djeseru

Mentuhotep had modelled his funerary monument, 'Glorious are the Seats of Nebhepetre', on the Old Kingdom pyramid complexes, and his was the first temple in Egypt to utilize terraces so that different parts of the building were constructed at different levels with the most sacred part of the temple cut directly into the Theban mountain. Unfortunately, the temple was ruined in antiquity and its original plan is now uncertain, although it seems that the sequence of terraces rose to a solid mastaba- or pyramid-like core. It was these terraces which first inspired the architects of Tuthmosis II, the initial 18th Dynasty developer of the site, and the original plans for the New Kingdom temple adhered fairly faithfully to the Middle Kingdom model. However, with the untimely death of Tuthmosis II, the building works were halted, the plans were redrawn on a far more ambitious scale, and *Djeser-Djeseru* became very much Hatchepsut's own monument, an architectural masterpiece providing a superb example of a manmade object designed to fit perfectly into its natural setting. The beauties of *Djeser-Djeseru* have inspired many egyptologists to flights of purple prose:

It is built at the base of the rugged Theban cliffs, and commands the plain in magnificent fashion; its white colonnades rising, terrace above terrace, until it is backed by the golden living rock. The ivory white walls of courts, side chambers and colonnades, have polished surfaces which give an alabaster-like effect. They are carved with a fine art, figures and hieroglyphs being filled in with rich yellow colour, the glow of which against the white gives an effect of warmth and beauty quite indescribable.[15]

Few who have enjoyed the privilege of visiting Deir el-Bahri would argue with this assessment, and today *Djeser-Djeseru* remains beyond doubt one of the most beautiful buildings in the world. It certainly occupies a unique place in the history of Egyptian architecture, and indeed the columned porticoes which provide a striking contrast of light and shade across the front of the building appear to many modern eyes more Greek than Egyptian in style, provoking anachronistic but flattering comparisons with classical temple architecture in its most pure form. Only Winlock, the long-term excavator of *Djeser-Djeseru*, has gone on record as expressing his doubts about the magnificence of the edifice, and even he reserves his criticism for its construction rather than its design:

Unquestionably, when it was completed the building was far more imposing than its eleventh dynasty model, and its plan had been adapted to fit its magnificent surroundings in a wholly masterful way. But whenever we have had occasion to examine its shoddy, jerry-built foundations, we have had an unpleasant feeling of sham behind all this impressiveness which up to that time had not been especially characteristic of Egyptian architects. Possibly Senenmut was a victim of necessity and speed was required of him – or perhaps there is some more venal explanation.[16]

The architect of this masterpiece is generally assumed to be Hatchepsut's favourite Senenmut, who numbers amongst his titles 'Controller of Works in Djeser-Djeseru'. However Senenmut never specifically claims the title of architect, a strange omission for one not normally shy of listing his own accomplishments, and it seems that the Chief Treasurer Djehuty, who '. . . acted as chief, giving directions, I led the craftsman to work in the works of Djeser-Djeseru', may well have played a major part in its development. Other high-ranking courtiers, including the Vizier (unnamed, but almost certainly Hapuseneb who is credited with the building of Hatchepsut's tomb) and the Second Prophet of Amen, Puyemre, also had some involvement in its construction; all of these officials are known to have been the recipients of so-called 'name stones', building blocks donated to the construction project by the ordinary citizens of Thebes. These roughly cut stones, recovered from the foundations of the Valley temple, all bear the cartouche of Maatkare plus an additional hieratic inscription detailing the date that they were sent to the building site, the name of the sender and the name of the recipient. Further bricks recovered from the Valley temple are stamped with the cartouches of Hatchepsut and Tuthmosis I, which appear side by side.

The name of Tuthmosis I is also to be found amongst the engraved scarabs which formed a part of the temple foundation deposits. These deposits – offerings intended to preserve the name of the builder and to ensure good luck in the founding of the temple – were buried with ceremony in small mud-brick-lined pits at every important point around the boundaries of the temple and its grounds.[17] They included a mixture of amulets, scarabs, foods, perfumes and miniature models of the tools which would be used in the building of the temple. The inscriptions all make it clear that Hatchepsut alone was to be regarded as the temple's founder:[18]

She made it as a monument to her father Amen on the occasion of stretching the cord over *Djeser Djeseru*, [the ritual laying out of the temple ground-plan] may she live forever, like Re!

Hatchepsut intended her new temple to house both her own mortuary chapel and, on a slightly smaller scale, that of her father, Tuthmosis I. The mortuary chapel in its most simple form, as provided for a private individual, was the place where the living could go to make the offerings of food, drink and incense which would sustain the Ka or soul of the deceased in the Afterlife. The cult-statue, a representation of the dead person which stood within the chapel, became the focus for these daily offerings as it was understood that the soul could actually take up residence within the statue. A royal mortuary chapel, however, was not simply a cafeteria for the deceased. The divine king, once dead, could become associated with a number of important deities, particularly Osiris and Re, both of whom represented a potential Afterlife; the king could choose whether to spend eternity sailing daily across the sky in the solar boat with Re, or relaxing in the Field of Reeds with Osiris. The royal mortuary chapels reflected these associations, providing a dark and gloomy shrine for the worship of Osiris and a light open-air court for the worship of Re. During the New Kingdom they also reflected the growing power of Amen. Amen now started to play a prominent role in the scenes which decorate the walls, and his shrine now formed the focus of the mortuary chapel.

All these elements were to be found at *Djeser-Djeseru*, which was designed as a multi-functional temple with a complex of shrines devoted to the worship of various deities. In addition to the mortuary temples of Hatchepsut and Tuthmosis I, there were twin chapels dedicated to the local goddess Hathor and to Anubis, smaller shrines consecrated to the memory of Hatchepsut's ancestors, and even a solar temple, its roof open to the cloudless Theban sky, dedicated to the worship of the sun god Re-Harakte. The main shrine was, however, devoted to the cult of Amen Holiest of the Holy, a variant of Amen with whom Hatchepsut would become one after death. It was as the focus of the Amen-based 'Feast of the Valley', an annual festival of death and renewal, that *Djeser-Djeseru* played an important part in Theban religious life.

The Feast of the Valley was celebrated at new moon during the second month of *Shemu* or summer. Amen normally dwelt in splendid isolation in the sanctuary of his own great temple at the heart of the Karnak complex. Here he spent the days and nights in his dark and lonely shrine, visited only by the priests responsible for performing the rituals of washing and dressing the cult-statue, and by those who tempted him daily with copious offerings of meat, bread, wine and beer. However, on the appointed day he would abandon the gloom of his torchlit home and, accompanied by the statues of Mut and Khonsu, would cross the river to spend the night with Hathor at *Djeser-Djeseru*.

With an escort of priests, musicians, incense-bearers, dancers and acrobats and doubtless an excited crowd of Thebans, and with his own golden barque carried high on the shoulders of his servants, Amen made his way in the bright sunlight along the processional avenue to the canal. Here he embarked on his barge, sailed in state across the Nile and navigated his way through the network of canals which linked the mortuary temples of the West Bank. He disembarked at the small Valley Temple situated on the desert edge (now entirely destroyed) and, after the performance of a religious rite, proceeded along the gently sloping causeway which, aligned exactly on Karnak, was lined with pairs of painted sphinxes. Along the route there was a small barque shrine where his bearers could pause if necessary before passing into the precincts of the temple proper. That same evening many Theban families would set off in procession for the West Bank where they too were to spend the night, not in a temple, but in the private tomb-chapels of their relations and ancestors. The hours of darkness were spent drinking and feasting by torchlight as the living celebrated their reunion with the dead. After the climax of the Feast, a religious rite performed at sunrise, Amen sailed back to his temple, and the bleary-eyed townsfolk returned home to bed.

The *Djeser-Djeseru* was surrounded by a thick limestone enclosure wall. Once through the gate, Amen passed immediately into a peaceful, pleasantly shaded garden area where T-shaped pools glinted in the sunlight and trees – almost certainly the famous fragrant trees from Punt – offered a tempting respite from the fierce desert sun. Looking upwards, Amen would have seen the temple in all its glory; a softly gleaming white limestone building occupying three ascending terraces set back against the cliff, its tiered porticoes linked by a long, open-air stairway rising through the centre of the temple towards the sanctuary. Amen's route lay upwards. Passing over the lower portico he reached the flat second terrace where his path was marked out by pairs of colossal, painted red-granite sphinxes, each with Hatchepsut's head, inscribed to 'The King of Upper and Lower Egypt Maatkare, Beloved of Amen who is in the midst of *Djeser-Djeseru*, and given life forever'.

The second imposing stairway continued upwards so that Amen entered the body of the temple on its upper and most important level. Amen passed from the bright desert light to the cool shade and, making his way between the imposing pairs of kneeling colossal statues which lined the path to the sanctuary, he reached his journey's end; the haven of his own dark shrine cut deep into the living rock of the Theban mountain. Here the secret, sacred rites would be performed by torchlight, and magnificent offerings would first be presented to the god and then shared out between his priests.

It is possible that Hathor too only spent a limited amount of time at *Djeser-Djeseru*. A much-damaged scene on the northern wall of the outermost room of the shrine depicts the arrival of the barque of Amen at the Valley temple. Hathor's barque is also shown, as indeed are three empty royal barges which seem to belong to the two kings Hatchepsut and Tuthmosis III and to their 'queen', the Princess Neferure. These three have presumably left their boats to join the festivities. The accompanying text suggests Hathor's visitor status:

Shouting by the crews of the royal boats, the youths of Thebes, the fair lads of the army of the entire land, of praises in greeting this god, Amen, Lord of Karnak, in his procession of the 'Head of the Year' . . . at the time of causing this great goddess [Hathor] to proceed to rest in her temple in *Djeser-Djeseru-Amen* so that they [Hatchepsut and Tuthmosis III] might achieve life forever.[19]

Hathor, 'Lady of the Sycamores', 'Mistress of Music' and patron of love, motherhood, and drunkenness, could take several forms. She could appear as the nurturing cow-goddess who suckled amongst others the

Fig. 6.4   Hatchepsut being suckled by the goddess Hathor in the form of a cow

infant Hatchepsut, as the serpent goddess, the 'living uraeus of Re' who symbolized Egyptian kingship, as a beautiful young woman or as a bloodthirsty lion-headed avenger. She could even, in her more sinister role as the 'Seven Hathors', become a goddess of death. Hatchepsut seems to have felt a particular devotion for Hathor, a devotion which may well have stemmed from her period as queen-consort. Throughout the dynastic period successive queens of Egypt were each closely identified with Hathor, and indeed during the Old Kingdom several queens had left the seclusion of the harem to serve as priestesses in her temple. This tradition had faded somewhat during the Middle Kingdom, but the strong queens of the late 17th and early 18th Dynasties had revived it, becoming firmly associated with the goddess in her dual role as divine consort and mother of a king. Our best-known example of a queen associated with Hathor comes from the smaller temple at Abu Simbel, Southern Egypt, whose colossal statues of Queen Nefertari, wife of Ramesses II, show her represented as the goddess. Contemporary depictions of Hathor show her wearing the customary queen's regalia so that the link between the queen and the goddess is made obvious to all.

Hatchepsut dedicated a number of shrines to Hathor in her various manifestations; these often took the form of a rock-cut sanctuary fronted by a colonnade or vestibule. The Speos Artemidos with its unfinished Hathor-headed pillars may be included amongst these, as Pakhet was a local version of Hathor's fierce lion-headed form. It is therefore not too surprising that Hatchepsut's mortuary temple, established on the site of a traditional Hathoric shrine and home to a chapel dedicated to Hathor, includes many representations of this goddess. Here she is not only shown as a cow feeding the baby Hatchepsut, she plays an important

Fig. 6.5   Hathor in her anthropoid form

role during Hatchepsut's birth and she even, in her role as 'Mistress of Punt', manages to gain a mention in the tale of Hatchepsut's epic mission. This link between Hatchepsut and a powerful, female-orientated mother-goddess is highly significant, suggesting as it does that Hatchepsut – principally known for her association with the male god Amen – may not have been averse to having her name linked with a predominantly feminine cult.[20]

Almost all New Kingdom cult temples were decorated with scenes intended to demonstrate the good relationship which existed between the king and his gods. The outer, more public parts of the temples (the pylon and courtyard) usually depicted the pharaoh in his most obvious

role, that of the warrior-king defending his land against the traditional
enemies of Egypt, while the inner, more private areas showed more
intimate scenes: here the king could be seen acting as high priest, or
making an offering before the cult statue. *Djeser-Djeseru* cannot be
classed as a typical New Kingdom temple. Not only did the building
have an unprecedented three-tiered design, its owner also had her own
unique propaganda message which she was determined to put across via
the walls of her temple. Nevertheless, and bearing these two important
differences in mind, the scenes found on the two lower porticoes do
seem to contain the same mixture of public and more private scenes
that we might expect to find at a more conventional temple site.[21]

The two broad stairways connecting the terraces effectively cut the
temple in two, so that the two lower porticoes which front the temple
are divided into four distinct sections. Here we find scenes depicting
significant events from Hatchepsut's life and reign, all chosen to emphasize her filial devotion to Amen. Along the bottom south (or left hand as
we face the temple) portico we see scenes of the refurbishment of the
Great Temple of Amen at Karnak, including the erection of the famous
obelisks, while on the opposite side of the same portico, which is now
unfortunately much destroyed, we are shown Hatchepsut in her role as
the traditional 18th Dynasty huntin', shootin' and fishin' pharaoh; she
takes the form of an awesome sphinx to trample the enemies of Egypt,
and appears as a king fowling and fishing in the marshes. The middle
portico tells the tale of Hatchepsut's divine birth and coronation
(northern side) and the story of the expedition to Punt (southern side).
At each end of this portico is a chapel, the northern chapel being
dedicated to Anubis, the jackal-headed god of embalming, and the
southern chapel, possibly the site of her original Deir el-Bahri shrine,
being dedicated to Hathor.

The uppermost level, the most important part of the temple, took the
form of a hypostyle hall fronted by an Osiride portico with each of its
twenty-four square-cut pillars faced by an imposing, twice life-sized,
painted limestone Osiriform statue of Hatchepsut staring impassively
outwards over the Nile Valley towards Karnak. These statues were
matched by the ten Osiride statues which stood in the niches at the rear
of the upper court, by the four Osiride statues in the corners of the
sanctuary and by the enormous Osiride statues – each nearly 8 m (26 ft)
tall – which stood at each end of the lower and middle porticoes. All

11. The standing obelisk of Hatchepsut at the heart of the Temple of Amen, Karnak.

12. a and b. (above and below) *Djeser-Djeseru.*

13. (left) Senenmut and the Princess Neferure.
14. (above) Senenmut and Neferure.

15. Osiride head of Hatchepsut.

16. The carefully erased image of Hatchepsut.

17. Tuthmosis III.

these statues showed the king with a white mummiform body and crossed arms holding the emblems of Osiris, the ankh or life sign and the *was*-sceptre, symbol of dominion, combined with the traditional emblems of kingship, the crook and flail. Her bearded face was painted either red or pink, her eyes were white and black and her eyebrows a rather unnatural blue, while on her head Osiris/Hatchepsut wore either the White crown of Upper Egypt or the double crown.

On the southern side of the upper portico was the mortuary chapel of Hatchepsut, a rectangular vaulted chamber with an enormous false-door stela of red granite occupying almost the entire west wall. The cult-statue of Hatchepsut would have stood directly in front of this stela. Next door was the much smaller chapel allocated to the cult of Tuthmosis I; the west wall of his chamber has been demolished and his false-door stela is now housed in the Louvre Museum, Paris. It is possible that there was originally an even smaller chapel dedicated to the cult of Tuthmosis II, although all trace of this has now been lost. On the opposite side of the upper portico was an open-air solar temple with a raised altar of fine white limestone dedicated to the sun god Re-Harakhte. There was also a small chapel dedicated to Anubis and to Hatchepsut's family; here her parents Tuthmosis I and Ahmose and her non-royal grandmother Senisenb all appear on the walls. The sanctuary itself, two dark, narrow interconnected rooms designed to hold the barque of Amen and the statue which represented the god himself, was carved with images of the celebration of the beautiful Feast of the Valley; Hatchepsut, Neferure, Tuthmosis I, Ahmose and Hatchepsut's dead sister Neferubity all appear on the walls to offer before the barque.

Hatchepsut's mortuary cult was abandoned soon after her death, and *Djeser-Akhet* took over as the site for the celebration of the Feast of the Valley. It is therefore highly likely that Senenu, High Priest of both Amen and Hathor at *Djeser-Djeseru* during Hatchepsut's lifetime, was both the first and last to hold this exalted post. However, the cult of Amen and, to a lesser extent, the cult of Hathor continued to be celebrated at *Djeser-Djeseru* until the end of the 20th Dynasty. By this time the Tuthmosis III temple *Djeser-Akhet* and the Mentuhotep II mortuary temple had been abandoned and both lay in ruins. The Hatchepsut temple, its upper level now badly damaged, continued to flourish as a focus for burials until, during the Ptolemaic period, it became the cult centre for the worship of two deified Egyptians, Imhotep the builder of the step-pyramid, and the 18th Dynasty sage and architect Amenhotep, son of Hapu. The Amen sanctuary was cleared of its rubble, extended and refurbished for their worship. The site then fell again into disuse until the fifth century BC when it was taken over by a Coptic monastery who also used the Amen sanctuary as a focus for their worship. The site was finally abandoned some time during the eighth century AD, apparently because rockslides had rendered the upper levels dangerous.

7

Senenmut: Greatest of the Great

ꜣꜥꜣ꜀꜀꜀꜀꜀

I was the greatest of the great in the whole land. I was the guardian of the secrets of the King in all his places; a privy councillor on the Sovereign's right hand, secure in favour and given audience alone . . . I was one upon whose utterances his Lord relied, with whose advice the Mistress of the Two Lands was satisfied, and the heart of the Divine Consort was completely filled.[1]

Amongst Hatchepsut's loyal supporters there is one who stands out with remarkable clarity. Senenmut, Steward of the Estates of Amen, Overseer of all Royal Works and Tutor to the Royal Heiress Neferure, played a major bureaucratic role throughout the first three-quarters of Hatchepsut's reign. As one of the most active and able figures of his time, Senenmut occupied a position of unprecedented power within the royal administration; his was the organizational brain behind Hatchepsut's impressive public building programme, and to him has gone the credit of designing *Djeser-Djeseru*, one of the most original and enduring monuments of the ancient world. And yet, in spite of a comprehensive list of civic duties successfully accomplished, it has almost invariably been Senenmut's private life which has attracted the attention of scholars and public alike. In effect, Senenmut's considerable achievements have not merely been blurred as we might expect by the passage of time, they have been distorted and almost effaced by a host of preconceptions and speculations concerning Senenmut's character, his motivation and even his sex life.[2] The traditional tale of Senenmut, a classic rags-to-riches romance with a moral ending warning the reader against the twin follies of over-ambition and greed, is generally told as follows:

Senenmut, the highly talented and fiercely ambitious son of humble parents, started his career in the army where his natural abilities soon became apparent. Driven by a burning desire to shake off his lowly origins, he rose rapidly through the ranks before quitting the army to join the palace bureaucracy. Here, once again, his remarkable skills soon became apparent and Senenmut enjoyed accelerated promotion to become a high-grade civil servant. As it became obvious that there was no immediate heir to the throne, the royal court started to buzz with intrigues and plotting. Senenmut now took the calculated decision to link his future totally with that of Hatchepsut. He became the female king's most loyal supporter within the palace as he worked ruthlessly and efficiently to ensure that, against all the odds, her reign would succeed. When his gamble paid off, and Hatchepsut finally secured her crown, Senenmut was amply rewarded for his loyalty. He was showered with a variety of secular and religious titles including the prestigious Stewardship of the Estates of Amen, a position which allowed him free access to the vast wealth of the Karnak temple. His most publicized role was, however, that of tutor to the young princess Neferure.

Our hero's golden future seemed assured. He had amassed great personal wealth, and had started to build himself a suitably splendid tomb in the Theban necropolis. His position at court appeared unassailable. Not only did he have effective control over the state finances, he was a close personal friend of the royal family and a major influence in the life of the heiress-presumptive to the Egyptian throne. Most important of all, he was Hatchepsut's lover, dominating the passive queen to the extent that she, dazzled by his charm and ignorant of his true nature, became totally dependent upon his judgement. From his unprecedented position of power, Senenmut was able to exert great influence over the land. Effectively, Senenmut was ruler of Egypt.

Unfortunately, in best story-book tradition, Senenmut did not remain content with his lot. Caught in the grip of an uncontrollable avarice and corrupted by a false sense of his own importance, he started to take advantage of his exalted position, plundering the royal coffers for his own ends and permitting himself privileges hitherto reserved for the pharaoh. Showing great daring he abandoned his traditional T-shaped Theban tomb and, diverting the royal workmen away from their official task, started to excavate, in secret, a new tomb within the precincts of Hatchepsut's own mortuary temple. Eventually Senenmut committed his most heinous crime of all: he ordered that his own name and image be hidden behind the inner doors of *Djeser-Djeseru*.

Inevitably Nemesis struck and the betrayal of trust came to light. Hatchepsut's revenge was swift and furious, as befits a volatile woman deceived. Senenmut was instantly stripped of all his privileges and disappeared in mysterious circumstances. His unused tombs were desecrated, his monuments were vandalized and his reliefs and statues were defaced in a determined attempt to erase both the name and memory of Senenmut from the history of Egypt. However, in her impulsive destruction of her lover, Hatchepsut effectively destroyed herself. Bereft of Senenmut's guidance and unable to function alone, she rapidly lost her grip on the crown, and within two years of Senenmut's fall, Tuthmosis III was sole Pharaoh of Egypt.

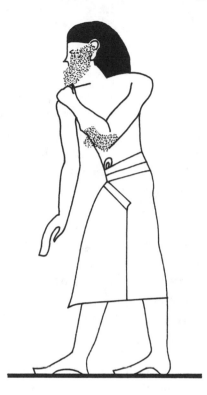

Fig. 7.1   The damaged figure of Senenmut from Tomb 353

So much for the popularly accepted biography of Senenmut which, with innumerable variations, was for a long time accepted as a true account of the spectacular rise and sudden fall of Hatchepsut's greatest supporter.[3] Any reader could choose whether to believe in Superman-Senenmut, the dashing hero and devoted lover, or Svengali-Senenmut, the cunning manipulator and malevolent power behind the throne; either way, it was always Senenmut's dominant relationship with the queen that was important; his actual achievements were a relatively insignificant part of their joint story. Recently, however, there has been a growing awareness that the cloud of suppositions which has almost invariably hovered around any discussion of Hatchepsut and her court has spread to engulf Senenmut, obscuring him from the cold light of objective assessment. A review of the known facts about Senenmut, uncoloured as far as possible by prejudgements and assumptions, presents

us with a less dramatic but equally fascinating portrait of an atypical
18th Dynasty man.

Archaeological evidence confirms that Senenmut hailed from
Armant (ancient *Iuny*), a medium-sized town lying approximately fifteen miles to the south of Thebes. Armant had originally been the
capital town of the Theban province; it was later to become well
known for its Ptolemaic buildings and its Bucheum, the necropolis of
the sacred Buchis bulls. The discovery of the shared tomb of Ramose
and Hatnofer, Senenmut's parents, confirms that Senenmut was not of
particularly high birth. Within his tomb Ramose, Senenmut's father,
was given the non-specific epithet 'The Worthy', a polite but somewhat
meaningless appellation invariably used for the respected dead. His
mother, Hatnofer, daughter of a woman named Sitdjehuty, was simply
identified as 'Mistress of the House', a very general title awarded to
married women. The ancient Egyptians did not suffer from any sense of
false modesty. They felt that their official titles were an important part
of the personality, and it was customary for all ranks and decorations, no
matter how trivial, to be recorded for posterity. An Egyptian would
only have considered omitting a lowly or unimportant title from his
parent's tomb if it had been superseded by a more prestigious accolade.
We must therefore assume that Ramose and Hatnofer, with their rather
modest epithets and undistinguished tomb, did not play a prominent
role in public life.

However, it would be entirely incorrect to assume that Senenmut
sprang from lowly peasant stock. We know that Senenmut was an able
and well-educated administrator, and from this we may deduce that his
father and grandfathers before him were members of the literate upper-
middle classes. Education was always the key to professional advancement in ancient Egypt, and never was it more important than during
the 18th Dynasty when the expanding empire created a constant
demand for bureaucrats to maintain the vast civil service. The rather
vague title of 'scribe', which could be applied to any literate Egyptian
regardless of occupation, was a prestigious accolade to be accepted with
pride. Literacy was, however, by no means widespread, and only the
more privileged of middle- and upper-class boys – possibly five per cent
of the total population – were educated. Most people remained illiterate
and unable to gain the foothold in the professions which would allow
them to advance up the social pyramid. Their lack of mobility was

reinforced by custom which demanded that sons should follow the trade or profession of their father, and by the tradition of marriage within the same family. To modern western eyes, accustomed to the idea of advancement through education, this acceptance of a static society may appear strange. However, in the ancient world, it was generally accepted that one had to be content with one's lot. As St Paul wrote, 'Let each man abide in the same calling wherein he was called.'

Senenmut must, therefore, have belonged to the top ten per cent of the population. He was probably the scion of one of the families which formed the literate provincial classes and from which a talented son could rise to national prominence. Such meteoric rises were by no means common in Egypt, but they were certainly not unknown. The Pharaoh Ay, successor to Tutankhamen, who ruled Egypt 250 years after Hatchepsut, seems to have come from a family who first became prominent in the southern city of Akhmim, while thirty years after Ay's reign the family of the great King Ramesses II had their origins in a comparative backwater of the Eastern Nile Delta.

We know that Senenmut came from a typically large Egyptian family; he had at least three brothers named Amenemhat, Minhotep and Pairy and at least two sisters, Ahhotep and Nofret-Hor. For a long time it was assumed, on the basis of a mistranslation, that Senenmut also had a fourth brother named Senimen. Senimen's existence is not open to doubt; he was a contemporary court official who rose to succeed Senenmut as tutor to Princess Neferure, who was depicted in Senenmut's Tomb 71 (but not in Tomb 353 where Senenmut's true siblings were shown together with their parents), and who was buried in Theban Tomb 252 which makes no mention of any family link with Senenmut. However, we now know that Senimen was the son of a woman named Seniemyah, not Hatnofer and, while it is possible that the two were half-brothers, there is no evidence to show that this was actually the case.[4]

Nor is there any evidence to suggest that Senenmut ever married; there is no mention of a wife or children in either of his tombs. If he did remain single, he must have been an oddity, one of the few bachelors living unwed in a country where married life and the fathering of many children was viewed as the ideal. Given the constant emphasis placed on family life, and the particular need for a son to perform the funeral rites of his dead parents, we might expect Senenmut to have married at the start of his career, and therefore to have been either divorced or widowed before he came to national prominence as a single man. However, had Senenmut ever been widowed, we would expect to find a reference to his dead wife within his tomb. Did his later involvement with the queen prevent him from referring to the fact that he had ever been married, no matter how briefly? It certainly is tempting to draw a parallel with the court of the English Queen Elizabeth I, albeit over 3,000 years later and in a different land, where, in turn, the Earl of Leicester and his stepson the Earl of Essex, both favourites of the queen, found it prudent to keep their inconvenient wives hidden in the country, away from the queen's unforgiving gaze.

Our meagre information about Senenmut's early life comes from the joint tomb of Ramose and Hatnofer. Careful excavation has shown that Ramose, aged about sixty, predeceased his wife and was buried in a relatively humble grave. This suggests that his children did not at the time of his death have the means to give their father a more splendid interment, as tradition decreed that it was a son's duty to bury his father in the best manner possible. When Hatnofer died of old age, during Year 6 or 7 of Hatchepsut's reign, Senenmut was in a far better position to provide for his mother's funeral. He had already chosen the site for his own final resting place and he decided to bury his mother on the same hillside, just below his own tomb. Here a relatively simple chamber was cut into the rock, and the expensively mummified body of Hatnofer was interred in a wooden anthropoid coffin together with a gilded mask, canopic jars and a selection of traditional grave-goods suitable for a woman. Ramose was then resurrected from his more lowly resting place, hastily re-bandaged, placed in a painted anthropoid coffin and re-united with his wife.

Hatnofer's tomb was also home to two further coffins housing the badly mummified remains of three anonymous women and three unknown children. The discoverers of the tomb saw these six bodies as the grisly evidence that Senenmut's immediate family had been struck by sudden catastrophe:

... that eight persons of the same family or group should have died so nearly at the same time that they could be buried together on one occasion is certainly extraordinary, but seems, nevertheless, to be what actually happened.[5]

It actually seems far more likely that these bodies represent members of Senenmut's immediate family who had previously been buried nearby; their decayed wrappings and disarticulated skeletons encrusted with mud suggest that they too had been retrieved from less impressive cemeteries. The re-burial of private individuals, while not common, was certainly not unknown at this time, and Senenmut's filial devotion would have met with general approval. Clearly, the parents of the few upwardly mobile children were able to enjoy the posthumous benefits of their offsprings' success.

There were three major career paths open to the educated and ambitious 18th Dynasty male: the army, the priesthood and the civil service. It is always possible that Senenmut chose to join the army, and a badly damaged fragment of what appears to be autobiographical text within his tomb (Tomb 71) lends some credence to this idea. The text, which includes the words 'capture' and 'Nubia', is positioned next to images of running soldiers. However, the remainder of the inscription is virtually unreadable and is therefore open to a variety of interpretations. His lack of military titles in later life, and his father's lack of any military titles, perhaps indicates that Senenmut selected a vocation more obviously suited to his organizational skills. The priesthood and the bureaucracy were very closely linked at this time, and it seems sensible to deduce that Senenmut rose to prominence as a local administrator working either for the royal bureaucracy or the temple, before being seconded to state administration at Thebes. Given Senenmut's subsequent plethora of Amen-based titles (for example, Overseer of Amen's Granaries, Storehouses, Fields, Gardens, Cattle and Slaves; Controller of the Hall of Amen; Overseer of the Works of Amen, etc.), the suggestion that he began his career as an administrator in the temple of Amen at Karnak appears entirely reasonable.

Our first concrete sighting of Senenmut, dating to the period before Hatchepsut's accession, finds him already busy at the palace with a variety of prestigious appointments including steward of the property of Hatchepsut and Neferure and tutor to the young princess. Unfortunately, we have no means of knowing when Senenmut had started his illustrious royal career. Our only clue is provided by a shrine built at the Gebel Silsila; this informs us that Senenmut was already 'Steward of the God's Wife and Steward of the King's Daughter' at the time of

construction. These two tantalizingly anonymous ladies have been tentatively identified as Queen Ahmose and Princess Hatchepsut, indicating
that Senenmut was in royal service during the reign of Tuthmosis I, but
it is perhaps more likely that the two women are Queen Hatchepsut
and Princess Neferure, and therefore that Senenmut was initially appointed either by Tuthmosis II or during the early part of Hatchepsut's
regency following the death of Tuthmosis II.

Gebel Silsila, forty miles to the north of Aswan, was both the location
of sandstone quarries and a cult centre for the worship of the Nile in
flood. Senenmut's shrine, which is of uncertain use and which has been
variously described as a grotto, cenotaph, temple and tomb, is one of a
number of such edifices built on the West Bank by the highest-ranking
civil servants of the 18th Dynasty, including Hapuseneb, the first
Prophet of Amen and architect of Hatchepsut's burial chamber, and
Neshi, the leader of Hatchepsut's celebrated expedition to Punt. The
monument therefore serves to emphasize Senenmut's prominent role
amongst the great and the good (and the influential) of his time.

Senenmut's shrine (Shrine 16) is situated high on the cliff and faces
east, towards the Nile. It was almost certainly designed to be reached
from the river at the time of high water. The shrine consists of a framed
doorway, cut into the sandstone cliff, leading into a square room
housing a seated statue of Senenmut, cut from the living rock. The walls
originally displayed a series of sunk relief scenes and inscriptions. These
are now badly damaged, although the flat ceiling still shows traces of its
original colourful pattern. Although most of the Gebel Silsila shrines
incorporate a fairly consistent funerary emphasis in their texts and
scenes, Senenmut's shrine omits the customary earthly and funerary
feasts and includes instead a depiction of Hatchepsut being embraced
by the crocodile-headed god Sobek and Nekhbet, the vulture goddess
of Upper Egypt, shown as a woman wearing a feathered vulture headdress. As other commentators have observed, 'the peculiar status of
Senenmut and the relationship between him and his monarch no doubt
account for these unusual features'.[6]

... I was promoted before the companions, knowing that I was distinguished
with her; they set me to be chief of her house, the palace, may it live, be
prosperous and be healthy, being under my supervision, being judge in the
whole land, Overseer of the Granaries of Amen, Senenmut ...[7]

Following Hatchepsut's rise to power, Senenmut dropped a number of his lesser titles, including that of tutor to Neferure, acquired a clutch of more prestigious accolades (such as Overseer of the Granaries of Amen and Overseer of all the Works of the King [Hatchepsut] at Karnak), and settled into his principal post as Steward of Amen. Although, as far as we are aware, he never held the title of First Prophet of Amen, arguably the most powerful position that a non-royal Egyptian could aspire to, the stereotypical and self-congratulatory propaganda text quoted above confirms the wide range of his official duties. Titles in ancient Egypt were not necessarily indicative of actual employment, but rather served to place a man in the social hierarchy; for example, the exact duties of the 'Sandal-bearer of the King' or the 'Royal Washerman' are unknown, but it is highly unlikely that they involved the performance of undignified personal services for the monarch, as both posts were held by men of rank and breeding. Winlock's intriguing suggestion that, in addition to his obvious public duties, Senenmut had 'held more intimate ones like those of the great nobles of France who were honoured in being allowed to assist in the most intimate details of the royal toilet at the king's levees'[8] appears very unlikely. Winlock based this remarkable conclusion on the fact that Senenmut bore what we now assume to be the purely honorary titles of 'Superintendent of the Private Apartments', 'Superintendent of the Bathroom', and 'Superintendent of the Royal Bedroom'.

Senenmut's plethora of epithets should, therefore, be taken as an indication of his general importance rather than a precise listing of his actual duties, and the exact amount of time that he was actually required to devote to his official posts remains unclear. His range of titles does, however, suggest that he might by now have been a relatively elderly man. As the average life expectancy for a high-ranking court official was between thirty and forty-five years, any official who lived past forty years could reasonably expect to become a much venerated and much decorated elder statesman, if only because death had removed almost all his contemporary competitors. The longer that Senenmut lived, and of course the longer that he continued in the queen's favour, the more titles he could expect to acquire. Thus we find Ineni, an equally long serving statesman, rejoicing in the titles of:

Hereditary Prince, Count, Chief of all Works in Karnak; the double silver-house was in his charge; the double gold house was on his seal; Sealer of all contracts in the House of Amen; Excellency, Overseer of the Double Granary of Amen.[9]

Unofficially, Senenmut seems to have acted as the queen's right-hand-man and general factotum. The rapid increase in his personal wealth at this time is obvious. Not only was Senenmut now rich enough to bury his mother with appropriate pomp, he was also able to start constructing his own magnificent tomb, acquire a quartzite sarcophagus and build his Silsila shrine.

In the absence of any contemporary written description of Senenmut, we must turn to his surviving images in an attempt to find clues to his character. What did the queen see when she turned to look at her faithful servant? Possibly not what modern observers have seen when studying Senenmut's somewhat unprepossessing physiognomy:

Whatever first attracted Great Royal Wife Hatchepsut to Senenmut, it certainly was not his good looks. . . . portraits show a pinch-featured man with a pointed high-bridge nose and fleshy lips that seem pursed; with a weak chin tending to jowliness and eyes that might be judged a bit shifty; and with deep creases or wrinkles about the cheeks, nose and mouth, and under the jaw.[10]

Winlock was also struck by Senenmut's 'aquiline nose and nervously expressive, wrinkled face. As for the wrinkles, they surely were the feature by which Senmut was known'.[11] However beauty, or in this case a shifty eye, wrinkles and a tendency towards 'jowliness', lies as always in the eye of the beholder, and others have been prepared to take a kinder view of his features:

The profile has the imperious outline of the Tuthmoside family. A slight fullness of the throat, with two strokes of the brush suggesting folds, the sparingly executed lines around the eyes, and a reversed curve from the eyes past nose and mouth indicate in masterful fashion the sagging plump features of the aging man of affairs.[12]

Each of these descriptions has been based on our four surviving ink sketches of Senenmut's face. Three of these portraits are on ostraca now

housed in the Metropolitan Museum of Art, New York, while the fourth
has survived undamaged on the wall of Tomb 353. All four show
Senenmut in profile, with a single eye and eyebrow facing forwards in
the conventional Egyptian style. His rather rounded face and double
chin certainly suggest a man used to enjoying the finer things in life,
while his crows' feet and wrinkles confirm that he was no longer in the
first flush of youth when the sketches were made. The striking similarity between these less-than-flattering sketches suggests that all four may
be actual depictions of Senenmut, drawn by people who actually knew
him. In contrast, our other more formal images of Senenmut, his statues
and his tomb illustrations, are merely conventional representations of a
'great Egyptian man' with little or no attempt at accurate portrayal.

. . . Grant that there may be . . . made for me many statues from every kind of
precious hard stone for the temple of Amen at Karnak and for every place
wherein the majesty of this god proceeds . . .[13]

At least twenty-five hard stone statues of Senenmut have survived the
ravages of time. This is an extraordinarily large number of statues for a

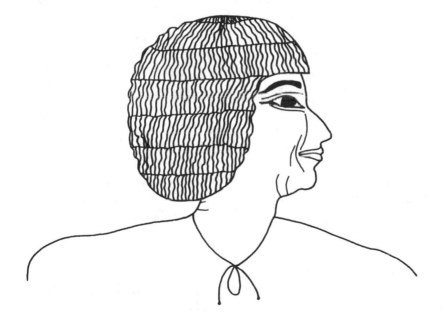

Fig. 7.2   Sketch-portrait of Senenmut from the wall of Tomb 353

private individual; no other New Kingdom official has left us so
many clear indications of his exalted rank and, as we must assume
that most, if not all, were the gift of the queen, his highly favoured
status. In ancient Egypt, statues were not simply designed to be *objets
d'art*, intended to enhance rooms or beautify gardens. All images were
automatically invested with magical or religious powers, and they were
commissioned so that they could replace either living people or gods
within the temple and the tomb. It seems likely, given his links with
Amen, that the majority of Senenmut's statues would have been placed
in the courtyard of the great temple of Amen at Karnak, although
Senenmut appears to have dedicated statues of himself in most of
the major temples around Thebes. Within the temple the statues
would have been positioned in ranks facing the sanctuary, ensuring
that the living Senenmut received the benefits of their proximity to the
god.

The artistic inventiveness of the Senenmut figures confirms the
innovative nature and general technical excellence of small-scale sculpture throughout Hatchepsut's reign. They depict Senenmut in his
various roles, most typically holding the infant Neferure in his arms,
a pose designed to stress Senenmut's importance rather than his
tender feelings towards his young charge. Some show him squatting
with the child's body wrapped in, and almost obscured by, his cloak,
while one shows Senenmut sitting with Neferure – stiff and unchild-
like – held at right angles in his lap, a position hitherto reserved for
women nursing children. The majority of the remaining statues show
Senenmut kneeling to present a religious symbol such as a sistrum or
a shrine. At least one statue, a 1.55 m (5 ft 1 in) high granite representation of Senenmut presenting a sistrum to the goddess Mut,
originally housed in the temple of Mut at Karnak, was so admired by
its subject that it was reproduced in black diorite on a smaller scale,
presumably so that it could be placed in a less public shrine and used for
private worship.

Not all contemporary representations of Senenmut were intended to
flatter, as crude graffiti from an unfinished Middle Kingdom tomb
show. This chamber, situated in the cliffs above Deir el-Bahri, was used
as a resting place by the gangs of workmen engaged in building Hatchepsut's mortuary temple. Here the builders idled away their rest breaks

by doodling and scribbling on the walls. Included amongst the doodles are a number of mildly pornographic scenes including depictions of naked, well-endowed young men. One sketch shows a tall, fully clothed, unnamed male who has variously been identified as both Senenmut and Hatchepsut, and who is apparently being approached by a smaller naked male with an improbably large erection. Although it is possible that the two figures represent entirely separate and unconnected doodles, they are close enough together for us to speculate whether Senenmut/Hatchepsut is about to become the subject of a homosexual encounter.

Homosexual intercourse for pleasure in ancient Egypt is not well attested. Instead, homosexuality was generally regarded as a means of gaining revenge on a defeated enemy. By implanting his semen the aggressor not only humiliated his victim by forcing him to take the part of a woman, but also gained a degree of power over him. If Senenmut is really being approached in this way, he is about to be thoroughly degraded. No disgrace ever attached to the aggressor performing the homosexual rape; the shame belonged entirely to the victim. Thus, in the New Kingdom story which tells of the seduction of the young god Horus by his uncle Seth, it is Horus who feels the shame of a woman. Seth is merely acting like any red-blooded male:

Now when evening had come a bed was prepared for them and they lay down together. At night Seth let his member become stiff, and he inserted it between the thighs of Horus. And Horus placed his hand between his thighs, and caught the semen of Seth.[14]

By catching the semen before it enters his body and subsequently throwing it into the marsh, Horus has effectively thwarted his uncle's evil plan to discredit him in the eyes of other males. Later, with the help of his mother, he is able to turn the tables on Seth. He sprinkles his own semen over the lettuces growing in the palace garden which he knows that Seth will eat. When the two gods are called to give an account of their deeds, although Seth claims to have done 'a man's deed' to Horus, the semen of Horus is discovered within Seth's own body and Seth is totally humiliated.

Nearby on the tomb wall (Fig. 7.3) are shown a couple, naked but for their idiosyncratic headgear, who are indulging in a form of sexual

Fig. 7.3   Hatchepsut and Senenmut? Crude graffito from a Deir el-Bahri tomb

intercourse which has modestly been described as 'a method of approach from the rear'.[15] As Manniche has noted:

Intercourse from behind ('dog fashion') . . . seems to have been rather popular in
Egypt, to judge from the number of extant representations of the position, the
man most frequently standing, with the woman bending over. Whether any of
these examples indicate anal intercourse cannot be determined from the representations alone, but it seems rather unlikely in that no practical purpose
would have been served . . .[16]

The more dominant male figure sports what has been described as an
overseer's leather cap, but which may actually be a bad haircut, while his
larger and curiously androgynous companion has a dark female pubic
triangle but no breasts. She is wearing what has been identified as a
royal headdress without the uraeus, and is generally acknowledged to
represent Hatchepsut. The whole scene has been interpreted, some
might say over-interpreted, as a contemporary political parody intended

to highlight the one way in which Hatchepsut could never be a true
king – she could never dominate a man in the way that she is now
being dominated.[17] Senenmut is shown quite literally taking his queen
for a ride.

Hatchepsut is by no means the first woman in a position of authority to be insulted by this type of graffiti. The deep-rooted feeling
that any female who rejects her traditional submissive role is both
unfeminine and unnatural has often led to wild charges of wanton
behaviour fired at dominant women. Accusations of sexual lust and
impropriety are perhaps the only way in which less powerful and
therefore, it has been argued, emasculated and frustrated men can
attack their more powerful mistresses. Nor is this type of assault the
prerogative of men. Women who have not themselves breached social
boundaries are often the first to condemn those who have and, as
women well know, an attack on a woman's reputation is the most
damaging attack of all. Certainly the influential females of history –
women who have dominated in a man's world – have consistently
attracted prurient speculation concerning their sexual behaviour.
These women, who range from Cleopatra of Egypt via Semiramis of
Assyria and Livia of Rome to Catherine the Great of Russia, were
routinely accused of sexual promiscuity of the grossest and most
vivid kind.

It seems that only by making a deliberate feature of her virtue and
chastity, often maintained under the most difficult of conditions, can
a powerful woman hope to avoid tales of her sexual depravity becoming her main contribution to her country's history. Thus Odys-
seus's faithful Penelope, Shakespeare's 'most unspotted lily' Elizabeth I
and Joan of Arc, 'the Maid of Orleans', all strong women, deliberately
made purity one of their main attributes. We should therefore not be
surprised to find that Hatchepsut's subjects, unused to the idea of a
strong female ruler, were prepared to speculate on the relationship
between the female king and Senenmut, her servant and their immediate boss. Humour would have been the only weapon that the
workmen could use to attack their superiors, and it would perhaps
be attaching too much importance to what appears to be a casual
scribble, were we to assume that it signifies anything other than a
crude attempt to depict Hatchepsut in her rightful female place:
being dominated by a man.

Fig. 7.4   Senenmut worshipping at Djeser-Djeseru

Nevertheless, the suggestion that Senenmut and Hatchepsut were more than just good friends is worthy of serious consideration. An intimate relationship with the queen would account for the rapid rise in Senenmut's fortunes and would explain why Senenmut chose to defy tradition and remain unmarried. It is certainly tempting to see Senenmut's unprecedented privileges, such as burial within the confines of *Djeser-Djeseru* and the linking of their two names within Tomb 353, as Hatchepsut's tacit acknowledgement of Senenmut's role as her morganatic partner, if not her consort. Queens, however great, are not immune from normal human feelings, and at times Hatchepsut may have found her position to be an intolerably lonely one. A trusted companion may have helped to ease the burden of state.

In theory, Hatchepsut and Senenmut, both unattached individuals, would have been free to enjoy an open sexual relationship without public censure. Dynastic Egypt was not an unduly prudish society and Hatchepsut, as king, would have been at liberty to choose her own partners just as other New Kingdom monarchs were free to fill their harems with the women of their choice. And yet Hatchepsut, firstly as a woman and secondly as a king with a rather tenuous claim to the throne, was in a very difficult position. Throughout her reign she endeavoured to emphasize her unique royal position as the daughter, wife and sister of a king. The enormous gulf which separated the divine pharaoh from the people is hard for us to understand but would have been very real to Hatchepsut. Marriage or a permanent alliance with a commoner would have compromised and damaged her position, making the aura of divinity with which she chose to cloak herself appear more transparent to those around her.

Senenmut is generally credited with being the political force behind Hatchepsut's assumption and exercise of kingship. While this assessment cannot be proved, it is probably correct.[18]

If Hatchepsut and Senenmut were not lovers, did they enjoy anything other than a purely professional relationship? Did Senenmut control Hatchepsut by the power of his personality? And if so, was he directly responsible for Hatchepsut's unprecedented decision to seize power? As Gardiner has noted: 'It is not to be imagined . . . that even a woman of the most virile character could have attained such a pinnacle of power without masculine support.'[19] Senenmut was one of Hatchepsut's most loyal servants at this time, and it is clear that he must have approved of her claim to the throne since he continued to work for the new regime. The suggestion that he masterminded the accession is far less feasible; it is an idea based less on the available archaeo-historical evidence (nil) than on the twin assumptions that Senenmut was a manipulative person and that Hatchepsut, possibly due to her femininity, was incapable of controlling her own destiny. It is certainly difficult to equate the strong and mature Hatchepsut of the Deir el-Bahri temple with the timid and passive Trilby or the childish Lady Jane Grey, and it seems impossible that any intelligent woman could have been persuaded to take such a momentous step against her will. Winlock, believing Senenmut and Hatchepsut to have been kindred souls and acknowledging that Hatchepsut's gender did not necessarily preclude intelligence, has summarized the situation:

. . . the only question is whether it was through infatuation for her [Hatchepsut] that Sen-Mut followed her in a course of her own designing, or whether through ambition for himself he was encouraging her to break with the customs of her people.[20]

It is clear that Senenmut's main strengths lay in his abilities as an organizer, administrator and accountant. In modern times there is a tendency to laugh at desk-bound civil servants; their work is seen as dull, repetitive and unnecessary, and those unfortunate enough to be employed as clerks or accountants are often perceived as boring, faceless nonentities. In ancient Egypt nothing could be further from the truth. The scribe enjoyed the most enviable of employments as, exempt from the need to perform degrading manual labour in the hot sun, he revelled in his exalted position. The importance of the efficient civil servant in a developing state should never be underestimated. Construction work in Egypt, without the benefits of modern machinery, was a lengthy and labour-intensive business requiring the co-ordination of vast numbers of workmen and their associated back-up facilities such as food, water, accommodation and equipment, and a tried and tested administrator would have been of great value to the queen.

The extent of his creative talents is perhaps more open to question. Senenmut is often credited with building all of Hatchepsut's monu-ments, although there is no evidence that he was actually an architect, and he himself is often rather vague when referring to his precise role in these operations. Nevertheless, he appears to have had a hand in various construction projects in and around Thebes. His main architec-tural achievements must remain the overseeing of *Djeser-Djeseru* and the erecting of the obelisks at Karnak. However, the unique astronomical ceiling in his Tomb 353 (discussed in further detail below), and the eclectic variety of texts and ostraca included in Tomb 71 (ranging from plans of the tomb itself through various calculations to the *Story of Sinuhe*), certainly suggests that Senenmut was a cultured and well-rounded man with a wide range of interests extending far beyond his official duties.

Thanks to his role as Overseer of Works at Deir el-Bahri, Senenmut was able to ensure that his connection with the queen and her monu-ment was preserved for eternity. Over sixty small representations of Senenmut, either kneeling or standing with outstretched arms, have been discovered concealed within the temple. These images had been carved on walls normally covered by the wooden doors of shrines and statue niches, so that they would have been completely hidden from public gaze while the doors were opened for worship. The accom-panying short inscriptions make it clear that Senenmut is engaged in worshipping both the god Amen and his mistress Hatchepsut 'on behalf of the life, prosperity and health of the King of Upper and Lower Egypt, Maatkare living forever'.

In Egyptian art, the image could always serve as a substitute for the person or thing being represented. Therefore, by placing his image near the god's sanctuary, Senenmut was actually placing himself in close proximity to the god, and was receiving unspecified benefits from this close association. However, being near to the gods was purely a royal prerogative, a privilege allowed only to the king who served as high priest of every Egyptian deity. Because he appeared to be usurping royal privileges, and because it was hitherto unheard of for a non-royal person to be included in any royal temple, many egyptologists deduced that Senenmut had commissioned the carving without obtaining the permission of the queen. This theory fitted with the then-current view of Senenmut as a devious and scheming manipulator, and has remained surprisingly popular despite the translation of a badly damaged text, also from the Deir el-Bahri mortuary temple, in which Senenmut states that he had royal permission to carve his image within the sacred precincts and indeed within every Egyptian temple. This text is worth quoting at length:

Giving praise to Amen and smelling the ground to the Lord of the gods on behalf of the life, prosperity and health of the King [i.e. Hatchepsut] of Upper and Lower Egypt, Maatkare, may he live forever, by the Hereditary Prince and Count, the Steward of Amen, Senenmut, in accordance with a favour of the King's bounty which was extended to this servant in letting his name be established on every wall, in the following of the King, in *Djeser-Djeseru* [Deir el-Bahri], and likewise in the temples of the gods of Upper and Lower Egypt. Thus spoke the King.[21]

This bold proclamation of royal authority was carved on the reveals of the doorway leading into the north-west offering hall of the temple, and was available for all who were exalted enough to enter the temple precincts to read. It confirms what common sense suggests, that the queen must have known about the 'secret' images. Senenmut would have experienced a great deal of difficulty in keeping scores of illicit carvings hidden and, given that a powerful man like Senenmut must have had many enemies, it seems inconceivable that no word of this treachery would have reached Hatchepsut's ears. An alternative theory, that Senenmut not only carved his images in secret, but also lied about receiving royal approval for his action, is more convoluted and perhaps less easy to accept. We now know that Senenmut was not the only 18th Dynasty official to include his own image within a royal monument. Neshi, Viceroy of Kush under Tuthmosis III, had himself depicted in

the act of praying on the reveals of some of the doorways in the temples of
Hatchepsut and Tuthmosis III at Buhen. Although Buhen, lying beyond
the southern border of Egypt, was far enough away from the court to
allow a certain amount of variation from standard Egyptian practices, it
is interesting that Neshi did not suffer in any way for his impertinence.

May the king give an offering: a thousand of bread, beer, cattle and fowl . . . that
they may grant abundance and he may be purified, for the Ka of the Steward
of Amen, Senenmut the justified.[22]

Senenmut was wealthy enough to provide himself with two funerary monuments on the West Bank at Thebes; Tomb 71, the 'first
tomb', conspicuously sited on top of the Sheikh Abd el-Gurna hill,
and Tomb 353, the 'second tomb', hidden beneath the precincts of
Djeser-Djeseru. Historians have consistently placed great emphasis on
these two tombs, concluding that it was his presumption in building
secretly within the precincts of the Deir el-Bahri temple which finally turned Hatchepsut against Senenmut. It is therefore worth considering the art and architecture of these two very different monuments in some detail.[23]

Senenmut selected a (then) little used area of the Theban necropolis
for his first tomb, securing a highly desirable, and highly visible, location
on the brow of the hill now known as the Sheikh Abd el-Gurna. His
choice of site was to prove well judged. He was soon joined by two of
his illustrious contemporaries, the steward Amenhotep (Tomb 73) and
the royal tutor Senimen (Tomb 252), and several lesser-ranking officials
quickly followed suit, making Gurna one of the most popular private
cemeteries on the West Bank during the reigns of Hatchepsut and
Tuthmosis III. Senenmut's own tomb ultimately served as a focal point
for a number of less important burials, and clearance of the hillside
below Tomb 71 in the 1930s revealed a scattering of subsidiary inhuma-
tions; an unknown woman in a cheap wooden coffin wearing a scarab
inscribed for the 'God's Wife Neferure', an unknown male wrapped in
reed matting, a boy named Amenhotep who may have been Senenmut's
much younger brother, a male singer named Hormose who was buried
with his lute beside him, two anonymous human bodies in anthropoid
coffins and the bodies of a horse and an ape, each mummified and in its
own coffin.

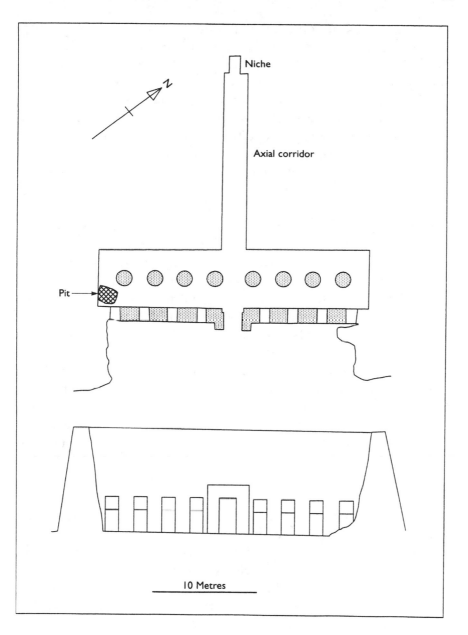

Fig. 7.5   Plan and reconstruction of the façade of Tomb 71

An ostracon fortuitously recovered from the forecourt of Tomb 71 fixes the exact date that work on the site commenced to 'Year 7 [of Hatchepsut's reign], spring, day 2: the beginning of work in the tomb on this day'. The steep slope at the summit of the hill presented Senenmut's architect with an immediate technical problem. The front wall of the tomb could be cut directly into the rock face, but in order to provide the tomb with the traditional forecourt it was necessary to construct an artificial terrace; this problem was solved by working on the terrace and the tomb simultaneously, recycling the debris being excavated within the tomb and using it to build a buttressed terrace extending eastward over the descending slope of the hill. A long but narrow forecourt was then sited on top of the terrace, and two deep pits of unknown purpose were excavated, one on each edge of the fore-court. When the collapsed terrace was investigated in 1935–6 the intact burial chamber of Ramose and Hatnofer was discovered. Wine labels dated to Year 7 within this tomb confirm the date that construction started on Tomb 71 as, given its position beneath the artificial terrace, this chamber must have been excavated before the major building work commenced.

The plan of Tomb 71 is that of a simple inverted T-shape extending into the Sheikh Abd el-Gurna, topped by a rock-cut shrine which was originally intended to house a statue of Senenmut holding the Princess Neferure. The imposing façade, cut from the sloping rock and extended by the use of stone walls so that the tomb rose above the natural slope of the hill, has a central doorway and eight almost square windows which admit light into the transverse entrance hall. This hall, with its eight faceted columns, its row of statue-niches set into the western wall and its distinctive decorated ceiling, makes a suitably impressive entrance for visitors to the tomb.

A tall but narrow axial corridor extends at right-angles out of the hall, running westwards into the cliff for almost 24 m (78 ft) and ending in a wall which originally housed a red quartzite false-door stela in-scribed with sections of Chapter 148 of the *Book of the Dead* '. . . may you give to the steward Senenmut life, prosperity, joy and endurance'. Above the false door was a small stone-lined statue niche designed to hold a statue of the deceased.

The walls and ceiling of the hall and corridor were originally coated with fine plaster and lavishly decorated with colourful murals and

painted hieroglyphic texts. Unfortunately, very little of the original art-
work now survives, although the colourful Hathor-headed frieze in the
hall is still clearly visible. One particular scene, depicting the presentation of a tribute by six Aegean men (now sadly reduced to three)
carrying a variety of distinctive vessels, is justly famous as a contemporary documentation of the links between Egypt and Minoan Crete
during Hatchepsut's reign.

The clearance of the tomb in 1930 led to the discovery of
Senenmut's once magnificent red-brown quartzite sarcophagus, now
smashed into over a thousand pieces and spread all over the interior
of the tomb and the surrounding hillside. Two fragments were recovered from the tomb of the 11th Dynasty Vizier Dagi, more than
100 m (328 ft) to the north of Senenmut's tomb, while some of the
more substantial pieces were found to have been re-cycled into grind-
ing stones and other useful objects by enterprising locals. Larger
fragments of the sarcophagus had already been collected and sold by
antiquities traders, and some had even made their way into private
European collections. It is perhaps not surprising, given these circumstances, that less than half of the sarcophagus and lid have yet been
recovered.[24]

Painstaking reconstruction has shown that the sarcophagus was originally an oblong box with rounded corners giving it a cartouche-shaped
plan-form. It measured 236 × 88 × 89 cm (7 ft 9 in × 2 ft 10 in × 2 ft 10
in). The kneeling figures of the goddesses Isis and Nephthys were
carved on the head and foot ends, while the four sons of Horus and two
manifestations of Anubis decorated the sides. Inside the sarcophagus was
carved the standing figure of Nut, her arms stretched wide and extending up the sides of the box. Funerary texts taken from the *Book of
the Dead* were inscribed on both the inside and the outside walls. The
exterior walls were originally polished and painted a dark red in an
attempt to enhance the natural colour of the stone, and touches of
yellow and blue paint were added to highlight details such as wigs,
bracelets and collars. In marked contrast, the lid was left plain and
unfinished.

The undamaged sarcophagus must have appeared highly similar to
the sarcophagus prepared for Hatchepsut in her role as king (see
Chapter 4). Many of the measurements are identical, although
Senenmut's sarcophagus is slightly shorter and has two rounded ends

rather than a rounded head end and a flat foot end. This similarity in plan-form is perhaps not surprising, given that Senenmut was responsible for commissioning and perhaps even designing Hatchepsut's funerary equipment, and given that there are only a limited number of practical variations on the basic sarcophagus theme. What is surprising is that Senenmut was able to acquire any form of hard stone sarcophagus. During the 18th Dynasty, burial for most wealthy private Egyptians involved placing the mummified body inside an anthropoid wooden coffin which was in turn placed within a large shrine-shaped wooden coffin. Multiple coffins were occasionally used in more elaborate interments, but even the multiple coffins of Yuya and Thuyu, the non-royal parents of Queen Tiy, were only of gilded wood. As has already been noted, Queens Ahhotep and Ahmose Nefertari were interred in wooden sarcophagi, and it is possible that the body of Tuthmosis I was also originally housed in a wooden shrine. A quartzite sarcophagus would have been a very valuable asset and, in theory at least, must have been the gift of the queen. It may even be that a rejected prototype royal sarcophagus was adapted for Senenmut's private use, with or without the permission of its official owner; this would explain why a few word-endings in the carved text have a feminine rather than a masculine form, suggesting that the text had originally been intended for a woman.

Quartzite, a compacted sandstone which was both far more precious and far harder to work than granite, occurs naturally at several sites in Egypt: at Gebel Ahmar, just outside modern Cairo, between Cairo and Suez, in the Wadi Natrun, in Sinai, at Gebelein, Edfu and Aswan. Unfortunately, it is not possible to pinpoint the exact source of the quartzite used in Senenmut's sarcophagus, but it is likely to have come from the Gebel Ahmar as this was the major quartzite quarry, and we know that blocks from this site were transported to Thebes during the 18th Dynasty. The pharaoh had a monopoly over the quarrying of all hard stone and, in the cashless economy of ancient Egypt, it was simply not possible – in theory at least – for a private individual to turn up at the quarry and purchase a block of stone for his own use. All stone was quarried on the order of the monarch and all the quarried stone belonged to the monarch, although Senenmut, in his role as overseer, would have been in a better position than most to commission his own

work. However, it is hard to see how the commissioning and trans-
porting of such a costly, heavy and labour-intensive object could ever
have been kept secret from the queen. The sarcophagus must have been
roughed out at the quarry before being transported up river by barge
to Thebes, a far more difficult task than the transport of granite down
river from Aswan as, if the quartzite originated at Gebel Ahmar, it had
to be moved against the flow of the river. On arrival at Thebes the
sarcophagus must have been dragged overland to Sheikh Abd el-Gurna
and hoisted up the steep slope to the tomb where, the unfinished state
of the lid suggests, the final carving was performed.

Beneath the public rooms of Tomb 71, two uneven passageways
run at an oblique angle, eventually uniting to form a chamber which
in turn leads into the tomb of Anen (Tomb 120). Anen, Second
Prophet of Amen and brother of Queen Tiy, built his tomb to the
north of Tomb 71 approximately one century after all work had
stopped on Senenmut's tomb. It was originally accepted that these
subterranean passageways must represent the corridors leading to
Senenmut's burial chamber, an interpretation which was based more
upon the current belief that Senenmut had fully intended to be
buried within his tomb – but where? – than on strict archaeological
evidence. There is now considerable doubt that these corridors were
ever deliberately linked to Tomb 71; the possibility that they represent tunnelling from the tomb of Anen which has weakened the
floor of the older tomb, causing it to collapse, is worthy of serious
consideration. It is certainly difficult to see how the passageways
could have been entered from Tomb 71, and there is now no trace
of an entrance or vertical pit in the surviving floor of the axial
corridor. Unfortunately, the passages cannot now be fully explored as
they have been completely blocked with debris.[25]

If the subterranean corridors are to be excluded from our consideration, where then should we look for the burial chamber? The fact that
Senenmut was prepared to go to a great deal of trouble to have his
precious sarcophagus delivered to Tomb 71 indicates that he was, at the
time the sarcophagus was commissioned, fully intending to be interred
there. Therefore we may conclude that he must have planned a burial
chamber within the tomb. The two deep pits excavated into the tomb
forecourt may possibly represent unfinished burial shafts but, given
their size and position, this seems unlikely. The northern pit is now

inaccessible and the southern pit, which is 7 m (22 ft 11 in) deep, shows
no trace of a burial chamber. A pit cut into the south-east corner of
the transverse hall is, however, worthy of further consideration.[26] The
pit descends for 1.9 m (6 ft 2 in) and then opens into a small room
measuring 3.5 × 1 × 1.05 m (11 ft 5 in × 3 ft 3 in × 3 ft 5 in). At first
sight it may be felt that the cramped size of this chamber makes it a very
unlikely final resting place for the great Senenmut, and more likely that
it was intended for the subsidiary burial of a member of his family.
However, it was not customary to inter 18th Dynasty private individuals
with large numbers of grave goods, and a burial chamber only needed
to be large enough to house the deceased's sarcophagus or coffin plus
his canopic jars. Traditionally it was the upper, public, part of the tomb
which needed to be both spacious and imposing; the actual burial
chamber was relatively unimportant and could be as small as was practically possible. In the absence of any more obvious burial shafts, we must
conclude that this small chamber was Senenmut's intended final resting
place.

Senenmut's tomb was substantially complete when all building
work ceased; only the burial chamber and the rock-cut shrine above
the tomb were obviously unfinished, and the latter may well already
have been abandoned due to flaws in the natural rock. At some point
following its completion, however, Tomb 71 suffered a great deal of
damage. Some of this, such as the collapse of the ceiling in the transverse hall and the extensive damage to the painted plaster walls, is a
natural result of the poor quality of the rock on the Sheikh Abd
el-Gurna. Other damage appears to have been entirely deliberate – a
determined if somewhat ineffective attempt to physically remove the
name and image of Senenmut from the tomb. For a long time it was
accepted that this desecration had occurred soon after Senenmut's
death, instigated by either Hatchepsut or Tuthmosis III. However, the
archaeological evidence is not entirely consistent with this theory.
While it is true that a deliberate attempt has been made to erase the
names of both Senenmut and Hatchepsut, the names 'Amen', 'Mut' and
'gods' have also been excised from sections of the ceiling, implying that
at least some of the damage may have occurred during the Amarna
period. Further odd spots of random vandalism – such as attacks on
the face of Hathor included in the wall frieze – remain undated, but
probably occurred during the Christian era.

As news arrived of the end of the Great Steward, orders were given to close up his presumptuous new tomb. The job was done as quickly as possible . . . Hastily gathering together bricks and stones at the mouth of the tomb, they started to wall it up, but the work did not go fast enough, and before they had finished their wall they gave it up and raked down dirt just enough to cover over the doorway.[27]

Senenmut's second tomb, Tomb 353, was a far more secretive affair with a concealed entrance sunk into the floor of the large quarry which was then being used to provide material for the construction of the *Djeser-Djeseru* causeway. This again proved to be a site well chosen for its purpose. After its abandonment the tomb, its unimposing entrance now blocked by mud-bricks and covered by layers of debris and desert sand, vanished from the historical record, only to be rediscovered by chance in 1927. Unfortunately, the newly discovered tomb was completely empty.

In plan, the tomb consists of three subterranean chambers linked together by three descending stepped passageways. The upper chamber (Chamber A) is the most complete, with the walls smoothed and preliminary designs sketched on the walls and ceiling. Chamber B, a rectangular room with a flat ceiling, was left with rough walls, while Chamber C, a vaulted chamber, has walls which have been dressed but not decorated. The northeast corner of Chamber C contains a vertical shaft 1.5 m (4 ft 11 in) deep, with two niches opening off the shaft. The northern niche, which has a vaulted ceiling, measures 0.9 m (2 ft 11 in) high, while the eastern niche had a flat ceiling and measures only 0.7 m (2 ft 3 in) in height.

The unfinished nature of the decoration, plus the presence of builders' rubble in Chambers A and B, implies that the architects employed at least two major building phases, and that Chamber A had been constructed and almost completed before it was decided to extend the tomb by building Chambers B and C. It would otherwise be difficult to explain why Chamber A was the more highly decorated room, as it would surely have been more sensible for the artists to work backwards towards the entrance; first decorating Chamber C, retreating to Chamber B and then finally to Chamber A. We have no date for the commencement of work at Tomb 353, but the stratigraphy of

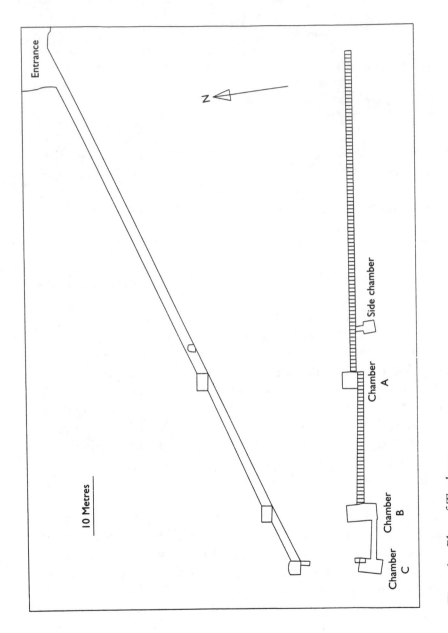

Fig. 7.6   Plan of Tomb 353

the quarry indicates that the first building phase was well underway by Year 16.

Unlike Tomb 71, Tomb 353 has suffered minimal disturbance over the centuries. There has been some slight natural damage caused by the extrusion of salt from the walls and ceilings, some ancient accidental damage which the original workmen have repaired with plaster, and some rather random attacks on faces on the walls of Chamber A. However, there has been no attempt to erase either text or the names of Senenmut or Hatchepsut, and Senenmut's image is still present in his tomb. The walls of Chamber A are decorated with columns of incised hieroglyphs recording a variety of spells and funeral liturgies designed to ease Senenmut's journey to the Field of Reeds: 'O you who are living in the two lands, you scribes and lector priests, you who are wise and who adore god, recite the transfiguration spells for the steward Senenmut.' There are also several representations of Senenmut, his brother Amenemhat and King Hatchepsut, and a false-door stela facing the entrance from the quarry. However, it is the decorated roof which has excited the attention of scholars, as this represents the earliest known astronomical ceiling in Egypt. It includes a calendar recording lunar months, representations of the northern constellations and illustrations of the planets Mars, Venus, Jupiter and Saturn.

The clearly differing nature of the two 'tombs' described above makes it unlikely that they were ever intended for the same purpose. Instead, it seems that Senenmut, although originally intending to be buried in Tomb 71 – to the extent that he ordered his precious sarcophagus to be delivered there – had finally elected to build himself a highly visible funerary chapel and a separate, hidden, burial chamber. The two monuments should therefore be properly regarded as forming the two halves of one whole. The typical 18th Dynasty private Theban tomb consisted of a T-shaped superstructure and a small burial chamber reached via a shaft which could be sited anywhere within either the funerary chapel or the chapel courtyard. The funerary chapel was the public part of the tomb where visitors could offer to the deceased, the burial chamber was completely private. This design had first been used by the ubiquitous architect Ineni, who had re-developed an old Middle Kingdom private tomb with a porticoed front, filling in the gaps between the pillars to make the desired T-shape.

Senenmut was certainly not the only official to experiment with a variation on Ineni's theme. The early 18th Dynasty was a period of innovation in private tomb architecture and, for example, his contemporary Amenemope also decided to separate the two distinct elements of his tomb, building a funerary chapel in the Theban hills and a separate burial chamber in the Valley of the Kings. Like Amenemope, Senenmut would have discovered clear advantages to the bi-partite tomb. Tomb 71 was built in a highly prestigious location with an excellent view over the necropolis, but not founded on good rock; tunnelling under the public rooms would have been both difficult and dangerous, and intricate wall carving was impossible. In direct contrast, Tomb 353 was built from firm rock, allowing safe tunnelling and detailed carving and with the additional benefit of being comparatively inconspicuous and therefore far more secure from the unwanted attentions of tomb robbers.

Given that Senenmut was not the only 18th Dynasty official to build himself an atypical tomb, it would appear unlikely that he could ever have been criticized for usurping a royal prerogative, particularly as it is now realized that the façade of Tomb 71 was by no means a straight copy of the façade of the Deir el-Bahri temple. He could certainly be criticized for tunnelling under the precincts of the Deir el-Bahri temple, and thereby linking his tomb with that of the queen, if anyone had realized that this was where his underground passages were tending. However, it is by no means certain that this was Senenmut's principal intention, as the passages follow a route which seem designed simply to exploit the local rock to best advantage. It must therefore be questioned whether Senenmut ever intended his plans for Tomb 353 to be kept secret from the queen. It would certainly have been very difficult, if not impossible, to undertake such a massive project without some word of illicit excavations reaching the palace and it seems far more logical to assume, in the face of any evidence to the contrary, that Hatchepsut both knew and approved of Senenmut's funerary arrangements.

The historical record is tantalizingly silent over the matter of Senenmut's death. All we know is that he retired abruptly from public life at some point between Hatchepsut's regnal Years 16 and 20, and was never interred in either of his carefully prepared tombs. What could have happened to him? The enigma of Senenmut's sudden disappearance is one which has teased egyptologists for decades, the lack of solid archaeological and textual evidence allowing the vivid imaginations of Senenmut-scholars to run wild, and resulting in a variety of fervently held solutions, some of which would do credit to any fictional murder/ mystery plot.[28]

As the most simple explanation, no matter how dull, is often the correct one, we might expect to find that Senenmut pre-deceased Hatchepsut, either dying of natural causes or, in a more melodramatic turn of plot, being killed by the agents of Tuthmosis III. If, as seems likely, he had started his royal career during the reign of Tuthmosis I, Senenmut would have been an elderly man of between fifty and seventy years of age by Year 16, and his death would not have been unexpected. Why then was he not buried in his intended tomb? Could Senenmut really have met his death abroad, or have been drowned in the Nile, or even been burned to death? Any of these unlikely tragedies would explain the lack of a body for burial, but would such a catastrophe really have passed unrecorded on any contemporary monument? Did Senenmut die before his burial chamber was completed, and was he therefore interred in a makeshift grave? Is it even possible that Senenmut had a third, even more secret tomb, still waiting to be discovered?

Speculation that the unexpected death of Princess Neferure caused Senenmut to lose all influence with the queen, leading to his gradual retirement from public life, appears less convincing, not least because there is no proof that Neferure predeceased her tutor. In any case, would anything as mild as early retirement from court have prevented Senenmut from being buried in his intended tomb?

More dramatic accounts of Senenmut's disappearance were popular during the late nineteenth and early twentieth centuries. These placed great reliance upon the fact that many of Senenmut's monuments were vandalized following his death, indicating that someone harboured a personal grudge against the powerful steward of Amen. This, set against the vivid background of a feuding royal court irretrievably split into irreconcilable factions, suggested that his fall from grace may have been the result of a major disagreement with the queen. If Senenmut was dismissed by Hatchepsut, it was argued, it was almost certainly due to his arrogant assumption of privileges hitherto reserved for royalty.

Certainly the queen had the power to dispose of her advisers as she wished but, as this chapter has shown, there is far less evidence for the usurpation of royal prerogatives than has previously been supposed. Could they have quarrelled over something more serious? Suggestions for such a quarrel have ranged from a lovers' tiff to Senenmut's defection to the rival political party of Tuthmosis III.

A variant on the vengeance theme has Senenmut surviving Hatchepsut, only to be killed by the supporters of Tuthmosis III. Less dramatic, and equally lacking in proof, is the suggestion that Senenmut outlived Hatchepsut and perhaps even continued to serve under Tuthmosis III before dying a natural death. The image of a vengeful Tuthmosis ruthlessly hounding his former co-regent's supporters has often featured in reconstructions of Senenmut's life. We now know that this thirst for vengeance may have been considerably overstated. At least some of Hatchepsut's principal advisers continued to serve under Tuthmosis III, including the architect Puyemre, the chief treasurers Tiy and Sennefer, and the chief steward Wadjet-Renpet. The recovery of a headless statue of Senenmut, engraved with the cartouche of Tuthmosis III and apparently housed for a time in *Djeser-Akhet*, the Deir el-Bahri temple of Tuthmosis III, indicates that the new king may not have wished to entirely obliterate the memory of an outstanding bureaucrat who served his country well.

Many of Senenmut's monuments were attacked following his death, when an attempt was made to delete his memory by erasing both his name and his image. It was originally assumed that these defacements were carried out soon after Senenmut's demise either by Hatchepsut – the unbalanced and irrational actions of a woman scorned – or by Tuthmosis III – the cool revenge of the displaced monarch. Following this line of reasoning, the vandalism must represent a frenzied personal attack aimed specifically against Senenmut. If this is the case, it is reasonable to assume that those responsible for the defacements may also have been responsible for Senenmut's sudden fall from power. However, realization is growing that the attacks on Senenmut's monuments may have been a minor part of a wider plan of defacement, aimed either at the memory of Hatchepsut or at the god Amen who was particularly linked with Senenmut. The assaults on Senenmut's name and image may therefore not be specifically linked to Senenmut's personal story, and may not have been perpetrated by those who schemed to bring

about his death. For this reason, it is not possible to discuss the defacement of Senenmut's monuments without also considering the attacks
against Hatchepsut's name and monuments which occurred at some
time following the death of the queen.

8

The End and the Aftermath

𓈖𓂧𓂆𓄿𓆱𓇋𓏏𓈖𓂋𓊃𓁢𓂧𓃀𓂋𓈖𓏏𓆓

*Now my heart turns this way and that, as I think what the people will
say. Those who shall see my monuments in years to come, and who shall
speak of what I have done.*[1]

After more than twenty years as ruler of Egypt Hatchepsut, by now an
'elderly' woman between thirty-five and fifty-five years of age, prepared
to die and live for ever in the Field of Reeds. Her funerary preparations
were well underway, her mortuary temple was already established, and
Hatchepsut was free to set her worldly affairs in order. Tuthmosis III
was her intended successor, and we start to see an obvious shift in the
balance of power as the fully mature king emerges from relative obscurity and starts to assume a more prominent role in matters of state. We
now find Tuthmosis standing beside rather than behind his stepmother,
acting in all ways as a true king of Egypt.[2] Tuthmosis, as commander-
in-chief of the army, assumed the onerous responsibility of defending
Egypt's borders. Egypt was already being troubled by sporadic outbreaks
of unrest amongst her client states to the east; these minor insurrections
were to culminate in the open rebellions which dominated much of
Tuthmosis' subsequent reign. Tuthmosis now found himself forced to
commit his troops to the first of the series of military campaigns which
would prove necessary to re-impose firm control on both Nubia and
the Levant.

Unfortunately, we have no Ineni to preserve a detailed record of
the passing of the female pharaoh but, in the absence of any evidence to the contrary, we must assume that Hatchepsut died a natural death, flying to heaven on the 10th day of the 6th month of
Year 22 (early February 1482 BC). The once popular idea that Tuthmosis, after more than twenty years of joint rule, might finally have
snapped and either killed or otherwise ousted his ageing co-ruler
seems unnecessarily melodramatic; Tuthmosis must have realized that

he had only to wait and allow nature to take her course. Hatchepsut
had already lived far longer than might have been expected, and time
was on the young king's side.

To Tuthmosis, as successor, fell the duty of burying the old king in
order to reinforce his own claim to rule as the living Horus. We may
therefore assume that Hatchepsut was properly mummified and allowed to rest with dignity, lying alongside her father in Tomb KV20.
Suggestions that Tuthmosis might have been vindictive enough to
deny Hatchepsut her kingly burial have often been made, but again
these theories have generally been based on the assumption of Tuthmosis' hatred for his co-ruler which, as we shall see below, has been
shown to be an oversimplification of events following Hatchepsut's
death.[3] Only one piece of material evidence has been put forward to
suggest that Hatchepsut's sarcophagus may never have been occupied.
When, in 1904, Howard Carter managed to force his way past the
rubble which blocked the entrance to the burial chamber of KV20,
he found that the tomb had already been ransacked. The two sarcophagi and the matching canopic chest were lying empty and the
remaining grave goods had been reduced to worthless piles of
smashed sherds and partially burned fragments of wood. The body of
Tuthmosis I had, in fact, been removed prior to the robbery by
workmen acting on the orders of Tuthmosis III, and had been transferred to the new tomb, KV38, which was itself in turn to be
robbed in antiquity. Inside KV20 the lid of Tuthmosis' sarcophagus
was left propped against the wall where the necropolis officials had
placed it in order to allow them sufficient room to manoeuvre the
body from the tomb. The lid of Hatchepsut's sarcophagus, supposedly
dislodged by the tomb robbers, was reportedly found lying intact and
face upwards over 5 m (16 ft 5 in) away from its base. This position is

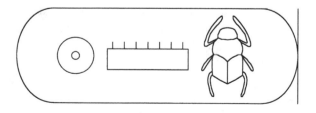

Fig. 8.1   The cartouche of King Tuthmosis III

somewhat unexpected; too heavy to simply lift, we might have expected to find evidence that the thieves used bars and wedges to
prise up the lid, allowing it to fall face downwards immediately by
the side of the sarcophagus.[4]

Could it be that the lid had never been placed on the sarcophagus,
and that Carter had in fact found it lying where the original 18th
Dynasty craftsmen had abandoned it? By extension, this would indicate
that Hatchepsut's body was never interred within KV 20. However, this
is a very slight and dubious piece of evidence on which to base a
reconstruction of events at Hatchepsut's death. We have no photograph
or plan of the tomb at the moment of re-entry, but examination of
Carter's painting of the interior of the burial chamber plainly shows
both the sarcophagus and its lid, which is not lying neatly on the floor
but is roughly displaced on top of what seem to be heaps of debris and
smashed grave goods.[5] Carter himself tells us that when he entered the
tomb 'the sarcophagus of the queen was open, with the lid lying at the
head on the floor . . . neither of the sarcophagi appeared to be *in situ*, but
showed signs of handling'. It would therefore appear most likely that it
was Carter or his workmen who moved the lid to its final resting place
while clearing out the chamber.

Fragments of Hatchepsut's anthropoid wooden coffin – a sure indication that she had indeed been accorded a decent burial – were eventually recovered from KV 4, the tomb of Ramesses XI, which had yielded
broken artifacts from the burials of several earlier pharaohs including, as
the excavators noted, 'numerous pieces of wood from the funeral furniture of some of the kings of the Eighteenth Dynasty . . . rendered into
small slivers that resembled kindling'.[6] It would appear that, during the
Third Intermediate Period, the tomb of Ramesses XI had been used as
a temporary workshop where the necropolis officials could restore or
re-wrap damaged mummies and process the artifacts recovered from
earlier burials, in particular those of Hatchepsut and Tuthmosis III.
Stripped of their most valuable recyclable aspects (for example, the
gilded–gesso surface of the coffin of Tuthmosis III was adzed clean; the
gold was presumably melted down and re-used, the coffin was still
functional although less decorative and was certainly less likely to attract
the attention of tomb robbers) the grave goods were sent together with
the bodies of their owners to the cache at Deir el–Bahri for permanent
storage.[7]

The remainder of Hatchepsut's funerary equipment is now lost, although a draughts-board and a 'throne' (actually the base and legs of a couch or bed), said to have been recovered from the Deir el-Bahri cache and presented to the British Museum by the Mancunian egyptological benefactor Jesse Howarth in 1887, have been identified as belonging to Hatchepsut on the basis of a wooden cartouche-shaped lid said to have been found with them. However, this identification is by no means certain; the Reverend Greville Chester, who obtained the artifacts on behalf of Mr Howarth, had himself acquired them from an Arab who had supposedly recovered them '. . . hidden away in one of the side chambers of the tomb of Ramesses IX [KV6], under the loose stones which encumber the place'.[8]

Hatchepsut's body has never been identified. However, the Deir el-Bahri cache which protected most of the 18th Dynasty royal mummies including Tuthmosis I(?), II and III, also included an anonymous and coffin-less New Kingdom female body together with at least one empty female coffin and a decorated wooden box bearing the name and titles of Hatchepsut and containing a mummified liver or spleen. We are therefore faced with the possibility that these female remains may include either all or part of the missing king. Further anonymous 18th Dynasty female remains have been recovered from the tomb of Amenhotep II (KV35), which was used as a storage depot for a collection of dispossessed New Kingdom mummies. This tomb yielded sixteen bodies including two unidentified women, either of them potential Hatchepsuts, who are now known as the 'Elder Lady' and the 'Younger Lady'. The Younger Lady is almost certainly too young to be Hatchepsut while the Elder Lady, thought to be a woman in her forties, was for a long time identified as the later 18th Dynasty Queen Tiy. However, recent X-ray analysis suggests that this lady may in fact have been less elderly than had been supposed; she appears to have died when somewhere between twenty-five and thirty-five years of age. It must be stressed that mummy-ages obtained by X-ray analysis do need to be treated with a degree of caution. The suggested X-ray age of thirty-five to forty years for the body of Tuthmosis III is, for example, plainly incompatible with the historical records which indicate that he reigned as king for over fifty years. However, if the analysis of the 'Elder Lady' is correct, it would appear that she too may have died too young to be Hatchepsut.

More intriguing is the suggestion that Hatchepsut may be identified with the body of the anonymous lady discovered in KV60, the tomb of the royal nurse Sitre. When it was discovered by Carter in 1903, this tomb still housed its two badly damaged female mummies, that of Sitre herself, and that of a partially unwrapped, obese middle-aged woman with worn teeth and red-gold hair. This lady had been approximately 1.55 m (5 ft 1 in) tall and had been mummified with her left arm across her chest in the typical 18th Dynasty royal burial position. Her obesity had apparently made it impossible for the embalmers to follow the usual custom of removing the entrails via a cut in the side, and she had instead been eviscerated through the pelvic floor. Carter had not been particularly interested in the tomb – he was looking for an intact royal burial which would please his sponsor, Lord Carnarvon – and, leaving things pretty much as he had found them, sealed it up again and departed. The English archaeologist Edward Ayrton had re-entered the tomb in 1906 and removed the lady Sitre and her wooden coffin to Cairo Museum, but the unknown lady had been left lying in a rather undignified position flat on her back in the middle of the burial chamber. The tomb entrance was subsequently resealed, and forgotten. When the American egyptologist Donald P. Ryan re-discovered the tomb in 1989, he provided the lady with a wooden coffin, and subsequently the burial was protected by fitting a door to the tomb. Several authorities have tentatively suggested that this unidentified lady might be none other than Hatchepsut who might have been removed from the nearby KV20 following a robbery and hidden for safety in KV60. Less likely is the theory that Tuthmosis III denied his stepmother an official burial and instead interred her alongside her old nurse.[9]

The funeral over, Tuthmosis III embarked upon thirty-three years of solo rule. He was immediately faced with revolt amongst a coalition of his Palestinian and Syrian vassals united under the banner of the Prince of Kadesh (a powerful city state on the River Orontes) and backed by the King of Mitanni, and he started a lengthy series of military campaigns designed to strengthen Egypt's position in the Near East. His aim, as he tells us, was to 'overthrow that vile enemy and to extend the boundaries of Egypt in accordance with the command of his father Amen-Re'. By Year 33 the weaker client states had all been subdued, and Tuthmosis was able to emulate his esteemed grandfather by crossing the River Euphrates, defeating the army of the King of Mitanni and then returning to Egypt via Syria where, in established Tuthmoside tradition, he enjoyed a magnificent elephant hunt. By Year 42, after twenty-one years of intermittent fighting, the boundaries of the empire were at last secure and Tuthmosis was able to relax into old age. His triumphs, however, were not to be forgotten. Tuthmosis shared Hatchepsut's love of self-promotion, and his campaigns were recorded for posterity and for the glory of Amen on the walls of the newly-built 'Hall of Annals' at Karnak, where:

His majesty commanded to record the [victories his father Amen had given him] by an inscription in the temple which his majesty had made for [his father Amen so as to record] each campaign, together with the booty which [his majesty] had brought [from it and the tribute of every foreign land] that his father Re had given him.[10]

Towards the end of his reign, his foreign problems now settled, Tuthmosis followed Hatchepsut in instigating an impressive construction programme; there was yet another phase of building at the Karnak temple complex while all the major Egyptian towns from Kom Ombo to Heliopolis plus several sites in the Nile Delta and Nubia benefited from his attentions. In private, Tuthmosis appears to have been a well-educated man of great energy – a real credit to his stepmother's upbringing. Not only was he an action man, a fearless warrior, skilled horseman and superb athlete, he was also a family man blessed with at least two principal wives, several secondary wives and a brood of children. In his spare time he composed literary works and his interests ranged from botany to reading, history, religion and even interior design.[11] Tuthmosis eventually appointed his son as co-regent, and some two years later it was it Amenhotep II, son of Meritre-Hatchepsut, who buried Egypt's greatest warrior king in Tomb KV 34 in the Valley of the Kings. Tuthmosis III had reigned for 53 years, 10 months and 26 days.

The mummy of Tuthmosis III, superficially intact and lying in its original inner coffin, was recovered from the Deir el-Bahri cache. The mummy was unwrapped and examined by Emile Brugsch in 1881, subsequently re-bandaged, and reopened by Maspero in 1886, who found that the body was covered in an unpleasant 'layer of whitish natron charged with human fat, greasy to the touch, foetid and strongly caustic'.[12] The mummy had, in fact, been badly damaged by tomb robbers, the head, feet and all four limbs had become detached and Maspero found that the body was actually held together by four wooden oars concealed beneath the linen bandages. The face was, however, undamaged, and Tuthmosis was revealed to have died in his fifties, almost completely bald, with a low forehead, narrow face, delicate ears and the buck teeth so often found in Tuthmoside family members.

At some point following Hatchepsut's death a serious attempt was made to deny her existence by physically removing her presence from the historical record. Gangs of workmen were set to work at the various monuments, and soon the name and figures of Hatchepsut had vanished; they had been completely hacked out – often leaving a very obvious Hatchepsut-shaped gap in the middle of a scene – as a preliminary to replacement by a different image or a new royal cartouche. At Karnak her obelisks were walled up and incorporated into the vestibule in front of pylon V, while at *Djeser-Djeseru* her statues and sphinxes were torn down, smashed and flung into rubbish pits. This was not merely a symbolic gesture of hatred; by removing every trace of the female king it was actually possible to rewrite Egyptian history, this time without Hatchepsut. If Hatchepsut's name was completely erased she would never have been, and the succession could now run from Tuthmosis I to Tuthmosis III without any female interference.

The removal of the name and image of a dead person, occasionally called a *damnatio memoriae*, served a dual purpose. Not only did it allow the rewriting of history, it was also a direct assault upon the spirit of the deceased. Theology dictated that, in order for the spirit or soul to live forever in the Field of Reeds, the body, the image or at least the name of the deceased must survive on Earth. If all memory of a dead person was lost or destroyed, the spirit too would perish, and there would come the much dreaded 'Second Death'; total obliteration from which there could be no return. The effects of the proscription on the dead Hatchepsut herself would therefore have been drastic. Every image and cartouche served as a re-affirmation of her reign, not merely a means of preserving her memory amongst her contemporaries and her future subjects, but a guarantee that she would live for ever in the Afterlife.

Until relatively recently the author of this proscription, and his motives, seemed obvious. Tuthmosis III had spent over twenty years seething with hatred and resentment against his co-ruler; what could be more natural than to indulge in one vindictive but eminently satisfying act of defiance against both Hatchepsut and those who had supported her in her work? However juvenile, his actions were entirely understandable:

Two more facts of which we may be perfectly certain are: 1) that Tuthmosis III obtained supreme control over Egypt only after many years of humiliating subordination to Hatchepsut and only as the result of a long and bitter struggle against his aunt and against the capable members of her party, and 2) that, as a result of this, he came to independent power with a loathing for Hatchepsut, her partisans, her monuments, her name and her very memory which practically beggars description.[13]

The shattering of Hatchepsut's monuments would presumably have brought about a cathartic release, and would have made Tuthmosis feel much, much better. Even to those who championed Hatchepsut and her actions, Tuthmosis' vandalism could not be condemned:

He had grown up a short, stocky young man full of a fiery Napoleonic energy, suppressed up to now but soon to cause the whole known world to smart. Long since he should have been sole ruler of Egypt but for Hatchepsut and we hardly have to stretch our imaginations unduly to picture the bitterness of such a man against those who had deprived him of his rights . . .'[14]

Nor is this action entirely foreign to modern ways of thinking. Indeed Winlock (writing in the 1920s) has compared the seemingly pointless destruction of Hatchepsut's monuments to the intensely patriotic period during the First World War when:

. . . the names of everything from Hamburger steaks to royal families were altered in a fervent desire to suppress memories of the enemy . . . Perhaps we are getting a little tamer than Tuthmosis III – but we can hardly pretend yet that his actions are entirely incomprehensible to us, when we find him destroying the statues of his mother-in-law.[15]

A more modern parallel may be drawn with the destruction of the statues of Lenin and other national leaders witnessed on the world's television following the collapse of the Communist regimes in the old Eastern-bloc countries.

But, however plausible, this theory of the brooding, vengeful

Fig. 8.2   Tuthmosis III being suckled by the tree-goddess Isis

Tuthmosis III is not entirely consistent with the image of the noble
scholar, historian and soldier suggested by the king's other monuments.
Naville, writing at the turn of the century, had already suggested that
Tuthmosis may not have started his reign with an immediate persecution of Hatchepsut's memory:

. . . all the recently discovered documents tend to prove that if Tuthmosis III was
the author of a few of these erasures, he did not begin by making them, and
they do not belong to the early years of his reign. The relations between aunt
and nephew were better than might be believed, and that excludes the idea
that Tuthmosis III was guilty of the death of Hatchepsut . . . the era of what has
been called the persecution, made not against the person of his aunt, but
against her memory, must be placed at the end of her reign.[16]

Naville based this suggestion on his own interpretation of a scene discovered on the remains of the dismantled Chapelle Rouge. Here a king, identified by Naville as Tuthmosis III, is shown offering incense before two (originally three) pavilions, each of which holds a sacred barque and shrine. Hatchepsut herself appears in the form of two (originally six) Osiride statues standing one on each side of the three shrines; an unmistakable indication to Naville that she is now dead. The living Tuthmosis III then steers his own barque, possibly containing the sacred emblems of Hatchepsut, towards Deir el-Bahri. Naville believed that these tableaux were intended to represent Tuthmosis III officiating at Hatchepsut's apotheosis as she became united with the god Amen. He used this interpretation to argue that, if Tuthmosis was prepared to complete the unfinished Chapelle Rouge with a scene showing the new king effectively worshipping the old – for by its nature this scene could only have been carved after Hatchepsut's death – it is unlikely that he was simultaneously erasing her name from other monuments.

Unfortunately, Naville's ingenious interpretation is now known to be incorrect. The Chapelle Rouge scene does indeed show a king offering incense before the barque of Amen, but that king is intended to be Hatchepsut. Although entirely male in appearance she is clearly named as 'The Good God, Lady of the Two Lands, Daughter of Re, Hatchepsut' and the text makes it clear that the offering is being made to Amen and not Hatchepsut. The whole scene is, in fact, a representation of Hatchepsut offering incense before the Chapelle Rouge itself, and we must assume that before this building was dismantled there were indeed two colossal mummiform statues standing one on either side of the shrine. These would certainly not be the only Osiride statues of Hatchepsut to be carved during her lifetime and indeed, as we have already seen, *Djeser-Djeseru* was originally decorated with over forty similar statues.

However, it appears that Naville may have been close to the truth when he suggested that the Chapelle Rouge might hold the key to the date of Hatchepsut's proscription. More recent analysis of the 18th Dynasty architecture of the Karnak temple, the so-called 'Hatchepsut suite' in particular, has shown that while the effacement of Hatchepsut's name did indeed occur during the reign of Tuthmosis III, it could not have occurred until relatively late in that reign, possibly not before Year 42.[17]

Naville was correct in his assumption that the Chapelle Rouge, far from being immediately defaced, was completed by Tuthmosis III, who added the topmost register of decorations in his own name and who then claimed the shrine as his own; an unlikely action for one who supposedly hated Hatchepsut's memory.

At about this time Tuthmosis was planning the construction of his own temple of Amen, *Djeser-Akhet*, which was to be built at Deir el-Bahri directly to the south of *Djeser-Djeseru*; at first sight, a rather perverse choice of site for one who could hardly bear the sight of Hatchepsut's name, although it is possible that the temple was built with the specific intention of reducing the importance of *Djeser-Djeseru*.[18] If so, the plan was successful, because once *Djeser-Akhet* was complete it took over as the focus for the celebration of the annual Feast of the Valley. *Djeser-Akhet* is now in a much damaged state, but it would appear that it was originally similar in design to *Djeser-Djeseru*. It too was built on a raised terrace and was approached by a broad causeway and ramp, although its geography dictated that it could have no rock-cut sanctuary. As it was built on higher ground, *Djeser-Akhet* must have dominated *Djeser-Djeseru* as its architects intended.

Some years later, Tuthmosis' own building projects at Karnak, including the construction of the Hall of Annals which from its texts can have occurred no earlier than Year 42, inadvertently concealed a few inscriptions and illustrations relating to Hatchepsut which should, had the proscription been in force by that time, already have been erased. Those parts of the scenes which were not protected by Tuthmosis' buildings were subsequently attacked, while the Chapelle Rouge was completely dismantled, its blocks put in storage for subsequent re-use and its granite doorways re-used in the Hall of Annals. The blocks of the Chapelle Rouge do show some rather random and incomplete erasures; either this destructive work was halted before it was fully underway or, more realistically, the attacks against the still-visible images of Hatchepsut occurred after the Chapelle had been dismantled and its blocks had been stacked[19] – it seems that the rather slapdash workmen did not take the trouble to examine every surface of every block, but simply erased all visible references to Hatchepsut. It is therefore a moot point whether the destruction of the Chapelle Rouge should actually be seen as a part of the persecution of Hatchepsut's memory; common sense would suggest that the building was simply demolished to make room for the even more magnificent granite shrine which Tuthmosis III intended to build in its place. As we have already seen, this rather drastic type of 'restoration' occurred with relative frequency at Karnak; the barque shrine of Tuthmosis III was itself later to be replaced by the barque shrine of Philip Arrhidaeus, the half-brother of Alexander the Great, who ruled Egypt as king but who never visited his adopted country.

Similarly, it is extremely doubtful whether the walling up of Hatchepsut's obelisks can be considered a serious attempt at concealing them from view. It is, after all, a very difficult task to hide successfully a 29.5 m (97 ft) tall pair of obelisks without lowering them to the ground. The bases of the obelisks, now shrouded in their masonry boxes, were destined to be incorporated in the new vestibule that Tuthmosis was already constructing in front of pylon V, and it seems that they, like the Chapelle Rouge, were simply being adapted to fit in with Tuthmosis' building plans. However, if some of the Hatchepsut 'desecrations' are now open to question, there can be no doubt about the thoroughness of others. Throughout his seasons of work at Deir el-Bahri, H. E. Winlock was fortunate enough to find the remains of scores of statue fragments, all of which had been torn from their sites in and around the temple and dumped in the convenient pits and hollows left by the contemporary building works at the site. Winlock was later to calculate that the temple and its processional way must originally have been home to some two hundred brightly coloured statues and sphinxes, each one a likeness of Hatchepsut herself. The 'Hatchepsut Hole' discovered by accident during the 1922–3 season beneath the dump of a late nineteenth-century excavation yielded dozens of limestone and granite statues and occupied the workforce of 450 workmen for half the season. Later, during the 1926–7 and 1927–8 seasons, more statue fragments turned up in the nearby 'Senenmut Quarry' where, as their excavator reported:

. . . we found a jumble of pieces of sculpture from the size of a finger-tip to others weighing a ton or more. There were large sections of the limestone colossi from the upper porch; brilliantly coloured pieces from the ranks of sandstone sphinxes which had lined the avenue . . . and fragments of at least four or five kneeling statues of the queen in red and black granite, over six feet high.[20]

Had these statues been merely thrown out of the temple, it would seem possible that they had been removed during a form of ancient spring clean so that Tuthmosis III, replacing them with statues of himself, could claim *Djeser-Djeseru* as his own. The erasure of the carved wall-images of Hatchepsut might then also be interpreted as a preliminary stage in Tuthmosis' plan to usurp Hatchepsut's role as founder and patron of the temple. However, as Winlock noted, the statues showed all the signs of a vicious personal attack:

They could only have been dragged out to their burial place slowly and laboriously and the workmen had plenty of opportunity to vent their spite on the brilliantly chiselled, smiling features. On the face of an exquisitely carved red granite statue a fire had been kindled to disintegrate the stone, and the features of the statue brought to the museum have been battered entirely away and the uraeus on the forehead, the symbol of royalty, completely obliterated. Tuthmosis III could have had no complaint to make on the execution of his orders, for every conceivable indignity had been heaped on the likenesses of the fallen queen.[21]

Other statues had undergone at least two distinct stages of vandalism. First the uraeus, symbol of kingship, had been knocked off the royal head-dress, and then the face had been disfigured, the nose being broken and the eyes being carefully picked out with a chisel, before the statue was finally dragged from its base and smashed. Some of the larger fragments had later been converted by enterprising locals into querns and pestles.

The attempted obliteration of Hatchepsut's memory has invariably been linked with the attacks against Senenmut's name and monuments. Under the old theory, that of instant revenge against Hatchepsut and her acolytes, this was inevitable. The actual damage caused to the monuments of Senenmut is not, however, entirely consistent with this argument. Indeed, Senenmut's name and image seem to have suffered from several different types of damage without appearing to fit into any pre-organized plan. Occasionally it was only his name that was attacked while his image remained intact. At the other extreme some of his statues were smashed and physically thrown out of the temples. He seems, in fact, to have been unfortunate enough to attract the attentions of several diverse groups of campaigners: those who objected to him personally, perhaps because of his relationship with Hatchepsut, and who therefore disfigured both his entire name and his image; those who were devoted to the worship of the Aten and who took exception to certain elements of his name (which contains the name of the goddess Mut, wife of Amen); those early Christian and Islamic iconoclasts who routinely objected to all pagan images. Others of his monuments have merely suffered the unavoidable ravages of time and have, for example, been reused during later periods. There was, as far as we can tell, no intense, systematic campaign against the monuments of Senenmut as there was against the monuments of Hatchepsut. Therefore, although a study of the defacement of the monuments of Senenmut may tell us a great deal about the attitude of later generations to their heritage, it tells us less than we might hope about the persecution of Hatchepsut's memory.

One striking aspect of the campaign against Hatchepsut's memory, and one which will probably have already become apparent, is the fact that it was both relatively short-lived and somewhat erratic in execution. Throughout the 18th Dynasty, the removal of an old name or image and the renewal of a wall in preparation for the carving of the new scene followed three well-established stages. First, the old scene was hacked out with a broad chisel. Next, a fine implement was used to smooth the rough surface and remove the raised ridges and, finally, the wall was polished and re-carved.[22] In many cases, however, we find that Hatchepsut's cartouche and figure were merely removed and not replaced, while her name was sporadically preserved at Armant, on the blocks of the Chapelle Rouge, at the Speos Artemidos where there is no sign of Tuthmoside erasures although there is some damage caused by the 'restorations' of Seti I, and in Tomb KV 20 where the workmen who removed the body of Tuthmosis I seem to have made no attempt to deface Hatchepsut's own inscribed sarcophagus, although it is, of course, possible that the body of Tuthmosis I was removed before the proscription took effect. At *Djeser-Djeseru* it was even possible to read some of the 'erased' inscriptions which had supposedly been hacked off the temple walls.

All this evidence leaves the very strong impression that the vindictive campaign, whatever its original purpose, was never carried out to its logical conclusion. Either the desired results had been achieved before the obliteration had been completed, or the impetus behind the campaign had been removed. It is perhaps not too fanciful a leap

of the imagination to suggest that Tuthmosis III, having started the
persecution relatively late in his reign, may have died before it was
concluded. His son and successor Amenhotep II, with no personal
involvement in the campaign, may have been content to allow the
vendetta to lapse. It may therefore be that Hatchepsut's subsequent
omission from the 19th Dynasty king lists of Seti I and Ramesses II
does not necessarily have a sinister motive; perhaps those who compiled the lists genuinely believed her to have been a queen-consort
or queen-regent rather than a full king. Ironically, it is ultimately that
fact that Hatchepsut had been content to share her reign with Tuthmosis III which allowed future generations to forget her name. Had
she ruled alone – having discreetly removed her young co-regent –
her name must have been preserved or else there would have been
an unaccountable gap in the king lists. As she always, in theory,
ruled alongside Tuthmosis III it was a simple matter to drop her
name from the historical record.

   This casts a whole new light on the reasons underlying the proscription of Hatchepsut; while it is possible to imagine and even empath-
ize with Tuthmosis indulging in a sudden whim of hatred against his

Fig. 8.3   Tuthmosis III and his mother Isis, boating through the Underworld

stepmother immediately after her death, it is far harder to imagine him overcome by such a whim some twenty years later. Indeed, if we can no longer be certain that Tuthmosis hated his stepmother as she lay on her deathbed, can we be certain that he ever hated her during her lifetime? There is certainly no other evidence to support the assumption that he did. Similarly, we must question whether Tuthmosis' primary motive in erasing the name of Hatchepsut was the persecution of her memory leading to the death of her soul, or whether this was merely an unfortunate side-effect of his wish to rewrite history by making himself sole ruler. In order to be fully effective, a *damnatio memoriae* required the complete obliteration of all cartouches and all images intended to represent the deceased. The spirit of the dead person could linger on if even one name was left intact, and Tuthmosis would have been well aware of this. Yet, as we have seen, the attacks against Hatchepsut's name and images were lackadaisical, to say the least. Of course, this begs the obvious question – if hatred was not the prime motivation behind the attacks on Hatchepsut's monuments, what was? What had Hatchepsut done to deserve this intensive persecution?

Tuthmosis III was clearly an intelligent and rational monarch. All that we know of his character suggests that he was not given to rash, impetuous acts and it seems logical to assume that throughout his life Tuthmosis was motivated less by uncontrollable urges than by calculated political expediency. We must therefore divorce his private emotions from his political actions, just as we must separate the person of Hatchepsut the woman from her role as Egypt's female pharaoh. Whatever his personal feelings towards his stepmother, Tuthmosis may well have found it advisable to remove all traces of the unconventional female king whose reign might possibly be interpreted by future generations as a grave offence against *maat*, and whose unorthodox co-regency might well cast serious doubt upon the legitimacy of his own right to rule. Hatchepsut's crime need be nothing more than the fact that she was a woman. Wounded male pride may also have played a part in his decision to act; the mighty warrior king may have balked at being recorded for posterity as the man who ruled for twenty years under the thumb of a mere woman.

Furthermore, Tuthmosis had always to consider the possibility that the first successful female king might establish a dangerous precedent. Until now this had not been a danger. Admittedly there had already

been one dynastic queen-regnant, but her reign was generally acknowledged to be a brave failure; a failure which had served to underline the
traditional view that a woman was basically incapable of holding the
throne in her own right. Queen Sobeknofru had ruled at the very end
of a fading Dynasty, and from the very start of her reign the odds had
been stacked against her. She was therefore acceptable to the conservative Egyptians as a patriotic 'Warrior Queen' who had failed, and few
would have seen reason to repeat the experiment of a female monarch.

Hatchepsut, however, was a very different case. By establishing a
lengthy and successful reign in the middle of a flourishing dynasty she
had managed to demonstrate that a woman could indeed become a
successful king, and therefore she posed more than a temporary threat
to both established custom and to the conservative interpretation of
maat. It should not be assumed that Hatchepsut was the only strong-
willed lady at the Tuthmoside court – indeed, Tuthmosis' refusal to
reinstate the position of 'God's Wife of Amen' suggests that he may
have been wary of granting his womenfolk additional power – and with
the end of his life rapidly approaching Tuthmosis may have felt it necessary to reinforce the tradition of male succession before he died. By
removing the most obvious signs of Hatchepsut's reign he could effectively delete the memory of the co-regency, and Tuthmosis himself
would emerge as sole successor to Tuthmosis II. Without an obvious
role-model, future generations of potentially strong female kings might
remain content with their traditional lot as wife, sister and eventual
mother of a king. It therefore becomes highly significant that it is only
the images of Hatchepsut as king which have been defaced. Hatchepsut
as queen consort – the correct place for a female royal – is still present
for all the world to see. Whether Tuthmosis deliberately left a few
hidden and undamaged images of his stepmother and mentor, granting
her the priceless gift of eternal life, we will never know.[23]

But, in spite of all Tuthmosis' efforts, Hatchepsut was not destined to
be Egypt's final female king, nor indeed her only conspicuous queen.
Although his own queen, Meritre-Hatchepsut, was nowhere near as
prominent as her illustrious predecessors, the subsequent queens of the
18th Dynasty continued to play an important and highly visible role in
public life. Queen Tiy, the commoner wife of Amenhotep III, was
politically active during the reign of both her husband and her son,

Akhenaten, while Queen Nefertiti, Akhenaten's consort, appeared
for a time to be almost as powerful
as the king himself. Their daughter, Ankhesenamen, widow of
Tutankhamen, was independent
enough to attempt to arrange her
own marriage with the son of a
foreign ruler. With the end of the
18th Dynasty the importance of
the queens diminished slightly although Nefertari, chief wife of
Ramesses II, appears in a prominent role on many monuments.
Two hundred and fifty years after
the death of Hatchepsut, at a time
of widespread civil unrest when
Egypt was moving perilously close
to a total breakdown of law and
order, the final Egyptian queen-
regnant, Twosret, came to power.
Unfortunately, such disturbed and
maat-less periods tend to be very

*Fig. 8.4   The High Priestess of
Amen-Re, Hatchepsut*

badly documented, and we have little archaeological or historical evidence with which to flesh out the bare bones of Twosret's reign.

Twosret had been the principal wife of the 19th Dynasty King Seti II
and, while not a member of the immediate royal family, is likely to have
been of royal blood. She bore her husband no living son and, after a
brief reign of no more than six years, Seti died and was succeeded on
the throne by Ramesses Siptah (later known as Merenptah Siptah), his
natural son by a Syrian secondary wife named Sutailja. History was
starting to repeat itself as Twosret found herself required to act as regent
to a young king who was not her own flesh and blood and whose physical weakness, the legacy of the childhood polio which had withered
one of his legs, made him an ineffectual ruler. Once again the inevitable happened. Gradually the already powerful dowager queen
started to take control, easing herself into the position of consort and
co-ruler. Whether or not she actually married her ward in order to

consolidate her position is unclear; on the wall of her tomb she is depicted standing behind Siptah in a typical wifely pose, but the young king's name has been erased and that of her actual husband Seti II has been substituted.

Following Siptah's early death a wave of discontent spread over the country and Twosret saw her opportunity. With no obvious successor to challenge her authority she clung on to her role as co-regent, reinforcing her position by adopting the full titulary of a male king of Egypt. She undertook the now traditional expeditions to Sinai and Palestine and commenced building works at Heliopolis and Thebes, but her solo rule was destined to be brief, possibly less than two years. She disappeared into obscurity, to be replaced by the rather nondescript pharaoh Sethnakht, founder of the 20th Dynasty, who later claimed to have 'driven out the usurper'. Manetho preserved the name of a King Thuoris as the final king of the 19th Dynasty.

At first sight there are many obvious points of similarity between the stories of these two female kings. Both were married to relatively short-lived and somewhat ineffectual kings, both failed to produce a male heir to the throne, both were required to act as regent to an unrelated minor and, while neither had a living husband, both came under the influence of a dominant court official (Hatchepsut was supported by Senenmut; Twosret had a less certain relationship with a mysterious individual known as the Great Chancellor Bay). Both must also have been strong-minded and forceful women capable of fighting against well-established traditions and holding their own against the male-dominated establishment. However, there are also some important dissimilarities between the two reigns. Twosret, like Sobeknofru before her, came to power as the last resort of a decaying dynasty lacking any more suitable (that is, male) monarch. In spite of Sethnakht's claim she was never, as far as we know, widely perceived as a usurper, and could even be congratulated on her valiant attempt to prolong a dying line. Furthermore, Twosret's reign was not a spectacular success. It was brief, undistinguished, and left Egypt in a worse political state than it had been before she came to power. It therefore posed no threat to subsequent male rulers. This seems to have made her in many ways far more acceptable as a monarch and, although Sethnakht usurped her tomb and attempted to remove her name and image from its walls, it seems that Twosret was never subjected to the persecution inflicted on Hatchepsut's memory.[24]

Queen, or King, Twosret was the last native-born Egyptian queen regnant. However, over one thousand years later Egypt was again to be ruled by a handful of dominant and short-lived women, this time the Greek queens of the Ptolemaic royal family. The last of these, Cleopatra VII, has entered the public imagination not only as the archetypal Egyptian queen but as one of the most widely recognized women of all times. Her story, an intriguing cocktail of incest, passion, and tragedy played out against a louche oriental setting, was fascinating to her more strait-laced Roman contemporaries, while the fact that her actions had a direct effect on the development of the Roman Empire ensured that her history would be recorded for posterity. Plutarch, writing a good many years after her death, was clearly intrigued by reports of the queen's physical charms:

The contact of her presence, if you lived with her, was irresistible; the attraction of her person, joining with the charm of her conversation, and the character that attended all she said or did, was something bewitching. It was a pleasure merely to hear the sound of her voice, with which, like an instrument of many strings, she could pass from one language to another.[25]

The story of Hatchepsut, a far more successful ruler but one who was less well documented, who was less interestingly 'wanton' in her behaviour, and who played little or no part in the development of western society, has never had the power to compete with the myths and legends which have grown up around Cleopatra, beautiful 'Serpent of the Nile'.

Cleopatra was, in spite of the legend, a rather plain woman, a direct descendant of Ptolemy I, the Macedonian general who had been made King of Egypt following the death of Alexander the Great. She ruled over one of the most fertile countries in the Mediterranean world, but it was a dissatisfied Egypt once again torn by civil unrest, chafing under Greek rule and directly influenced by the political infighting endemic in Roman politics. The royal family, heavily in debt, was in a constant state of violent feud, and Cleopatra only became queen following the untimely deaths of her father Ptolemy XII, her sister Cleopatra VI and a second sister Berenike. Her third sister Arsinoe rebelled against her rule and was eventually killed, her brother and co-regent Ptolemy XIII drowned, and her second brother–husband died in mysterious circumstances soon after their marriage. Cleopatra, the family survivor, proclaimed her infant son Caesarion (allegedly the child of Julius Caesar) co-regent, effectively making herself sole ruler of Egypt. Her reign brought a brief period of internal peace and economic stability. However, her decision to support Mark Anthony, the father of three of her children, in his power struggle with Octavian spelt disaster for Egypt. When Octavian's troops reached Alexandria in 30 BC Cleopatra and Anthony committed suicide, and Egypt was absorbed into the Roman Empire.

Long before Cleopatra's ill-fated reign, Hatchepsut had been all but forgotten by her people. Although *Djeser-Djeseru* continued to be recognized as a potent religious centre the name of its founder was now a distant memory, and Hatchepsut had been omitted from the king lists of Abydos and Sakkara where the succession was recorded as passing from Tuthmosis I to Tuthmosis II and then directly to Tuthmosis III. Similarly, she was excluded from the celebration of the festival of Min depicted on the wall of the Ramesseum, where again the procession of royal ancestors shows Tuthmosis I, II and III in sequence. This was not solely a royal vendetta; Hatchepsut was also missing from the non-royal tombs dating to the time of Tuthmosis III which might reasonably have been expected to include her name, and she is not even to be found amongst the 19th and 20th Dynasty private monuments of Deir el-Medina which recorded a host of far more ephemeral Tuthmoside princes and princesses. However, her memory must have lingered somewhere – possibly included on king lists which have not survived – as Manetho, writing his history of the kings of Egypt in approximately 300 BC, was able to include a female ruler named Amense or Amensis, sister of Hebron and mother of Mishragmouthosis (Tuthmosis III) as the fifth ruler of the 18th Dynasty. He accorded this female ruler a reign of either 21 years 9 months (Josephus version) or 22 years (Africanus).

As the centuries passed and all knowledge of hieroglyphic writing faded, Hatchepsut sank even deeper into obscurity. Her name was to be lost for almost two thousand years, during which time her monuments with their unreadable cartouches stood in mute testimony to their founder. Eventually, however, *Djeser-Djeseru*, now ruined and to a large extent buried under dunes of wind-blown sand and piles of rocks fallen from the cliff above, started to attract the attention of the western tourists who were becoming increasingly fascinated by Egypt's ancient past.[26] By the middle of the eighteenth century, Deir el-Bahri had been proved to be a prolific source of mummies, papyri and other exotic oriental desirables, and trade in the stolen antiquities was both brisk and lucrative. A steady trickle of distinguished visitors now started to arrive at the site, and *Djeser-Djeseru* was recorded by the British cleric Richard Pococke (1737), by the Napoleonic Expedition (1798–1802) and by William Beechey and the ex-circus strongman turned antiquarian Giovanni Battista Belzoni (1817). With the decipherment of hieroglyphics in 1822 came the first breakthrough in attempts to reconstruct the history of the temple. In 1828, the distinguished philologist and principal decoder of hieroglyphics, Jean François Champollion, paid a visit to Deir el-Bahri. Champollion was able to recognize the cartouche of Tuthmosis III, whom he called Moeris, and he realized that this king's cartouche usurped that of an earlier king whose partially erased name he misread as Amenenthe or Amonemhe.

Champollion firmly believed that his Amenenthe was a man. This caused him endless puzzlement as he noted that the name of the supposedly male king was consistently accompanied by feminine titles and forms. His words on this subject – fascinating to those of us blessed with hindsight – are worth quoting at length as they provide a good illustration of how a subconscious assumption or prejudice on the part of the excavator or translator may have a drastic effect on the interpretation of archaeological evidence:

If I felt somewhat surprised at seeing here, as elsewhere throughout the temple, the renowned Moeris, adorned with all the insignia of royalty, giving place to this Amenenthe, for whose name we may search the royal lists in vain, still more astonished was I to find on reading the inscriptions that wherever they referred to this bearded king in the usual dress of the Pharaohs, nouns and verbs were in the feminine, as though a queen were in question. I found the same peculiarity everywhere. Not only was there the prenomen of Amenenthe preceded by the title of sovereign ruler of the world, *with the feminine affix*, but also his own name immediately following on the title of 'Daughter of the Sun'. Finally, in all the bas-reliefs representing the gods speaking to this king, he is addressed as a queen, as in the following formula: 'Behold, thus saith Amen-Re, Lord of the Thrones of the World, to his daughter whom he loves, sun devoted to the truth: the building which thou hast made is like to the divine dwelling.'[27]

In order to explain this extraordinary situation, Champollion proposed the existence of an 18th Dynasty heiress-queen Amense, a sister of Tuthmosis II, who had first married a man named Tuthmosis and then, after his death, married the mysterious Amenenthe. Both these men ruled Egypt in Queen Amense's name. Following the death of Amense, Amenenthe retained his crown, becoming co-regent with the young Tuthmosis III, who turned out to be a somewhat ungrateful ward who was to spend much of his subsequent solo reign attempting to efface the name of his co-ruler from the walls of the Deir el-Bahri temple.

Niccolo Rosellini, Professor of Oriental Languages at the University of Pisa and a close personal friend of Champollion, published a description of *Djeser-Djeseru* in 1844. Rosellini put forward a variant on Champollion's theme; his succession passed from Tuthmosis I to Tuthmosis II, then to his wife Queen Amoutmai, her sister Queen Amense, and finally to Tuthmosis III. At the same time John Gardiner Wilkinson, another distinguished linguist and the first to classify and number the tombs in the Valley of the Kings, took up residence on the West Bank of Thebes where he had plenty of time to read the hieroglyphs for himself. Wilkinson tentatively suggested that the mysterious king should be re-named Amenneitgori or Amun-Noo-Het and should be re-classified not as a man but as a woman 'not in the list; a queen?'[28] It was left to Karl Richard Lepsius, leader of the Prussian expedition of 1842–5, to make some sense of the muddle by confirming that the clue to the king's identity was not to be found in her appearance, which as all agreed was entirely masculine, but in her inscriptions:

In the outermost angle of this rock-cove [Deir el-Bahri, called el-Asasif by Lepsius] is situated the most ancient temple-building of Western Thebes, which belongs to the period of the New Egyptian Monarchy, at the commencement of its glory . . . It was queen Numt-Amen, the elder sister of Tuthmosis III, who accomplished this bold plan . . . She never appears on her monuments as a woman, but in male attire; we only find out her sex by the inscriptions. No doubt at that period it was illegal for a woman to govern;

for that reason, also, her brother, probably still a minor, appears at a later period as ruler along with her. After her death her Shields [cartouches] were everywhere converted into Tuthmosis Shields, the feminine forms of speech in the inscription were changed, and her names were never adopted in the later lists along with the legitimate kings.[29]

Lepsius was the first to publish the name of 'Hat . . . u Numt-Amen' although he assigned her to the 17th Dynasty.

However, the situation was still far from clear, and Samuel Sharpe, writing in 1859 and relying on secondary sources including Manetho, Herodotus and Eratosthenes for his information, was fairly typical of many of his fellow authors in his confusion. He knew of the existence of the female Egyptian king, and he even knew many of the salient facts of her reign, but he had her dates and even her name hopelessly jumbled:

. . . Tuthmosis II followed the first of that name on the throne of Thebes; but he is very much thrown into the shade by Amun-Nitocris, his strong-minded and ambitious wife. She was the last of the race of Memphite sovereigns, the twelfth or eleventh in succession from the builders of the great pyramids; and by her marriage with Tuthmosis, Upper and Lower Egypt were brought under one sceptre. She was handsome among women, and brave among men, and she governed the kingdom for her brother with great splendour . . . Tuthmosis III, on coming to the throne was a minor: queen Nitocris, who had before governed for her husband, now governed for his successor, and even when the young Tuthmosis came of age, he was hardly king of the whole country till after the death of Nitocris . . . in her sculptures she is always dressed in men's clothes to indicate that she was a queen in her own right, and not a queen consort . . .[30]

Sharpe correctly credits Hatchepsut with building works at Karnak, the erection of a pair of obelisks and the construction of the Deir el-Bahri temple, but he also believed that she had built the third pyramid at Giza, misreading her name Maatkare and confusing her with both King Menkaure of the 4th Dynasty and Queen Menkare-Nitocris, the 6th Dynasty female ruler of Egypt whose story has become entangled with a host of myths and legends and whose beautiful naked ghost – this time confused with the fictional courtesan and queen, Rhodolphis – is said to haunt the pyramids.

★

A mere twenty-five years later, with a greater understanding of the hieroglyphic language, much of the confusion had been cleared away. Hatchepsut's name, titles and principal monuments were now known, and she even had her own entry in a dictionary of Egyptian archaeology published in 1875:

Hatsou . . . queen of the 18th Dynasty. Her *prenomen* is *Ra-ma-ka* [Maatkare read backwards]. Her father, Thouthmes I, proclaimed her queen in preference to her two brothers, who reigned later under the names of Thouthmes II and Thouthmes III. However she shared power with Thouthmes II, who died a short time after. Again Hatchepsut reigned alone . . . Next she associated herself with her second brother Thouthmes III, and it was not until the fifteenth year of his reign that she eventually decided to give up the throne. She is represented on the monuments as a king, with a bearded face.[31]

From this time on it was the work of the archaeologists patiently excavating in and around Luxor and on the West Bank at Thebes which was to add factual flesh to the bare bones of Hatchepsut's history. Mariette, Naville, Carter, Winlock, Lancing, Hayes and the Polish Mission, to name but a few, have all made substantial contributions to our increasing understanding of her unusual reign, an understanding which is, through necessity, based almost entirely on Hatchepsut's own surviving monuments and monumental inscriptions – her own propaganda in stone. Hatchepsut had always intended that her monuments should be read as eternal testimonies to her own grandeur. It is perhaps only fitting that they should now, some three thousand years after their conception, start to slowly reveal the story of her rule as the king herself wished it to be told. Hatchepsut's mummified body may be lost to us but her name, temporarily forgotten but now forever linked with the beautiful *Djeser-Djeseru*, is once again spoken in Egypt.

Historical Events

Years Before Christ	LOCAL CHRONOLOGY	EGYPT
3000	Archaic Period (Dynasties 1–2)	Unification of Egypt
2500	Old Kingdom (Dynasties 3–6)	Djoser step-pyramid at Sakkara Great Pyramid of Khufu at Giza
2000	First Intermediate Period (Dynasties 7–11)	
	Middle Kingdom (Dynasties 11–13)	Theban kings re-unify Egypt Queen Sobeknofru
1500	Second Intermediate Period (Dynasties 14–17)	Hyksos kings in Northern Egypt
	New Kingdom (Dynasties 18–20)	**Hatchepsut** Tutankhamen Ramesses II Queen Twosret
1000	Third Intermediate Period (Dynasties 21–25)	Kings at Tanis Nubian kings
500	Late Period (Dynasties 26–31)	
	Ptolemaic Period	
A.D. 0		Egypt part of Roman Empire

Notes

Introduction

1 Extract from the Speos Artemidos inscription of King Hatchepsut, translation given by Gardiner, A. (1946), The Great Speos Artemidos Inscription, *Journal of Egyptian Archaeology* 32: 43–56.

2 Budge, E. A. W. (1902), *Egypt and Her Asiatic Empire*, London: 1.

3 Naville, E. (1894), *The Temple of Deir el-Bahari: its plan, its founders and its first explorers: Introductory Memoir*, 12th Memoir of the Egypt Exploration Fund, London: 15.

4 Budge, E. A. W. (1902), *Egypt and Her Asiatic Empire*, London: 4.

5 Naville, E. (1906), Queen Hatshopsitu, her life and Monuments, in T. M. Davis (ed.), *The Tomb of Hatshopsitu*, London: 1.

6 Gardiner, A. (1961), *Egypt of the Pharaohs*, Oxford: 184.

7 Hayes, W. C. (1973), Egypt: Internal Affairs from Tuthmosis I to the Death of Amenophis III, in I. E. S. Edwards *et al.*, (eds), *Cambridge Ancient History*, 3rd edition, Cambridge, 2.1: 317.

8 Drioton, E. and Vandier, J. (1938), *L'Égypte: Les Peuples de l'orient méditerranéen II*, Paris: 398.

9 O'Connor, D. (1983), in Trigger, B. G. *et al.*, (eds), *Ancient Egypt: a social history*, Cambridge: 196. The abstract concept of *maat* was personified in the form of an anthropoid goddess, the daughter of the sun god, Re. This lady was always depicted as a slender young woman wearing a single tall ostrich feather tied on her head by a hair-band.

10 Consult Lichtheim, M. (1973), *Ancient Egyptian Literature I: the Old and Middle Kingdoms*, Los Angeles: 149–63, for a full translation and discussion of this text.

11 Naville, E. (1894), *The Temple of Deir el-Bahari: its plan, its founders and its first explorers: Introductory Memoir*, 12th Memoir of the Egypt Exploration Fund, London: 9.

Chapter 1   Egypt in the Early Eighteenth Dynasty

1   Extract from the Speos Artemidos inscription of King Hatchepsut, translation given by Gardiner, A. (1946), The Great Speos Artemidos Inscription, *Journal of Egyptian Archaeology* 32: 47–8.

2   In a tradition which started during the Old Kingdom, many Egyptian men of rank made permanent records of their achievements in the form of stylized autobiographies which were preserved on the walls of their tombs.

3   For these, and many other Middle Kingdom texts in translation, plus a discussion of the development of Old and Middle Kingdom literature, consult Lichtheim, M. (1973), *Ancient Egyptian Literature I: the Old and Middle Kingdoms*, Los Angeles. See also Parkinson, R. B. (1991), *Voices from Ancient Egypt: an anthology of Middle Kingdom writings*, London.

4   Quoted in Gardiner, A. (1961), *Egypt of the Pharaohs*, Oxford: 155. Josephus claims to be quoting directly from Manetho himself. His explanation of the name 'Hyksos' is now known to be incorrect; Hyksos is actually the corrupted Greek version of an Egyptian phrase meaning 'The Chiefs of Foreign Lands'. We have no knowledge of the precise origins of the Hyksos peoples.

5   The 13th Dynasty Brooklyn Papyrus 35.1446 gives some indication of the numbers of these migrants when it records that 45 out of a total of 79 recorded domestic servants were 'Asiatic' in origin.

6   As the dynasties represent lines of ruling families or related individuals rather than successive chronological periods it was possible for Egypt, at times of disunity, to be ruled by two or more dynasties at the same time. Thus, the 14th Dynasty appears to have been contemporary with the 13th Dynasty, and Dynasties 15, 16 and 17 were also contemporary, each dynasty ruling over its own, exclusive, territory.

7   Gardiner, A. (1961), *Egypt of the Pharaohs*, Oxford: 167–8.

8   Gardiner, A. (1961), *Egypt of the Pharaohs*, Oxford: 155–6.

9   Extract from The Quarrel of Apophis and Seknenre, translated in Simpson, W. K., ed. (1973), *The Literature of Ancient Egypt: an anthology of stories, instructions and poetry*, New Haven: 77–80.

10   Smith, G. E. (1912), *The Royal Mummies*, Cairo.

11   Gardiner, A. (1961), *Egypt of the Pharaohs*, Oxford: 167.

12   For a full discussion of this stela, see Habachi, L. (1972), *The Second Stela of Kamose and his Struggle against the Hyksos Ruler and his Capital*, Gluckstadt.

13   All extracts from the autobiography of Ahmose, son of Ibana, are translated by S. R. Snape. For a published translation of this work, consult

Lichtheim, M. (1976), *Ancient Egyptian Literature II: the New Kingdom*, Los Angeles: 12–15.

14 For a basic description of Egyptian army life, consult Shaw, I. (1991), *Egyptian Warfare and Weapons*, Risborough. Shaw provides a more specialized reading list.

15 Extract from the obelisk inscription of King Hatchepsut, Karnak.

16 Wosret was a relatively obscure Upper Egyptian goddess.

17 Homer, *Iliad*, Book IX. Homer refers to the Egyptian Thebes as 'hundred-gated' to distinguish it from the Greek 'seven-gated' city of Thebes.

18 Keen, M. (1990), *English Society in the Middle Ages 1348–1500*, London: 161. Keen cites as an example the household of Earl Gilbert of Clare who moved on average every two to three weeks.

19 The English Queen Elizabeth I undertook similar tours of her country as a deliberate cost-cutting exercise, staying with local dignitaries in order to save the expense of maintaining a permanent court in London. A visit from the queen and her entourage could prove to be a ruinously expensive honour for a loyal subject.

20 Quoted in Kitchen, K. (1982), *Pharaoh Triumphant: the life and times of Ramesses II*, Warminster: 122.

21 Herodotus, *Histories*, II: 14.

22 Breasted, J. H. (1905), *A History of Egypt*, New York: 334.

23 For a full translation, consult Lichtheim, M. (1976), *Ancient Egyptian Literature II: the New Kingdom*, Los Angeles: 168.

24 Stevenson Smith, W., *The Art and Architecture of Ancient Egypt*, revised and edited by W. K. Simpson (1981), New Haven: 225.

25 Herodotus, *Histories*, II: 164.

Chapter 2   A Strong Family

1 Extract from the stela of King Ahmose, translated by S. R. Snape.

2 Some slight doubt has been cast over the royal parentage of Queen Ahmose Nefertari by an inscription recovered from Karnak which appears to read, 'He [the king] clothed me [Ahmose Nefertari] when I was a nobody.' However, the precise translation, and exact meaning of the translation, is by no means certain, and it is entirely possible that 'nobody' should be read as 'orphan'. This matter is discussed in further detail in Redford, D. B. (1967), *History and Chronology of the Eighteenth Dynasty of Egypt: seven studies*, Toronto: 30–31.

3   There is no direct proof that Meryt-Neith ever ruled Egypt as an inde-
     pendent king, but there is a strong body of circumstantial evidence which
     certainly points that way. This evidence is reviewed in detail in Tyldesley,
     J. A. (1994), *Daughters of Isis: Women of Ancient Egypt*, London: Chapters 6
     and 7.

4   A division of labour which became formalized in the artistic convention
     which, despite the fact that Egypt was a racially well-mixed African
     country, decreed that men should always be depicted with a tanned
     brown skin, women with an indoor pallor.

5   Ever since the nineteenth-century Scottish lawyer McLennan published
     his *Primitive Societies*, in which he outlined a theory that all kinship and
     marriage patterns passed through the same four evolutionary stages –
     promiscuity, matriarchy, patriarchy and cognatic monogamy. The publica-
     tion of J. G. Frazer's *The Golden Bough* (1914), London, also had a deep
     influence on his contemporaries working in the fields of archaeology and
     egyptology.

6   For a full explanation of all these terms, consult Fox, R. (1967), *Kinship
     and Marriage*, London.

7   Extract from the *Instructions of King Amenemhat I*; for a full translation of
     this text, see Lichtheim, M. (1973), *Ancient Egyptian Literature I: the Old
     and Middle Kingdoms*, Los Angeles: 135–9.

8   Extract from the New Kingdom Inscription of Scribe Any. For a full
     translation of this text, consult Lichtheim, M. (1976), *Ancient Egyptian
     Literature II: the New Kingdom*, Los Angeles: 135–46.

9   Tylor, J. J. and Griffith, F. L. (1894), *The Tomb of Paheri at el-Kab*, 11th
     Memoir of the Egypt Exploration Society, London: 25.

10   Redford, D. B. (1967), *History and Chronology of the Eighteenth Dynasty of
     Egypt: seven studies*, Toronto: 65.

11   Consult Lerner, G. (1986), *The Creation of Patriarchy*, Oxford: 93. The same
     parallel is cited in Robins, G. (1993), *Women in Ancient Egypt*, London: 28.

12   From the marriage scarab of Amenhotep III.

13   Quoted in Robins, G. (1993), *Women in Ancient Egypt*, London: 30.

14   Lane, E. B. (1836), *Manners and Customs of the Ancient Egyptians*, London.

15   This image certainly affected those late nineteenth-century egyptologists
     who went to Egypt determined to uncover a multitude of concubines
     and Ottoman-style harems; find them they did, mistakenly classifying
     many innocent servant girls, housekeepers and secondary queens in their
     quest for the elusive, erotic, ancient Egyptian whore of their dreams.

16   Blanch, L. (1959), *The Wilder Shores of Love*, London: 220.

17   See, for example, Shaarawi, H., translated by M. Badran (1986), *Harem
     Years: the memoirs of an Egyptian feminist (1879–1924)*, London. For an

account of a happy childhood spent in a traditional Islamic harem in Morocco, read Mernissi, F. (1994), *The Harem Within*, London.

18 This point is discussed in further detail in Dodson, A. (1990), Crown Prince Djhutmose and the royal sons of the Eighteenth Dynasty, *Journal of Egyptian Archaeology* 76: 87–96. An appendix lists the few known royal princes of the 18th Dynasty.

19 James, T. G. H. (1973), Egypt: from the expulsion of the Hyksos to Amen-ophis I, in I. E. S. Edwards *et al.* (eds), *The Cambridge Ancient History*, 3rd edition, Cambridge, 2.1: 305.

20 James, T. G. H. (1973), Egypt: from the expulsion of the Hyksos to Amen-ophis I, in I. E. S. Edwards *et al.* (eds), *The Cambridge Ancient History*, 3rd edition, Cambridge, 2.1: 306.

21 Gardiner, A. (1961), *Egypt of the Pharaohs*, Oxford: 130.

22 Extract from the autobiography of Ahmose, son of Ibana, translated by S. R. Snape. For a published translation of this work, consult Lichtheim, M. (1976), *Ancient Egyptian Literature II: the New Kingdom*, Los Angeles: 12–15.

23 Several historians claim, without citing any concrete evidence, that Tuth-mosis I belonged to a collateral branch of the royal family; see for ex-ample Grimal, N. (1992), translated by I. Shaw, *A History of Ancient Egypt*, Oxford: 207.

24 Gardiner, A. (1961), *Egypt of the Pharaohs*, Oxford: 130.

25 For a detailed study of this subject, consult Murnane, W. J. (1977), *Ancient Egyptian Coregencies*, Chicago.

26 Translation taken from Watterson, B. (1991), *Women in Ancient Egypt*, Stroud: 56 and 60. For a full translation of this story, consult Lichtheim, M. (1980), *Ancient Egyptian Literature III: the Late Period*, Los Angeles: 127–8.

27 Translation taken from Watterson, B. (1991), *Women in Ancient Egypt*, Stroud: 56 and 60. For a full translation of this story, consult Lichtheim, M. (1980), *Ancient Egyptian Literature III: the Late Period*, Los Angeles: 127–8.

28 Wilkinson, J. G. (1837), *The Ancient Egyptians: their life and customs 2*, London: 224.

Chapter 3   Queen of Egypt

1 Extracts from the biography of Ineni, translated in Breasted, J. H. (1906), *Ancient Records of Egypt*, vol. 2, Chicago: 108, 116.

2   Extract from the autobiography of Ahmose, son of Ibana, translated by S. R. Snape. For a published translation of this work, consult Lichtheim, M. (1976), *Ancient Egyptian Literature II: the New Kingdom*, Los Angeles: 12–15.

3   Breasted, J. H., *Ancient Records of Egypt*, vol. 2, Chicago: 106.

4   Figures suggested by Hopkins, K. B. (1983), *Death and Renewal: sociological studies in Roman History*, 2, Cambridge.

5   See Baines, J. and Eyre, C. J. (1983), Four Notes on Literacy, *Goettinger Miszellen* 61: 65–96.

6   For a discussion of Prince Ramose, see Snape, S. R. (1985), Ramose Restored: a royal prince and his mortuary cult, *Journal of Egyptian Archaeology* 71: 180–83. There is virtually no evidence to support the existence of a further three sons (named Binpu, Nekenkhal and Ahmose) who are occasionally cited as royal princes but who, were they truly the sons of Tuthmosis and Ahmose, must have died in early childhood before they could make any impact on the historical record.

7   Egyptology is by no means an exact science, and it remains a possibility that we may be muddling up two Mutnofrets, one the concubine of Tuthmosis I and mother of Tuthmosis II, and one a royal princess, the daughter of Tuthmosis I and sister of Tuthmosis II and Hatchepsut.

8   Cartouche is the name given to the rectangular enclosure, intended to represent a tied loop of rope, always drawn around the two principal names of the kings of Egypt.

9   Sethe, K. (1896), *Die Thronwirren unter den Nachfolgern Königs Tuthmosis I, ihr Verlauf und ihre Bedeutung*, Leipzig.

10 This story is told more fully in Davies, W. V. (1982), Thebes, in T. G. H. James (ed.), *Excavating in Egypt: the Egypt Exploration Society 1882–1992*, London: 6. It was evidently Mme Naville who posed the threat to the continuation of the archaeological work; bereft of her kitchen, she demanded that she and her husband return immediately to Switzerland. It is tempting to speculate that it was Naville's relationship with his forceful wife which stimulated his interest in Hatchepsut, another forceful woman.

11 Edgerton, W. F. (1933), *The Tuthmoside Succession*, Chicago.

12 Hayes, W. C. (1935), *Royal Sarcophagi of the XVIII Dynasty*, Princeton.

13 Winlock, H. E. (1932), The Egyptian Expedition 1930–31, *Bulletin of the Metropolitan Museum of Art New York* 32.2: 5–10.

14 Carter himself initially believed that the two women might be the nurses of Tuthmosis IV.

15 Gardiner, A. (1961), *Egypt of the Pharaohs*, Oxford: 180.

16   Winlock, H. E. (1928), The Egyptian Expedition 1925–1927, *Bulletin of the Metropolitan Museum of Art New York* 23.2: 47.

17   Hayes, W. C. (1973), Egypt: Internal Affairs from Tuthmosis I to the death of Amenophis III, in I. E. S. Edwards *et al.* (eds), *Cambridge Ancient History*, 3rd edition, Cambridge, 2.1: 316.

18   Budge, E. A. W. (1902), *Egypt and her Asiatic Empire*, London: 4. Budge is by no means the only author to assume that Hatchepsut ruled on behalf of her weaker brother; see, for example, Hayes, W. C. (1935), *Royal Sarcophagi of the XVIII Dynasty*, Princeton: 145. Hayes cites several earlier references.

19   Carter, H. (1917), A Tomb Prepared for Queen Hatshepsuit and other recent discoveries at Thebes, *Journal of Egyptian Archaeology* 4: 114.

20   Carter, H. (1917), A Tomb Prepared for Queen Hatshepsuit and other recent discoveries at Thebes, *Journal of Egyptian Archaeology* 4: 118.

21   Hayes, W. C. (1935), *Royal Sarcophagi of the XVIII Dynasty*, Princeton: 67.

22   Sethe, K., Helck W. *et al.* (1906–58), *Urkunden der 18. Dynastie*, Leipzig and Berlin: 34.

23   Discussed in Robins, G. (1993), *Women in Ancient Egypt*, London: 49.

24   Hayes, W. C. (1973), *Royal Sarcophagi of the XVIII Dynasty*, Princeton: 316.

25   Maspero, G. (1896), *The Struggle of the Nations*, London: 242–3.

26   Smith, G. E. (1912), *The Royal Mummies*, Cairo: 29.

27   Carter, H. and Newberry, P. E. (1904), *The Tomb of Thoutmosis IV*, London.

28   For a review of the various caches, consult Reeves, C. N. (1990), *Valley of the Kings: the decline of a royal necropolis*, London: Chapter 10.

29   Brugsch's words quoted in Wilson, E. (1887), Finding Pharaoh, *The Century Magazine*. Brugsch was apparently concerned that his candle might cause a conflagration in the dry and dusty chamber. John Romer, who also quotes from Brugsch, devotes a chapter to the circumstances surrounding the finding of the Deir el-Bahri cache in Romer, J. (1981), *Valley of the Kings*, London.

30   Dawson, W. R. (1947), Letters from Maspero to Amelia Edwards, *Journal of Egyptian Archaeology* 33: 70.

31   See, however, Reeves, C. N. (1990), *Valley of the Kings: the decline of a royal necropolis*, London, Chapter 10: 18–19. Reeves believes that Tuthmosis II was not interred in the Valley of the Kings, but in a lesser tomb at Deir el-Bahri.

32   See, for example, Gardiner, A. (1961), *Egypt of the Pharaohs*, Oxford: 181 '. . . from its neglect one might conjecture that no one cared very much what was his fate'; Hayes, W. C. (1935), *Royal Sarcophagi of the XVIII Dynasty*, Princeton: 144 '. . . one could hardly have expected her to have

had either the inclination or the opportunity to make elaborate preparations for Tuthmosis II's burial.'

33   Sethe, K., Helck, W. *et al.* (1906–58), *Urkunden der 18. Dynastie*, Leipzig and
      Berlin: 180, 8–12.

34   This is discussed further in Redford, D. B. (1967), *History and Chronology
      of the Eighteenth Dynasty of Egypt: seven studies*, Toronto: 74–6.

35   Consult Gabolde, L. (1987), La chronologie du règne de Thoutmosis II,
      ses conséquences sur la datation des momies royales et leurs répercussions
      sur l'histoire du développement de la Vallée des Rois, *Studien zur Altägyp-
      tischen Kultur* 14: 61–81. The problem of Hatchepsut's age is discussed in
      Bierbrier, M. L. (1995), How old was Hatchepsut?, *Goettinger Miszellen* 144:
      15–19.

36   Naville, E. (1894), *The Temple of Deir el-Bahari: its plan, its founders and its
      first explorers: Introductory Memoir*, 12th Memoir of the Egypt Exploration
      Fund, London: 14.

Chapter 4   King of Egypt

1   Extract from the biography of Ineni, translated in Breasted, J. H. (1906),
      Ancient Records of Egypt: historical documents, vol. 2, Chicago: 341.

2   Lichtheim, M. (1973), *Ancient Egyptian Literature I: the Old and Middle King-
      doms*, Los Angeles: 220.

3   Sethe, K and Helck, W. (1906–58) *Urkunden der 18. Dynastie*, Leipzig and
      Berlin, 4.219, 13–220, 6. Breasted, J. H. (1988), *Ancient Records of Egypt*,
      2nd edition, 2, Chicago: 187–212.

4   Naville, E. (1896), *The Temple of Deir el-Bahari Part 2*, 14th Memoir of the
      Egypt Exploration Fund, London: 15.

5   Naville, E. (1896), *The Temple of Deir el-Bahari Part 2*, 14th Memoir of the
      Egypt Exploration Fund, London: 17.

6   Naville, E. (1898), *The Temple of Deir el-Bahari Part 3*, 16th Memoir of the
      Egypt Exploration Fund, London: 5–6.

7   The partially erased inscription with a similar theme carved on the upper
      northern colonnade at the Deir el-Bahri mortuary temple and already
      discussed in Chapter 3 is also best disregarded as pure fiction, and contrib-
      utes little to our search for the date of Hatchepsut's accession.

8   A donation stela recovered from North Karnak, apparently erected by
      Senenmut in Year 4, seems at first sight to offer proof of a co-regency by
      Year 4 as it refers to Tuthmosis III as king, describes Hatchepsut as
      'Maatkare', and mentions the mortuary temple of Deir el-Bahri which

can only have been built following Hatchepsut's accession. However, this stela was badly damaged soon after it was carved and, although it has undergone extensive restoration during the 19th Dynasty, we cannot now be certain that our reading of the year date is accurate. References to Senenmut's tomb suggest that the stela was carved some time after Year 7.

9   For further details concerning this cult, consult Bell, L. (1985), Luxor Temple and the Cult of the Royal *Ka, Journal of Near Eastern Studies* 44: 251–94.

10 Translation given by Dorman, who examines the evidence for the accession date of Hatchepsut in minute detail, giving valuable references to earlier and more specialized publications. Consult Dorman, P. F. (1988), *The Monuments of Senenmut: problems in historical methodology*, London, Chapter 2: 22.

11 As McDowell has pointed out: 'It is at any rate suspicious that the god Amen's wishes so often coincided with the manifest desire of the King or the High Priest . . . although this may have been the result of some subconscious influence on those who interpreted the god's will rather than the more crass manipulation of the proceedings.' McDowell, A. (1990), *Jurisdiction in the Workmen's Community of Deir el-Medina*, Leiden: 107.

12 The celebration of the *heb-sed* forms the basis of William Golding's ancient Egyptian novella *The Scorpion God* (1971), London.

13 See Uphill, E. P. (1961), A joint *sed*-festival of Thutmose III and Queen Hatchepsut, *Journal of Near Eastern Studies* 20: 248–51.

14 Hayes, W. C. (1935), *Royal Sarcophagi of the XVIII Dynasty*, Princeton: 144.

15 Hayes, W. C. (1935), *Royal Sarcophagi of the XVIII Dynasty*, Princeton: 146.

16 Harem plots and palace intrigues were rarely included in the official Egyptian records as they were classed as grievous offences against *maat* and as such were considered best ignored, but they did exist.

17 Winlock, H. E. (1928), The Egyptian Expedition 1927–1928, *Bulletin of the Metropolitan Museum of Art New York* 23.2: 8.

18 From the statue-base of Inebny, now housed in the British Museum, quoted and discussed in Murnane, W. J. (1977), *Ancient Egyptian Coregencies*, Chicago: 41.

19 It is, of course, always possible that he did indeed do so, but this begs the question why wait until Hatchepsut was a relatively old woman (aged between thirty-five and fifty-five) before having her killed?

20 The whole question of the proscription of Hatchepsut's memory is considered in detail in Chapter 8.

21 Gibbon, E. (1896), J. B. Bury (ed.), *The History of the Decline and Fall of the Roman Empire*, London, 1: 149.

22 Breasted, J. (1906), *Ancient Records of Egypt: historical documents*, vol. 2, Chicago: 342, 343.

23 Ray, J. (1994), Hatchepsut the female pharaoh, *History Today* 44.5: 28.

24 The Deir el-Bahri mortuary temple, *Djeser-Djeseru*, is considered in more detail in Chapter 6.

25 Christie, A. (1945), *Death Comes as the End*, Glasgow. The identification of the path is made in Romer, J. (1981), *Valley of the Kings*, London: 135.

26 Romer, J. (1974), Tuthmosis I and the Biban el-Moluk, *Journal of Egyptian Archaeology* 60: 119–33.

27 Winlock, H. E. (1929), Notes on the reburial of Tuthmosis I, *Journal of Egyptian Archaeology* 15: 64.

28 Davis, T. M. (ed.) (1906), *The tomb of Hatshopsitu*, London: xiii.

29 Carter, H., (1906), Description of the finding and excavation of the tomb, in Davis, T. M. (ed.) (1906), *The tomb of Hatshopsitu*, London: 80.

30 Hayes, W. C. (1935), *Royal Sarcophagi of the XVIII Dynasty*, Princeton: 98.

31 See, for example, Robins, G. (1983), Natural and canonical proportions in ancient Egyptians, *Goettinger Miszellen* 61: 17–25. Robins's figures are based on pre-New Kingdom skeletal remains.

32 Hayes, W. C. (1935), *Royal Sarcophagi of the XVIII Dynasty*, Princeton: 139–140. Hayes believed that Tuthmosis I had originally been buried in KV 38, and that Tuthmosis III was merely restoring his grandfather to his rightful tomb. It is perhaps somewhat unfair to criticize Hatchepsut's meanness in providing her father with a second-hand sarcophagus, as such rare a piece of craftsmanship, even second-hand, would have been immensely valuable.

33 Winlock, H. E. (1929), Notes on the reburial of Tuthmosis I, *Journal of Egyptian Archaeology* 59.

34 Maspero, G. (1896), *The Struggle of the Nations*, London: 582.

35 While it is not entirely impossible that Tuthmosis I died young, and indeed his highest recorded regnal year is only Year 4, the historical evidence would suggest that he enjoyed a longer life. For a discussion of the reign lengths of Tuthmosis I and Tuthmosis II, consult Wente, E. F. and Van Siclen, C. C. (1977), A Chronology of the New Kingdom, *Studies in Honor of George R. Hughes*, Chicago: 217–61. The problem of using X-ray analysis to age mummies is discussed in more detail in Robins, G. (1981), The value of the estimated ages of the royal mummies at death as historical evidence, *Goettinger Miszellen* 45: 63–8.

36 The first mortuary chapel of Tuthmosis I is considered in further detail in Quirke, S. (1990), Kerem in the Fitzwilliam Museum, *Journal of Egyptian Archaeology* 76: 170–74.

Chapter 5   War and Peace

1   Winlock, H. E (1928), The Egyptian Expedition 1925–1927, *Bulletin of the Metropolitan Museum of Art New York* 23.2: 47. Winlock is quoting from Hatchepsut's own less than modest description of herself.

2   Buttles, J. R. (1908), *The Queens of Egypt*, London: 90. Buttles is again quoting directly from Hatchepsut's monuments.

3   Benson, M. and Gourlay, J. (1899), *The Temple of Mut in Asher*, London: 160.

4   Hayes, W. C. (1959), *The Scepter of Egypt*, 2, New York: 100.

5   For a full discussion of Hatchepsut's statuary and its significance consult Tefnin, R. (1979), *La Statuaire d'Hatshepsout: portrait royal et politique sous la 18e dynastie*, Brussels.

6   Naville, E. (1898), *The Temple of Deir el-Bahari Part 3*, 16th Memoir of the Egypt Exploration Fund, London: 5.

7   See, for example, Gardiner, A. (1961), *Egypt of the Pharaohs*, Oxford: 183: 'Twice before in Egypt's earlier history a queen had usurped the kingship, but it was a wholly new departure for a female to pose and dress as a man.'

8   Margetts, E. L. (1951), The masculine character of Hatchepsut, Queen of Egypt, *Bulletin of the History of Medicine* 25: 559.

9   Margetts, E. L. (1951), The masculine character of Hatchepsut, Queen of Egypt, *Bulletin of the History of Medicine* 25: 561.

10 Warner, M. (1981), *Joan of Arc: the image of female heroism*, London, 145–6.

11 Deuteronomy 22: 5. It is interesting that by the late twentieth century, most societies will accept a woman wearing traditional men's clothing, but the sight of a man in a dress is still perceived as deviant sexual behaviour.

12 This is discussed further in Tefnin, R. (1979), *La Statuaire d'Hatshepsout: portrait royal et politique sous la 18e dynastie*, Brussels.

13 For this, and other examples of imagery in Elizabethan art, consult Strong, R. (1977), *The Cult of Elizabeth*, London.

14 Extract from the obelisk inscription of Hatchepsut, translated by S. R. Snape.

15 Gardiner, A. (1961), *Egypt of the Pharaohs*, Oxford: 189. Gardiner is by no means the only egyptologist to have represented Hatchepsut's reign as an entirely peaceful one without offering much evidence in support of his assumption. Donald Redford has given a detailed examination of all the available evidence for Hatchepsut's wars in Redford, D. B. (1967), *History and Chronology of the Eighteenth Dynasty: seven studies*,

Toronto: Chapter 4. Redford concludes that Hatchepsut's military campaigns have in fact been significantly understated.

16 Budge, E. A. W. (1902), *Egypt and her Asiatic Empire*, London: x.

17 Winlock, H. E. (1928), The Egyptian Expedition 1925–1927, *Bulletin of the Metropolitan Museum of Art New York* 23.2: 52.

18 Murray, M. (1926), Queen Hatchepsut, in W. Brunton, *Kings and Queens of Ancient Egypt*, London: 63.

19 Wilson, J. (1951), *The Burden of Egypt*, Chicago.

20 Wolf, N. (1990), *The Beauty Myth*, London: 207.

21 Dio Cassius, translated by E. Carey, *Dio's Roman History Book L*, London, 33.

22 Fraser, A. (1988), *The Warrior Queens: Boadicea's Chariot*, London: 9.

23 Naville, E. (1898), *The Temple of Deir el-Bahari Part 3*, 16th Memoir of the Egypt Exploration Fund, London: 11.

24 Naville quoted and discussed in Redford, D. B. (1967), *History and Chronology of the Eighteenth Dynasty: seven studies*, Toronto: 59.

25 Translation given in Habachi, L. (1957), Two graffiti at Sehel from the reign of Queen Hatchepsut, *Journal of Near Eastern Studies* 16: 99.

26 Naville, a fervent supporter of Hatchepsut, first posed this question in 1906 (see Davis, T. M. (ed.), *The tomb of Hatshopsitu*, London: 74). However, those more critical of Hatchepsut have often taken the opposite view, seeing her reign as a backwards step in the expansion of the empire, and occasionally being highly critical of Hatchepsut herself for denying Tuthmosis III an even longer and more glorious reign.

27 Gardiner, A. (1946), The Great Speos Artemidos Inscription, *Journal of Egyptian Archaeology* 32: 46.

28 Tomb inscription of the Old Kingdom Overseer Harkhuf, who is himself quoting from a letter written by the child-king Pepi II. Translation based on that given by James, T. G. H. (1984), *Pharaoh's People: scenes from life in imperial Egypt*, Oxford: 29.

29 Naville E. (1906), The Life and Monuments of the Queen, in T. M. Davis (ed.), *The tomb of Hatshopsitu*, London: 28–9.

30 Naville, E. (1898), *The Temple of Deir el-Bahari Part 3*, 16th Memoir of the Egypt Exploration Fund, London: 14.

31 Naville, E. (1906), in Davis, T. M. (ed.) *The tomb of Hatshopsitu*, London: 73–4.

32 Naville, E. (1898), *The Temple of Deir el-Bahari Part 3*, 16th Memoir of the Egypt Exploration Fund, London: 13.

33 Naville, E. (1898), *The Temple of Deir el-Bahari Part 3*, 16th Memoir of the Egypt Exploration Fund, London: 14.

34 Naville, E. (1898), *The Temple of Deir el-Bahari Part 3*, 16th Memoir of the Egypt Exploration Fund, London: 14.

35 Quoted in Kitchen, K. A. (1971), Punt and how to get there, *Orientalia* 40, 184–207: 190.

36 Naville, E. (1898), *The Temple of Deir el-Bahari Part 3*, 16th Memoir of the Egypt Exploration Fund, London: 16–17.

Chapter 6   Propaganda in Stone

1   Extract from the obelisk inscription of Hatchepsut, translated by S. R. Snape.

2   Winlock, H. E. (1928), The Egyptian Expedition 1925–1927, *Bulletin of the Metropolitan Museum of Art New York* 23: 53.

3   For a full translation of the interior texts of the Speos Artemidos, from which these three extracts are taken, see Fairman, H. W. and Grdseloff, B. (1947), Texts of Hatchepsut and Sethos I inside Speos Artemidos, *Journal of Egyptian Archaeology* 33: 15.

4   Gardiner, A. (1946), The Great Speos Artemidos Inscription, *Journal of Egyptian Archaeology* 32: 47–8.

5   Discussed in detail in Bjorkman, G. (1971), *Kings at Karnak: a study of the treatment of the monuments of royal predecessors in the Early New Kingdom*, Acta Universitatis Upsaliensis, Uppsala.

6   Extract from the obelisk inscription of Hatchepsut, translated by S. R. Snape.

7   Translation after James, T. G. H. (1984), *Pharaoh's People: scenes from life in imperial Egypt*, Oxford: 34.

8   This obelisk is uninscribed and therefore cannot be definitely attributed to Hatchepsut. However, it is known to date to the Tuthmoside period, and Hatchepsut seems to be the most likely owner.

9   Pliny, *Natural History*, Book 36: 14.

10 Habachi, L. (1957), Two Graffiti at Schel from the reign of Queen Hatshepsut, *Journal of Near Eastern Studies* 16: 90.

11 Extract from the obelisk inscription of Hatchepsut, translated by S. R. Snape.

12 Habachi, L. (1957), Two Graffiti at Schel from the reign of Queen Hatshepsut, *Journal of Near Eastern Studies* 16: 99.

13 Naville, E. (1894), *The Temple of Deir el-Bahari: its plan, its founders and its first explorers: Introductory Memoir*, 12th Memoir of the Egypt Exploration Fund, London: 1.

14 See Dodson, A. (1989), Hatshepsut and her 'father' Mentuhotpe II, *Journal of Egyptian Archaeology* 75: 224–6.

15   Buttles, J. R. (1908), *The Queens of Egypt*, London: 85.

16   Winlock, H. E. (1928), The Egyptian Expedition 1925–1927, *Bulletin of the Metropolitan Museum of Art New York* 23: 55–6.

17   The foundation deposits were intended to ensure that all would go well with the building; a parallel may be drawn with the modern practice of formally laying foundation stones.

18   Over three hundred engraved seals have been recovered from the foundation deposits of *Djeser-Djeseru*; these are mostly inscribed with the regal name of Hatchepsut but they also give the names of Hatchepsut the queen (35), Tuthmosis II (31), Princess Neferure, 'King's Daughter, King's Sister and God's Wife' (18), Tuthmosis I (2) and Amen (18). Most of these scarabs can now be found in the collections of the Metropolitan Museum of Art, New York.

19   Text is quoted in Brovarski, E. (1976), Senenu, High Priest of Amun, *Journal of Egyptian Archaeology* 62: 70.

20   See, for example, Donohue, V. A. (1992), The goddess of the Theban Mountain, *Antiquity* 66: 881: '. . . the maternally generative emphasis in her own [i.e. Hatchepsut's] mythic personality that so intense a celebration of this goddess confirms goes far to modify the prevailing view that it was in masculine terms alone that Hatchepsut sought to authenticate her supremacy.' See also Roberts, A. (1995), *Hathor Rising: the serpent power of Ancient Egypt*, Totnes. Roberts also stresses what she sees as the important link between Hathor and Hatchepsut.

21   To some observers, however, the tripartite nature of the temple is of great importance. See, for example, Roberts, A. (1995), *Hathor Rising: the serpent power of Ancient Egypt*, Totnes: Chapter 116.

Chapter 7   Senenmut: Greatest of the Great

1   An extract from Senenmut's fictional *curriculum vitae*, composed by Winlock and based on various original sources. See Winlock, H. E. (1942), *Excavations at Deir el-Bahri, 1911–1934*, New York: 16.

2   Peter Dorman discusses early approaches to Senenmut in some detail before taking a fresh look at the archaeological and historical evidence for his life and achievements. Consult Dorman, P. F. (1988), *The Monuments of Senenmut: problems in historical methodology*, London and New York. For an earlier study of Senenmut, see Meyer, C. (1982), *Senenmut: eine prosopographische Untersuchung*, Hamburg.

3   For a fictionalized account of the life of Senenmut, read Gedge, P. (1977), *Child of the Morning*, New York. This historical romance tells

how the teenage priest Senmut rescues the Princess Hatchepsut from an untimely death by drowning in the Sacred Lake of the Karnak temple. This leads to a lifelong bond between the pair, which is only broken when the now powerful Senmut is assassinated by the agents of the displaced King Thothmes. The grieving Hatchepsut, setting a precedent for Egyptian queens, chooses to commit suicide rather than face life without her lover.

4   This matter is discussed further in Roehrig, C. H. and Dorman, P. F. (1987), Senimen and Senenmut: a question of brothers, *Varia Aegyptiaca*, 3: 127–34.

5   Lansing, A. and Hayes, W. (1937), The Egyptian Expedition 1935–36, *Bulletin of the Metropolitan Museum of Art New York* 32.2: 31–21.

6   Caminos, R. and James, T. G. H. (1963), *Gebel Es-Silsilah 1: The Shrines*, London: 5.

7   Extract from the text carved on the base of a block statue of Senenmut now housed in the British Museum. After James, T. G. H. (1984), *Pharaoh's People: scenes from life in imperial Egypt*, Oxford: 32.

8   Winlock, H. E. (1928), The Egyptian Expedition 1925–1927, *Bulletin of the Metropolitan Museum of Art New York* 23.2: 36.

9   Extract from the autobiography of Ineni, Breasted, J. H. (1906), *Ancient Records of Egypt: historical documents*, vol. 2, Chicago: 43.

10 Forbes, D. (1990), Queen's Minion Senenmut, *KMT* 1: 1, 16. This article gives a brief but highly readable review of the life and major works of Senenmut.

11 Winlock, H. E. (1928), The Egyptian Expedition 1925–1927, *Bulletin of the Metropolitan Museum of Art New York* 23.2: 36.

12 Stevenson Smith, W., *The Art and Architecture of Ancient Egypt*, revised and edited by W. K. Simpson (1981), New Haven: 226.

13 Part of an inscription recording Senenmut's appeal to Hatchepsut for permission to have his statue placed within the Karnak temple, after Dorman, P. F. (1988), *The Monuments of Senenmut: problems in historical methodology*, London and New York: 125.

14 For a full translation of the story consult Lichtheim, M. (1976), *Ancient Egyptian Literature II: the New Kingdom*, Los Angeles: 214–23.

15 Wente, E. R. (1984), Some Graffiti from the Reign of Hatchepsut, *Journal of Near Eastern Studies* 43: 47–54.

16 Manniche, L. (1977), Some Aspects of Ancient Egyptian Sexual Life, *Acta Orientalia* 38: 22.

17 The ancient Romans took the view that man's desire for sexual intercourse made him weak and effeminate; sex therefore gave women power over men. The ancient Egyptians took entirely the opposite view.

18   Simpson, W. K. (1984), Senenmut, *Lexikon der Ägyptologie*, Wiesbaden, 5: 850.

19   Gardiner, A. (1961), *Egypt of the Pharaohs*, Oxford: 184.

20   Winlock, H. E. (1928), The Egyptian Expedition 1925–1927, *Bulletin of the Metropolitan Museum of Art New York* 23.2: 36.

21   Hayes, W. C. (1957), Varia from the Time of Hatchepsut, *Mitteilungen des Deutschen Archäologischen Instituts Abteilung Kairo* 15: 84.

22   Extract from the list of funerary offerings recorded in Tomb 353, after Dorman, P. F. (1991), *The Tombs of Senenmut*, New York: 138.

23   Both Senenmut tombs were investigated in the first half of this century by H. E. Winlock, working on behalf of the Metropolitan Museum of Art, New York. The previously unknown Tomb 353 was discovered in 1927, and this led to renewed interest in Tomb 71, which was cleared during the 1930–31 season.

24   The reconstructed sarcophagus has been published in Hayes, W. C. (1950), The Sarcophagus of Sennemut, *Journal of Egyptian Archaeology* 36: 19–23.

25   Dorman, P. F. (1991), *The Tombs of Senenmut*, New York: 29, notes that: 'Today these corridors have been refilled with debris up to the level of the floor of Tomb 71 and cannot be reinvestigated without considerable clearance. The present writer was unable to enter the tomb of Aanen to investigate the passage from the other end.'

26   Although there is always the possibility that this pit represents an unrelated secondary burial cut into the floor of the hall some time after the tomb had fallen into disuse.

27   Winlock's interpretation of the sealing of Tomb 353 following the unexpected death of Senenmut. See Winlock, H. E. (1928), The Egyptian Expedition 1925–1927, *Bulletin of the Metropolitan Museum of Art New York* 23.2: 58.

28   For a detailed discussion of Senenmut's mysterious disappearance, plus a useful list of other publications on this subject, consult Schulman, A. R. (1969–70), Some Remarks on the Alleged 'Fall' of Senmut, *Journal of the American Research Center in Egypt* 8: 29–48.

Chapter 8   The End and the Aftermath

1   Extract from the obelisk inscription of King Hatchepsut, translated by S. R. Snape.

2   The stela of Nakht from Sinai, for example, dated to Year 20 of the joint

reign, shows the two kings as equals, Hatchepsut on the right and Tuthmosis on the left, making parallel offerings to local deities.

3   See, for example, Edgerton, W. F. (1933), *The Tuthmoside Succession*, Chicago: 34: 'If I were to hazard my personal guess, I should say that Hatchepsut's body was probably disposed of in the same manner as the bodies of Senta's children in the demotic tale – that the dogs and cats ate her.'

4   See, for example, Hayes, W. C. (1935), *Royal Sarcophagi of the XVIII Dynasty*, Princeton: 151.

5   Published in Davis, T. M. (ed.) (1906), *The tomb of Hatshopsitu*, London: un-numbered plate opposite page 78.

6   Ciccarello, M. and Romer, J. (1979), *A Preliminary Report of the Recent Work in the Tombs of Ramesses X and XI in the Valley of the Kings*, San Fransisco: 3.

7   For a discussion of the tomb of Ramesses XI and its contents see Reeves, N. (1990), *Valley of the Kings: the decline of a Royal Necropolis*, London: 121–3.

8   Petrie, W. M. F. (1924), *A History of Egypt during the XVIIth and XVIIIth Dynasties*, 2, London: 92.

9   Donald P. Ryan describes the circumstances behind the rediscovery of this tomb, and discusses the Hatchepsut hypothesis, in Ryan, D. P. (1990), Who is buried in KV60?, *KMT*, 1: 34–63.

10   Extract from the Annals of Tuthmosis III. Lichtheim, M. (1976), *Ancient Egyptian Literature II: the New Kingdom*, Los Angeles: 30.

11   Tuthmosis III – a Leonardo-like 'Renaissance Man' ahead of his time – is supposed to have designed the furnishings intended for the temple of Amen.

12   Maspero, G. (1889), *Les Momies Royales de Deir el-Bahari*, Paris: 547–8.

13   Hayes, W. C. (1935), *Royal Sarcophagi of the XVIII Dynasty*, Princeton: 138.

14   Winlock, H. E. (1928), The Egyptian Expedition 1925–1927, *Bulletin of the Metropolitan Museum of Art New York*, 23.1: 58.

15   Winlock, H. E. (1928), The Egyptian Expedition 1927–28, *Bulletin of the Metropolitan Museum of Art New York*, 23.2: 9.

16   Naville, E. in T. M. Davis (ed.) (1906), *The tomb of Hatshopsitu*, London: 71, 72.

17   Nims, C. F. (1966), The Date of the Dishonouring of Hatchepsut, *Zeitschrift für Ägyptische Sprache und Altertumskunde*, Leipzig: 97–100. The whole question of the defacement of Hatchepsut's monuments is discussed in great detail, with all relevant references, in Dorman, P. F. (1988), *The Monuments of Senenmut: problems in historical methodology*, London: Chapter 3.

18   See Lipinska, J. (1967), Names and History of the Sanctuaries built by
      Tuthmosis III at Deir el-Bahri, *Journal of Egyptian Archaeology* 35: 25–33.

19   See Van Siclen, C. (1989), New data on the date of the defacement of
      Hatchepsut's name and image on the Chapelle Rouge, *Goettinger Miszellen*
      107: 85–6.

20   Winlock, H. E. (1928), The Egyptian Expedition 1925–1927, *Bulletin of
      the Metropolitan Museum of Art New York*, 23.1: 46. Further details of the
      finding of statue-fragments at Deir el-Bahri are included in the Bulletin
      Volumes 18, 23 and 24.

21   Winlock, H. E. (1928), The Egyptian Expedition 1925–1927, *Bulletin of
      the Metropolitan Museum of Art New York*, 23.1: 46.

22   Unpublished work by the late Ramadan Saad, quoted in Dorman, P. F.
      (1988), *Monuments of Senenmut: problems in historical methodology*, London:
      Chapter 3.

23   A question already posed by Redford, D. B. (1967), *History and Chronology
      of the 18th Dynasty: seven studies*, Toronto: 87: 'Standing alone before the
      image of the queen, Tuthmosis relented. She was, after all, his own flesh . . .
      In the darkness of the crypt, in the stillness of the cella, her cold statues,
      which never vulgar eye would again behold, still conveyed for the king
      the warmth and awe of a divine presence.'

24   It could, however, be argued that, because of the brief and disturbed
      nature of Twosret's reign, she was unable to build the inscribed monu-
      ments which would have preserved the evidence of such a persecution.
      Twosret's monuments may not have been defaced simply because they
      did not exist.

25   Plutarch, *The Lives of the Noble Grecians and Romans*, translated by Sir
      Thomas North (1927), Oxford.

26   The history of the temple, which is inextricably bound up with Hatch-
      epsut's own history, has been recorded by several authors; see for example
      Naville, E. (1894), *The Temple of Deir el-Bahari: its plan, its founders and its
      first explorers: Introductory Memoir*, 12th Memoir of the Egypt Exploration
      Fund, London; Wysocki, Z. (1979), *The Temple of Queen Hatchepsut: Re-
      sults of the investigations and conservation works of the Polish-Egyptian archaeo-
      logical Mission 1968–72*, Warsaw.

27   Naville, E. (1894), *The Temple of Deir el-Bahari: its plan, its founders and its
      first explorers: Introductory Memoir*, 12th Memoir of the Egypt Exploration
      Fund, London: 3.

28   Wilkinson, J. G. (1835), *Topography of Thebes and General View of Egypt*,
      London.

29   Lepsius, K. R., translated by L. and J. R. Horner (1853), *Letters from Egypt,
      Ethiopia, and the Peninsula of Sinai*, London: 255–6.

30 Sharpe, S. (1859), *The History of Egypt: from the earliest times till the conquest by the Arabs AD 640*, London.

31 Pierret, P. (1875), *Dictionnaire d'Archéologie Égyptienne*, Paris: 248. Translation, author's own.

Further Reading

The references listed below include the more basic and accessible publications with preference given to those written in English; all these works include bibliographies which will be of interest to those seeking detailed references on specific subjects. More specialized references to points raised in the text have been included in the notes.

Aldred, C. (1980), *Egyptian Art*, London.

Baines, J. and Malek, J. (1980), *Atlas of Ancient Egypt*, Oxford.

Breasted, J. H. (1906), *Ancient Records of Egypt: historical documents*, 5 volumes, Chicago.

Dorman, P. F. (1988), *The Monuments of Senenmut: problems in historical methodology*, London.

Dorman, P. F. (1991), *The Tombs of Senenmut*, New York.

Gardiner, A. (1961), *Egypt of the Pharaohs*, Oxford.

Grimal, N., *A History of Ancient Egypt*, translated by I. Shaw (1992), Oxford.

Harris, J. E. and Wente, E. F. (1980), *An X-Ray Analysis of the Royal Mummies*, Chicago and London.

Hayes, W. C. (1935), *Royal Sarcophagi of the XVIII Dynasty*, Princeton.

Hayes, W. C. (1959), *The Scepter of Egypt Vol II*, Cambridge, Mass.

Hayes, W. C. (1973), Egypt: internal affairs from Tuthmosis I to the death of Amenophis III, in I. E. S. Edwards *et al.* (eds), *The Cambridge Ancient History*, 3rd edition, Cambridge, 2.1: 313–416.

James, T. G. H. (1973), Egypt: from the expulsion of the Hyksos to Amenophis I, in I. E. S. Edwards *et al.* (eds), *The Cambridge Ancient History*, 3rd edition, Cambridge, 2.1: 289–312.

Kemp, B. J. (1989), *Ancient Egypt: anatomy of a civilization*, London.

Lichtheim, M. (1976), *Ancient Egyptian Literature II: the New Kingdom*, Los Angeles.

Manetho, translated by W. G. Waddell (1956), Cambridge, Mass. and London.

Naville, E. (1895–1908), *The Temple of Deir el-Bahari*, 7 volumes, London.

Ratie, S. (1979), *La Reine Hatchepsout; sources et problèmes*, Leyden.

Redford, D. B. (1967), *History and Chronology of the Eighteenth Dynasty: seven studies*, Toronto.

Reeves, C. N. (1990), *Valley of the Kings: the decline of a royal necropolis*, London.

Robins, G. (1993), *Women in Ancient Egypt*, London.

Shafer, B. E., ed. (1991), *Religion in Ancient Egypt: gods, myths and personal practices*, London.

Smith, G. E. (1912), *The Royal Mummies*, Cairo.

Stevenson Smith, W., *The Art and Architecture of Ancient Egypt*, revised and edited by W. K. Simpson (1981), New Haven.

Trigger, B. G., Kemp, B. J., O'Connor, D. and Lloyd, A. B., eds (1983), *Ancient Egypt: a social history*, Cambridge.

Troy, L. (1986), *Patterns of Queenship in Ancient Egyptian Myth and History*, Boreas.

Tyldesley, J. A. (1994), *Daughters of Isis: women of ancient Egypt*, London.

Watterson, B. (1991), *Women in Ancient Egypt*, Stroud.

Index

Figures in italic refer to a picture caption on that page.

DATE DUE

OCT 18 2006			
GAYLORD			PRINTED IN U.S.A.